G000109852

IRELAND 1922

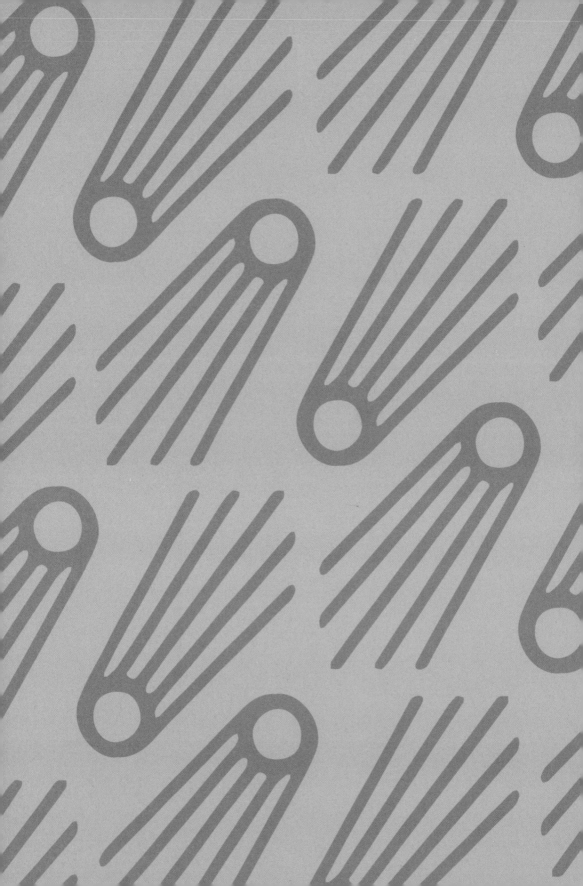

IRELAND
19
22

INDEPENDENCE, PARTITION, CIVIL WAR

Edited by DARRAGH GANNON and FEARGHAL McGARRY

Acadamh Ríoga na hÉireann
Royal Irish Academy

Ireland 1922. Independence, partition, civil war

First published 2022
Royal Irish Academy, 19 Dawson Street, Dublin 2
www.ria.ie

ISBN 978-1-911479-79-6 (HB)
ISBN 978-1-911479-91-8 (pdf)
ISBN 978-1-911479-92-5 (epub)

British Library Cataloguing in Publication Data. A CIP catalogue record for this book is available
from the British Library.

Edited by Helena King
Book design by Fidelma Slattery
Index by Lisa Scholey

Printed in Poland by L&C Printing Group

Royal Irish Academy is a member of Publishing Ireland, the Irish book publishers' association

5 4 3 2 1

Published with key support from the Department of Tourism, Culture, Arts, Gaeltacht, Sport and Media
under the Decade of Centenaries 2012–2023 Programme.

An Roinn Turasóireachta, Cultúir,
Ealaíon, Gaeltachta, Spóirt agus Meán
Department of Tourism, Culture,
Arts, Gaeltacht, Sport and Media

A NOTE FROM THE PUBLISHER
We want to try to offset the environmental impacts of carbon produced during the production of our books
and journals. For the production of our books this year we will plant 45 trees with Easy Treesie. The Easy
Treesie – Crann Project organises children to plant trees. Crann – 'Trees for Ireland' is a membership-based,
non-profit, registered charity (CHY13698) uniting people with a love of trees. It was formed in 1986 by Jan
Alexander, with the aim of 'Releafing Ireland'. Its mission is to enhance the environment of Ireland through
planting, promoting, protecting and increasing awareness about trees and woodlands.

Opposite: 'An oasis!'; pro-Treaty handbill conveying Michael Collins's view of the settlement as a stepping-stone to full independence.

AN OASIS!

¶ "Mr. de Valera compares Ireland to a party that had set out to cross a desert. 'We have come to a green spot,' he says, 'and there are some who say lie down and stay here.'"

¶ "Yes, we have come by means of the Treaty to a green oasis, the last in the long weary desert over which the Irish Nation has been travelling. Oases are the resting places of the desert, and unless the traveller finds them and refreshes himself he never reaches his destination."

¶ "Ireland has been brought to the last one, beyond which there is but an easy stretch to go. The Nation has earned the right to rest while it renews its strength and restores its vigour."

—*Michael Collins, 5/3/22.*

Support the Treaty

Irish Labour, Irish Paper and Irish Ink.

This is the kind of
" FREEDOM "
The TREATY gives you

The BLACK and TANS wore
it in their caps

Opposite: 'This is the kind of "Freedom" the Treaty gives you'; anti-Treaty handbill depicting the British crown above the Irish harp.

Opposite: 'The rejected suitor'; originally published in *London Opinion*, this treatyite handbill depicts the Irish electorate's rejection of anti-Treaty Sinn Féin.

THE REJECTED SUITOR.

Drawn by Bert Thomas.

Miss Erin (to De Valera): "Arrah, be off wid yez—it's Michael Collins I'm after marrying."

Opposite: 'This is what the Treaty gives you'; anti-Treaty handbill depicting a field gun, adorned with union flag, and a fallen patriot with the Irish tricolour.

MACHINE MADE BREAD

FOREWORD

Fifty essays. Fifty contributors. One seminal year.

The year 1922 marked the beginning of the final phase in Ireland's revolution: it saw the ratification of the Anglo-Irish Treaty; the establishment of the Irish Free State; the outbreak of the civil war; and the consolidation of partition as Northern Ireland opted out of the Free State settlement.

In fifty short essays, the contributors to this volume attempt to capture the breadth of events, issues and debates that marked the year. Building on their own expertise and on the wealth of recent scholarship provoked by the Decade of Centenaries, each contributor chooses one topic that illuminates a key aspect of Ireland in 1922 and how the revolutionary period would shape the formation of a new state. Together, these contributions create a mosaic of a year that would prove to be a turning point in Irish history; one whose legacy remains controversial a century on.

Ruth Hegarty,
Royal Irish Academy

Opposite: Two boys, one armed with a rifle, protect a horse-drawn bread van in Dublin.

REMEMBERING 1922

All Dublin was agog with anticipation. From early morning a dense crowd collected outside the gloomy gates in Dame Street...members of the Provisional Government went in a body to the Castle, where they were received by Lord FitzAlan, the Lord Lieutenant. Michael Collins produced a copy of the Treaty, on which the acceptance of its provisions by himself and his colleagues was endorsed...The Lord Lieutenant... expressed the earnest hope that under their auspices the idea of a happy, free, and prosperous Ireland would be attained.

The Times, 17 January 1922

Ireland's future lay unwritten at the outset of 1922, but the pageantry marking what Michael Collins, revolutionary-turned-statesman, provocatively termed 'the surrender of Dublin Castle' proved deceptive. Like King George V's opening of the Northern Irish parliament in Belfast the previous summer, the ritual obscured the reality that violent forces were driving political developments. Behind the scenes, British officials burned files as they hurriedly made arrangements to leave the country. Symbolising the seizure of the machinery of the state, the handover of Dublin Castle on 16 January masked a revolutionary event in constitutional form; its hasty improvisation reflecting the lack of

Opposite: Michael Collins, Kevin O'Higgins and Éamonn Duggan leave Dublin Castle after the transfer of power to the Provisional Government, 16 January 1922.

'precedent for British withdrawal from her colonies'.[1] Following soon after the republican split over the Anglo-Irish Treaty, the agreement that had facilitated the departure of Crown forces from southern Ireland, it marked the beginning of a power vacuum rather than an orderly transfer of sovereignty. In this 'grey area between the building of new states and the collapse of the old, all kinds of fanatical paramilitaries, political radicals and armed idealists' would flourish.[2] Across the recently drawn border, Belfast experienced the most intense communal violence of the revolutionary period during the first six months of 1922, which abated only with the descent of southern Ireland into a bitter civil war that summer.

As 1922 drew to a close, pro-Treaty politicians were preoccupied more with the survival than with the prosperity of the Irish Free State. They gathered in the Dáil on 6 December, dressed in military uniform or 'obviously ill-at-ease in civilian attire', to observe its formal inauguration. Few others witnessed the ceremony as the parliament, ringed by armed men, had been closed to the public. The occasion was marked, not by public celebration, but by 'an uncanny absence of shots' on Dublin's streets that night, *The Irish Times* reported.[3] The following day, both houses of the Northern Irish parliament convened to inform King George V of his loyal subjects' decision to opt out of the Irish Free State, formalising the partition of Ireland.

That same afternoon, IRA gunmen shot dead a pro-Treaty deputy, Seán Hales, as he made his way to the Dáil. They had failed to kill their intended victim: the Deputy Speaker of the Dáil, Pádraig Ó Máille—targeted for supporting the government's policy of executing anti-Treaty combatants—was shot in the spine. Regretting the death of Hales, the IRA officer who ordered the attack, Frank Henderson, had his son, a priest, offer Masses over the next sixteen years for the repose of his soul.[4] Meeting afterwards in emergency session, the Irish Free State government agreed, as one of its first acts, to execute four IRA prisoners, one from each province. One Cabinet minister subsequently recalled their decision as 'an act of counter-terror'.[5] One of the victims of this grim reprisal, Rory O'Connor, had been best man for Kevin O'Higgins, the government minister who confirmed the death sentences. The IRA retaliated by killing O'Higgins's father, Thomas, in front of his wife and daughter, and burning the family home in 1923: four years later, O'Higgins was assassinated in a final act of vengeance.

By 1922, 'murder, rioting, martyrdom, and expulsion had all become common currency in Ireland'.[6] The violence that so effectively undermined British power during the Irish revolution resulted in two embryonic Irish states whose survival would rest on their ability to use the same means to

impose their authority on their own alienated
minorities.[7] 'Ultimately all government is based on
force', Kevin O'Higgins informed the Dáil can-
didly on 8 December, and 'must meet force with
greater force if it is to survive.' The only way to
safeguard the state, W.T. Cosgrave insisted in the
same debate, was to strike 'terror' into its enemies.[8]

Wedding of Bridget
Cole and Kevin
O'Higgins. Also
pictured are (left)
Éamon de Valera and
(right) Rory O'Connor,
27 October 1921.

Over time, as both jurisdictions gained the stability that comes with
endurance, memories of the violence that accompanied their birth receded
in the public consciousness. A century later, how do we make sense of the
violence of 1922? This introductory essay sets 1922 in context: it outlines the
key political events of the year; considers how these were later remembered;
and analyses how historiographical assessments of responsibility for the divisions of 1922 have developed over the past century. It concludes by assessing
how the new sources, methods and perspectives that have emerged over the
Decade of Centenaries enable us to reconsider long-familiar narratives.

THE YEAR OF DIVISION

To chronicle the Irish revolution is to generate historical debate. One hundred years after the facts,
the Irish revolution remains open to historical
enquiry. Where, and when, did it begin: Covenant
(1912), Rising (1916), first Dáil (1919)? How,
and when, was it ultimately brought to an end: Treaty (1921), civil war
(1923), Boundary Commission (1924–25)? The Irish government's Expert
Advisory Group on Centenary Commemorations has catalogued the centenaries of the era by theme: labour (1913), suffrage (1918), violence (1920).
How then should we mark 1922, with its historically divisive and commem-
oratively challenging seminal events, in the historical calendar? By any academic or commemorative standard, it was the year of division. The establishment of the Irish Free State acknowledged the legislative independence
of Dáil Éireann from Westminster; the Belfast administration's secession
from the Free State ensured the continued partition of Ireland; while the
political repudiation of both polities by Irish republicans heralded a bitterly
fought civil war. Republican publicist Frank Gallagher famously ascribed
the end of the Irish revolution to 'the passing of the Treaty which saw Irish
unity melt away…the four glorious years were over'.[9] A year is a long time
in revolutionary politics; 1922 is deserving of renewed attention.

Years of intra-nationalist tensions, and weeks of intensive political
debate in Dáil Éireann, were brought to breaking point on 7 January 1922.
In the final vote on the Anglo-Irish Treaty, the agreement was passed by
sixty-four votes to fifty-seven. A consequent vote on the position of
'President of Dáil Éireann' saw Arthur Griffith defeat Éamon de Valera by
sixty votes to fifty-eight, prompting the departure of de Valera and anti-
Treaty TDs from the Dáil. Under the terms of the Treaty, meanwhile,
Michael Collins became chairman of the Provisional Government; the
Irish Free State would not take legal effect until 6 December 1922. In the
interim, Collins attempted to mediate political differences with the putative
Irish state, north and south. In March, he agreed a pact with the prime minister of Northern Ireland, James Craig, providing for greater protection
for Catholics in loyalist Belfast and bilateral discussions on the future of
the Irish border. In May, Collins and de Valera agreed a pact to allow pro-
and anti-Treaty Sinn Féin candidates to stand on a coalition ticket for the
June 1922 general election. Disillusioned by these concessions to the anti-
Treaty minority, Griffith would distance himself from 'Mr. Collins' in the

Opposite: Poster
advertising a pro-
Treaty election rally
in Naas, Co. Kildare,
16 April 1922.

SAORSTÁT NA h-ÉIREANN.

COME TO THE
GREAT LEINSTER RALLY
IN SUPPORT OF THE
FREE STATE,
AT
NAAS
On SUNDAY, APRIL 16th,
At 3 p.m. (Summer Time).

MR. MICHAEL COLLINS
WILL SPEAK; also
Mr. JOSEPH McGRATH, T.D.; Alderman M. J. STAINES, T.D.; Mr. C. M. BYRNE, T.D.; Mr. KEVIN C. HIGGINS, T.D.; Mr. GEAROID O'SULLIVAN, T.D.

Special Trains for Naas, at greatly Reduced Fares, will leave:---

Tullow at 11.15 a.m.
Maryborough at 11.5 a.m.
Bagenalstown at 11.10 a.m.
Calling at intermediate Stations.

Return Trains will leave Naas at about 7 p.m.   For full time-tables see Railway Company's posters.

Go Saoraid Dia Éire.

"The Leinster Leader Ltd." Printing Works

final months of their lives. Anti-Treaty republicans were placated further with the promise of a 'republican' constitution. The Provisional Government attempted to elide the trappings of empire, such as the 'oath of allegiance', by devising a Free State constitution with a republican ethos. The final draft

Soldiers remove field artillery following the National Army landing at Passage West, Co. Cork, 2 August 1922.

of the constitution, published on the morning of 16 June ('election day') following close inspection from the British government, adhered more closely to the terms of the Treaty than hoped. At the polls, pro-Treaty Sinn Féin secured 38% of the vote (58 seats) while anti-Treaty Sinn Féin secured 21% (36 seats). Contesting a general election for the first time, the Labour party secured an impressive 21% of the poll. The people had spoken in favour of the Treaty and the return of everyday socio-economic issues to Irish politics. Disillusioned by the failure to secure a republican constitution, and unwilling to swear the 'oath of allegiance', anti-Treaty Sinn Féin TDs refused to enter the Irish Free State parliament.

The IRA was divided both over the merits of the Treaty, and the necessity for military action. While the core of IRA GHQ went pro-Treaty,

forming the leadership cadre of the embryonic National Army, the majority of active Volunteers in Dublin and Munster were opposed to the Treaty. The evacuation of British-army barracks exposed a growing vacuum of military authority, almost precipitating the outbreak of civil war between rival factions in Limerick city in March. At the illegally assembled IRA 'Army Convention' held in Dublin later that month, those in attendance restored the allegiance of the Volunteers to the IRA Executive, rather than to Dáil Éireann. Anti-Treaty IRA leaders, however, differed in their attitudes to violence against the state. The Cork-based IRA Chief of Staff Liam Lynch worked with Richard Mulcahy to negotiate the terms of a continued truce between pro- and anti-Treaty IRA forces. Senior Dublin figures such as Rory O'Connor, Ernie O'Malley and Liam Mellows, escalated tensions by occupying the Four Courts. 'If a government goes wrong it must take the consequences', O'Connor proclaimed.[10] Pro- and anti-Treaty IRA were united from the spring of 1921 in a covert campaign to destabilise

A young boy, holding sword and scabbard, stands before the ruins of an imposing house.

Following pages: Jubilant National Army soldiers and civilian supporters.

the Northern Ireland regime, under the guidance of Collins, Lynch and O'Connor. Through this endeavour, the leaders of both IRA factions vied for the loyalty of the northern IRA in anticipation of the outbreak of civil war in the south.

Between April and June a series of joint IRA offensives by republicans (armed with weapons supplied by Britain to the Provisional Government) were carried out, leading to clashes with members of the Ulster Special Constabulary along the border around Belleek, Co. Fermanagh and Pettigo, Co. Donegal. Hundreds of IRA suspects in Northern Ireland would be interned under a new Special Powers Act. The repercussions of organised violence were most clearly felt in Belfast, wherein IRA attacks prompted loyalist reprisals on nationalist communities; over 250 civilians (mostly Catholics) were killed in the city between February and June. On 22 June, meanwhile, Sir Henry Wilson, security advisor to Craig's Cabinet, was assassinated by two IRA Volunteers in London. While Collins was suspected of involvement in the assassination, the British Cabinet focused its attention on the anti-Treaty IRA. Unbeknownst to the Provisional Government, British plans to carry out a combined air and ground attack on the Four Courts on 25 June were cancelled only that morning. Under severe pressure from the British government to confront the rebellious garrison, the Provisional Government seized on the anti-Treaty IRA's kidnap of National Army Deputy Chief of Staff J.J. 'Ginger' O'Connell as the basis for its ultimatum that the IRA evacuate the Four Courts, delivered to Rory O'Connor at 3.30 a.m. on 28 June. Forty-five minutes later, on Collins's orders, the artillery bombardment of the Four Courts began.

The fighting at the Four Courts would last three days, before O'Connor surrendered his garrison to the advancing National Army. The explosion at the Irish Public Record Office in the west wing of the Four Courts on 30 June was perhaps the defining event of the civil war in Dublin: historical records spanning over a thousand years would be destroyed in the blaze. Sporadic street fighting in the weeks that followed saw the deaths of prominent republicans such as Cathal Brugha and Harry Boland.

The forces of the anti-Treaty IRA, led by the redoubtable Liam Lynch, largely retreated south of the Shannon, towards the self-styled 'Munster Republic'. The National Army, led by Collins as commander-in-chief, used a combination of air, ground and naval forces to take the major anti-Treaty IRA strongholds of Waterford (20 July), Limerick (21 July) and Cork (10 August). IRA guerrilla attacks on National Army forces would continue throughout the year. Despite the setbacks experienced by anti-Treaty forces, the loss of the two leading figures within the pro-Treaty government threatened to undermine the political authority of the nascent Free State. On 12 August, Arthur Griffith died of a brain haemorrhage. Ten days later Michael Collins was killed in a guerrilla-style ambush at Béal na mBláth, Co. Cork. His funeral in Dublin was attended by over 500,000 Irish citizens.

'The Provisional Government was simply eight young men in the City Hall standing amidst the ruins of one administration, with the foundations of another not yet laid, and with wild men screaming through the keyhole.'[11] Kevin O'Higgins's vivid portrayal of state-building in 1922 captures the enormous political challenges faced by the leaders of the Irish Free State. In the aftermath of Collins's death, O'Higgins, and the newly installed chairman of the Provisional Government W.T. Cosgrave, prosecuted the civil war with rigour and severity. On 27 September a resolution was passed by the newly assembled third Dáil, granting the Provisional Government emergency powers, including the establishment of military tribunals with sanction to impose the death penalty for a number of military offences.

A series of state executions followed, notably that of Erskine Childers, who was shot by firing squad on 24 November for having in his possession a pistol gifted to him by Michael Collins. Eighty-one republicans would be officially executed by the National Army during the civil war, among them the tragically ill-placed Mountjoy internees: O'Connor, Mellows, Richard Barrett and Joseph McKelvey. In the field, the cycles of reprisal and counter-reprisal surpassed the violence of the War of Independence for callousness. Most infamously, the killing of five Free State army soldiers by a mine at Knocknagoshel, Co. Kerry on 5 March 1923, prompted the arrest and torture of nine republican prisoners the following evening. Shattered by hammer-blows, they were tied to a tree and blown apart by a mine. The men selected for this atrocity were reportedly considered to be 'anonymous, no priests or nuns in the family, those that'll make the least noise'.[12] One of the victims, Stephen Fuller, was blown away from the scene of the blast and miraculously survived to tell the tale; he later became a Fianna Fáil TD. Nine more anti-Treaty prisoners were murdered in Kerry over the next days. Such reprisals haunted the reputation of the pro-Treaty Fine Gael party for decades.

Five months after the legislative establishment of the Irish Free State, and Northern Ireland's formal decision to opt-out of the polity, the IRA finally brought the civil war to an end. In a message to republicans accompanying the order to 'dump arms' in May 1923, Éamon de Valera declared: 'military victory must be allowed to rest for the moment with those who have destroyed the Republic. Other means must be sought to safeguard the nation's right.'[13] The long war of words had just begun.

REMEMBERING

How have these formative events been remembered? That the Irish Free State emerged from a tainted treaty, which negated the republic proclaimed in 1919 and triggered a bitter civil war, explains why Ireland remains one of few states without an independence day. A century on, continuing sensitivities around the question of when Irish statehood began can be discerned from the circumspect formulation offered by the Expert Advisory Group on Centenary Commemorations:

> Unlike the United States of America, the independence initially proclaimed did not coincide in terms of extent or status with the state that emerged post conflict. The transfer of power took place over the course of 1922, beginning with the handing over of Dublin Castle on 16th January 1922 and ending with the formal coming into being of the Irish Free State on 6th December 1922, in the midst of civil war. There is unbroken political continuity with the Irish State that exists today, notwithstanding many important transformations since. There is another, even longer, institutional continuity going back to January 1919—the existence of the Dáil, which is the link between the revolution and the state and is, in a real sense, the founder of the state.[14]

A crisis of legitimacy was evident from the outset. Pro-treatyites never convincingly demonstrated that the new state embodied, as W.T. Cosgrave claimed, an 'almost unlimited measure of freedom and independence'.[15] The first duty of deputies at the inauguration of the Irish Free State parliament was to swear an oath to the British monarch, symbolising, for many, a humiliating subordination to empire. Foreshadowing de Valera's belated pragmatism, the Labour party leader Tom Johnson protested that the Treaty's terms 'are accepted by us, as they are accepted by the people generally, under protest, having been imposed upon Ireland by the threat of superior force'.[16]

The legitimacy of the state was further tarnished by the brutality of the civil war fought to preserve it. Although their role in founding the state, and defending it from republican violence, would become an important part of their political identity,[17] treatyite politicians proved more reticent than their opponents in commemorating the civil war. Dedicated to Griffith, Collins and O'Higgins, the dilapidated Leinster Lawn Cenotaph symbolised a wider neglect of the treatyite dead.[18] Remembering the civil war proved less useful for politicians seeking to legitimise the state than for their anti-Treaty opponents, for whom it provided a rallying cause and a refuge from demoralisation.

Forgetting, as the Expert Advisory Group has noted, offered one response to the challenges of remembering: 'there was nothing ignoble in the many silences that followed the Irish civil war—they were a better alternative to simplistic, polarised narratives and myth-making'.[19] The general amnesty introduced in 1924, however, was intended to indemnify the state from accountability for crimes committed in its name rather than to facilitate reconciliation.[20] With the civil war recalled, even by its victors, as a source of disillusionment, and the gradual abandonment of Collins's vision of the Treaty as a 'stepping stone' to full independence, the legacy of the Easter Rising appeared to offer greater potential to construct a unifying identity for the new state. In contrast to the legalistic text of the Treaty, which codified the state's formal links to the empire, the 1916 Proclamation's idealistic rhetoric symbolised the emancipatory potential of independence.[21] Boycotted by anti-Treaty republicans, however, ceremonies marking the events of 1916 would form part of the 'chronicle of embarrassment' that was political commemoration in the Irish Free State.[22]

Faced with similar challenges, state-builders in Northern Ireland adopted much the same commemorative strategies. The pre-war struggle against Home Rule, centring on a foundational declaration that rivalled the Proclamation—the Ulster Covenant—offered a more usable history on which to focus than the pragmatic calculations that saw unionists in six Ulster counties prioritise their interests above those of kith and kin in the rest of the province and throughout the rest of the island. Moreover, partition—a process rather than an event—had, by 1922, not concluded, causing ongoing uncertainty about the future of the Northern Ireland state. Like their southern republican counterparts, northern unionists also identified their state with a mythologised blood sacrifice in 1916, rather than with the less heroic violence that determined its actual formation.[23] Remembrance of the Battle of the Somme, rooted in Orange rituals, conflated Northern Irish citizenship with loyalty to Britain and to Ulster's Protestant heritage, eliding the awkward presence of the territory's large Catholic minority. The unveiling of First World War memorials peaked in Northern Ireland in 1922: 'it was these memorials, as opposed to any attempt to commemorate the birth of the state' that provided the focus of that state's foundational rituals.[24]

Two collective memories of state-formation emerged in Northern Ireland: a unionist narrative of a state under siege that preserved Ulster for Britain and empire, and a nationalist communal memory centred on the violence known as the 'Belfast Pogrom'. The collapse of the northern IRA, many of whose members fled south, and a sense of abandonment by the Irish Free State ensured that 1922 was recalled by northern Catholics as a traumatic year. On both sides of the border, violence complicated official remembrance of state formation. Atrocities such as the killing by policemen of members of the McMahon family in north Belfast (24 March 1922)—and the massacre of Protestants in Bandon Valley (26–28 April) and Altnaveigh (17 June) by republicans—could not easily be reconciled with the narratives of sacrifice promoted by both states. Nor could draconian methods such as internment, floggings and executions, which demonstrated greater ruthlessness by the leaders of the new states than that shown by their British predecessors.

Following the quashing of the Boundary Commission in 1925, which left intact the existing Irish border despite its patent oddities, neither state would seek to address the flaws of the 1922 settlement for almost half a century. Although frequently instrumentalised for political purposes on both sides of the border, partition itself was rarely memorialised. Despite 'its profound impact on the shape of modern Ireland', Robert Lynch notes, 'there are no monuments to partition, only those which reflect other state-sponsored narratives of revolution and resistance'.[25] Partition may have facilitated the establishment of Northern Ireland, but there was little appetite to commemorate a border that cut across unionist and Protestant communities and institutions, including the Orange Order and the Protestant Churches, as indiscriminately as Catholic and nationalist ones. A century on, sensitivities remain acute on both sides of the border, as demonstrated by the controversy arising from President Higgins's decision not to attend a religious service marking the centenary of partition.

The election of Fianna Fáil in 1932 was followed by de Valera's constitutional reforms, which swiftly dismantled the unlamented Free State. The enduring nature of the divisions of 1922, it became apparent, owed something to the small differences between both sides. If de Valera was the man who treatyite politicians could never forgive, anti-Treaty attitudes to the Irish Free State were complicated by an awareness that the sovereignty skilfully advanced by de Valera built on the solid foundations laid by his predecessors. Fianna Fáil's electoral dominance from 1932, however, ensured that the achievements of 1922 were overlooked. As the political correspondent of *The Irish Times* observed when de Valera chose not to mark the Treaty's twenty-fifth anniversary in 1946: 'the fact that the Oireachtas is able to assemble in Leinster House and direct the government of the country stems essentially from the Treaty'. Little had changed by 1971 when the refusal of Taoiseach Jack Lynch to commemorate the Treaty's fiftieth anniversary was denounced by the opposition as 'pigmy-minded pettiness'.[26]

Overleaf: Cartoon by O'Raghallaigh depicting how British prime minister David Lloyd George threatened force to secure Irish acceptance of the Anglo-Irish Treaty.

In recent decades, as an increasingly liberal and prosperous Irish state embraced a long-postponed modernity, the memory of 1922 has been tainted by a growing belief that independence fell short of the emancipatory ideals of the revolution. Ken Loach's influential film, *The wind that shakes the barley* (2006), vividly depicts 1922 as a wrong turn that saw British rule replaced by home-grown forms of repression. Michael Moran, the disillusioned protagonist of John McGahern's powerful 1990 novel *Amongst women*, reflected angrily on the outcome of his fight for freedom:

> what did we get for it? A country, if you'd believe them. Some of our own johnnies in the top jobs instead of a few Englishmen. More than half my own family work in England. What was it all for? The whole thing was a cod.[27]

In an earlier era, the miserable childhood evoked by Frank McCourt's 1996 memoir *Angela's ashes*—'the poverty; the shiftless loquacious alcoholic father; the pious defeated mother moaning by the fire; pompous priests; bullying schoolmasters; the English and the terrible things they did to us for eight hundred long years'—would have met with censorship rather than popular acclaim.[28] Grounded more in contemporary perspectives than the values of the revolutionary era, these cultural critiques nonetheless articulated uncomfortable truths, which historians were slower to record, and politicians and the public to concede, about the limits of liberty achieved in 1922.

How the Trea

Read "The R

y was Signed

A CHRONICLE OF DISAPPOINTMENT?

Consigned to a forgetful public remembrance (explored by Guy Beiner in the epilogue to this volume), the formative events of 1922 were also neglected by historians. Compared to that dealing with the struggle for independence, a much smaller body of work has analysed state-building, partition and civil war. The limited scholarship focusing on Ulster, whereby only in recent years has the role of the IRA been analysed, is particularly striking.[29] The roots of this neglect date back to 1922. Northern republicans, unlike their southern counterparts, were not keen to recollect a struggle that ended in failure and loss. In contrast to the southern state, which established the Bureau of Military History to preserve republican testimony, the northern state made little effort to record loyalist experiences of northern state-formation. The history of the Ulster Special Constabulary remains largely unwritten, while its archive in the Public Record Office of Northern Ireland is still closed to the public.[30]

Unionists faced the challenging task of fashioning a narrative to legitimise a state they had never sought. Mirroring nationalist historiography, which conflated the 'story of Ireland' with the dispossession and persecution experienced by Catholics since early-modern colonisation, popular unionist histories such as Ronald McNeill's *Ulster's stand for Union* (1922) depicted Northern Ireland as the inevitable consequence of the Ulster Plantation, which laid the cultural and political foundations for 'two nations in Ireland'.[31] By the late 1920s, this 'unenviable' state-building project was bolstered by geographers, archaeologists, folklorists and historians at the Queen's University of Belfast, who

> set to work constructing a distinctive six-county Ulster identity, seeking to give a more scientific, academic solidity to a boundary that ironically was one of the most artificial in the history of partition. The many histories of Ulster published in the wake of partition, bypassed the turmoil, violence and artificiality of the recently drawn border, imagining instead permanence and inevitability.[32]

Such assertions of Ulster distinctiveness often sat uneasily with the desire of unionist politicians to depict Northern Ireland as an integral part of the United Kingdom—as British as Finchley, to paraphrase a later Conservative prime minister.

From the late 1970s, scholarly accounts of northern state-formation were less forgiving. Setting the tone for much that followed, the first archival study of the establishment of Northern Ireland was titled *The factory of grievances*. Although its author was disposed favourably to partition at the outset of his research, the title reflects his 'distaste and despair' on completing his work.[33] With few exceptions, such as the revealingly-titled *A state under siege*,[34] accounts of northern state-formation emphasise sectarian violence and the politics of discrimination, locating the roots of the later Troubles in the failure of devolution.[35]

The early historiography of the Irish state was similarly grounded in division and disappointment. Much of it was written by revolutionary veterans who sought to attribute blame for the civil war. There was plenty to go round. P.S. O'Hegarty's influential account, *The victory of Sinn Féin*, published in 1924, argued that a zealous republican elite had prioritised abstract ideals over the interests of the Irish people. The national fall from grace that followed from the unnecessary use of violence after Easter 1916 had exposed the Irish as 'an uncivilised people with savage instincts'.[36] The opposing interpretation, exemplified by Dorothy Macardle's *The Irish republic* (1938), argued that the threat of British violence, and the treatyite betrayal of the democratic mandate for the republic achieved in 1918, were responsible for the civil war.[37]

The first wave of scholarly publications appearing in the 1970s broadly endorsed treatyite interpretations. F.S.L. Lyons's influential *Ireland since the Famine* described Cumann na nGaedheal's establishment of sound administration in the midst of civil war as 'an astonishing performance'.[38] Joseph Curran's *The birth of the Irish Free State, 1921–23* also emphasised the party's state-building achievements, questioning its rivals' democratic credentials: the civil war, Curran suggested, determined whether the new state would 'be ruled by the people or by a revolutionary junta'.[39] The next decades saw the emergence of a scholarly consensus that treatyite ruthlessness had been necessary to preserve democracy in 1922.[40] The civil war was attributed not merely to the Treaty split, but to a broader clash between modern, constitutionally minded pragmatists and elitist separatists.[41] For Joe Lee, the Treaty was 'the occasion, not the cause' of the civil war: 'The cause was the basic conflict in nationalist doctrine between majority right and divine right'.[42] In *1922: the birth of Irish democracy*, the most robust articulation of this interpretation, Tom Garvin argued that the civil war marked the triumph of 'the democratic impulse in Irish life' over 'the cult of the virtuous minority'.[43]

This historiographical consensus reflected the strong democratic credentials of the pro-Treaty position, endorsed as it was by a majority of the Cabinet, the Dáil and the electorate in 1922. But, given that de Valera had proved that Collins was right to argue that the Treaty could lead to full independence, it was also shaped by hindsight. More contentiously, sympathetic accounts of the treatyite position were influenced by contemporary sensitivities as a new generation of republicans set about killing for the republic. In weighing competing interpretations of revolutionary violence, Ronan Fanning subsequently reflected, 'Political imperatives prevailed, as they invariably do, over historical truth in the revisionist debate'.[44] By exaggerating treatyite democratic credentials, and eliding the British origins of the independent state, the historian John Regan charged that this 'statist historiography' advocated a democratic 'foundation myth' to serve the Irish political establishment's needs, re-orientating 'its nationalism away from irredentism, towards the conscious accommodation of partition'.[45]

The idea of 1922 as the triumph of Irish democracy has now given way to more nuanced interpretations. Although acknowledging that the Treaty did expose ideological divisions between rival traditions within Sinn Féin, Bill Kissane has argued that there was nothing inevitable about the civil war, which was brought about by British coercion rather than antidemocratic republicanism. Anti-treatyites had argued not that the Irish people had no right to accept the Treaty, but that they had the right to do so free from the threat of British violence. The conflict, in this reading, represents a clash between the irreconcilable rights of self-determination and majority rule rather than a struggle between opposing mentalities. Disturbing revelations, explored in this book, about the conduct of the civil war also undermined interpretations of the conflict as a clash between the forces of law and order and an unaccountable minority.[46] Whereas 1922 may not be remembered as his finest year, de Valera's subsequent actions were pivotal to the consolidation of democracy in the 1930s when Ireland became one of few post-war 'successor states' to avoid dictatorship.

An increasing emphasis on the state's conservatism has also taken some of the gloss off the legacy of 1922. Charles Townshend, for example, characterised the Irish Free State's replacement of the republican Dáil courts with a reversion to British legal principles as embodying 'a deeply counter-revolutionary impulse'.[47] Noting 'the sharply conservative aftermath of the revolution', Roy Foster has outlined how, after the revolution, 'nascent ideas of certain kinds of liberation were aggressively subordinated to the national project of restabilization (and clericalization)'.[48] In contrast, Anne Dolan has queried how disappointment has come to pervade accounts of early independence:

> Book after book describes a flat, narrow place that lost the courage of its own revolution's convictions, a cruel, timid place that was hard on its weakest and too much in thrall to those who preached right from wrong.[49]

To what extent, she asks, does this new scholarly consensus reflect frustration with the failure of independence to live up to contemporary expectations? 'As religious and institutional scandals made headlines this was...a history that an Irish public was willing at last to hear.'[50] Whatever their shortcomings, it seems fair to acknowledge that the state-builders of 1922 saw themselves as implementing revolutionary ideals as they understood them, and that many politicians and people on both sides of the Treaty divide shared conservative values that now elicit less admiration.

STORIES OF THE OTHER: NEW PERSPECTIVES

The official narratives of the revolutionary era, reinforcing the polarisation resulting from a decade of violence, served the needs of the majoritarian states that emerged from that conflict. The politics of partition, and of state-building, reified narrow conceptions of identity that failed to acknowledge the many 'varieties of Irishness' in existence.[51] Shaped by very different political circumstances, the pluralistic remembrance that characterises the current Decade of Centenaries has retrieved a broader range of historical experiences. Intended to 'foster deeper mutual understanding among people from different traditions on the island of Ireland', the Irish state's 'broad and inclusive' centenary commemorative programme has foregrounded social conditions, the Irish abroad, unionism, constitutional nationalism, and the First World War, alongside the republican perspectives that dominated previous anniversaries.[52] Even in Northern Ireland, where the memory of political violence retains the capacity to destabilise, the powersharing Executive has expressed (at least rhetorical) support for the commemorative principles of 'mutual respect, inclusiveness and reconciliation' in its New Decade, New Approach deal (2020).

This openness to reconsidering aspects of the past reflects broader impulses than instrumentalist state initiatives and post-conflict politics, not least the erosion of Catholicism as the most visible marker of Irish identity. The idea that the recent coalition between Fine Gael and Fianna Fáil marked the death of civil war politics exaggerates the divisive legacy of a conflict that had passed beyond living memory. The liberalisation of Irish society, by generating new identities, has created an appetite for stories that reshape how the past is understood by the public. The remarkable visibility of the role of revolutionary women,[53] among other novel aspects of the centenary commemorations of the Easter Rising in 2016, illustrates how changing social values continue to find expression through retellings of the national story to a degree that is unusual among modern states. Complicating the narrative, the opening of new archives, the democratisation of sources through digitisation, and the dissemination of scholarly research have, if belatedly, contributed to 'a more relaxed and inclusive definition of Irishness, and a less constricted view of Irish history'.[54]

In that spirit, this book explores 1922 in a manner intended to reflect greater awareness of the diversity of Irish experiences foregrounded by the Decade of Centenaries. Its fifty contributors, who differ in their approaches and interpretations, were asked to identify particular episodes that would make accessible some of the new interpretations of this era that have resulted from recent scholarship. Spanning cultural studies, heritage, history, design, film, gender, law, literature, memory, political science, and visual culture, their expertise grounds analysis of the political transformation of Ireland within its broad social, economic and cultural contexts. Innovative methodologies, such as those applied in the history of emotions, postcolonialism, and gender analysis, shed new light on familiar topics, as does the rich selection of accompanying illustrations, which enable consideration of visual and material culture alongside archival sources.

Political change is assessed in this book not only through consideration of landmark events such as the Treaty split or the outbreak of the civil war, but also by evaluating how these were moulded by social factors such as class and gender. In addition to assassinations, executions, hunger strikes and internment, overlooked forms of coercion—including arson, abduction and forced haircutting—that are less neatly categorised as political violence are considered. Forms of collective resistance, such as land agitation or the filling in of trenched border roads, highlight the radical impulses that often shaped local responses to revolution. Numerous essays illustrate poignantly how political violence was heavily mediated by gender, age, religion and class (exemplified by the targeting of wealthy landowners and prominent businessmen or—more disproportionately—the poor and marginal). Approximately 96% of the dead of the Irish revolution were male, while most combatants were aged in their late teens or early twenties when they died. Violence in Belfast, the most chaotic Irish city throughout 1922, was distinguished both by its high proportion of civilian fatalities and sectarian intercommunal character.[55] The complex and tragic circumstances surrounding individual deaths, and their traumatic impact, frequently challenge simplistic political narratives.

Activists from women's organisations, peace movements and other less well-remembered causes feature here alongside better-known politicians and gunmen. The prominence of subsequently marginalised figures, such as Mary MacSwiney, demonstrates how female activists played a more important role than was later acknowledged by accounts of the era shaped by post-revolutionary conservatism. The experiences of loyalists, disbanded policemen and religious minorities on both sides of the border, for whom political change represented disruption or terror rather than liberation, are also considered.

Everyday, and even mundane, experiences—such as shopping, trading, praying and playing—feature alongside the drama of high politics, which, then as now, often impacted on ordinary lives in unwelcome ways. The importance of cultural and economic thought, propaganda and masculinity in shaping the militaristic political discourses of 1922 receive attention. The striking extent to which the political divisions of the era were articulated in gendered, moralistic and exclusivist language would have implications for the construction of citizenship on both sides of the border.

Whether elevating or erasing traditions, revolution and independence reshaped Irish identities and even cultural and physical landscapes. Several contributors analyse how state-builders—seeking to create imagined communities as well as gaining the assent of existing ones—mobilised culture, whether through the promotion of emblems, symbols and statues; the patronage of artists; or the censorship of their work. The religious and political binaries constructed by the two Irish states extended to their opposing preferences for urban and rural imagery. Despite the role played by William Conor, John Lavery and W.B. Yeats in fashioning an iconography for the new regimes, most writers, musicians and artists did not find post-revolutionary Ireland a congenial environment for creative

endeavour. This was particularly the case in the Irish Free State, where the censorious mentality that would scar Irish cultural life was evident by 1922. Many Irish writers and intellectuals, like vast numbers of people from ordinary backgrounds, consequently chose to live elsewhere. The exodus included many of the revolution's losers on both sides of the border: a broad category ranging from well-heeled landowners, and other loyalist 'refugees', to servants of the Crown, northern republicans, and anti-Treaty veterans. Their fate provoked little concern on either side of the Irish sea: 'Minorities must be left to stew in their own juice', Churchill concluded, reflecting the 'brutal realpolitik' of the times.[56]

A large influx of Catholic refugees from Belfast had arrived in Dublin by June 1922. Many were housed in unionist-owned properties, such as the Freemasons' Hall, that were commandeered by the anti-Treaty IRA.

Reflecting a shift towards transnational and global perspectives that has characterised recent research on modern Ireland, this book addresses the experiences of these and other Irish people beyond the island.[57] The revolution witnessed an unprecedented mobilisation of the Irish diaspora, which met with considerable success in terms of fund-raising, diplomacy and propaganda. The fleeting prominence of the Irish question not only impacted profoundly on the lives and identities of Irish people across America and the British empire, it also generated international links with anti-imperial and other radical activists. Consequently, the confusion and demoralisation resulting from the splintering of republican unity in 1922 was not confined to the island; one of the civil war's less-recognised consequences was the diminished salience of Irish identity and activism among the diaspora.

The mosaic resulting from the fifty snapshots of Irish life gathered here does not lend itself to the kind of master narratives or definitive judgements associated with early accounts of independence. Representing 'the Irish revolution as a multilayered story, one that can be accessed from many different perspectives', President Michael D. Higgins has observed, 'challenges us to remember the events of a hundred years ago with an openness to the voices and stories of those we might constitute as "the other", the stranger, the enemy of yesterday.'[58] For contemporaries, 1922 marked something more disorienting and unfathomable than the end of the revolution, the dawn of a conservative era, or some other retrospectively imposed interpretation. For some, the momentous political events of the year barely intruded into more pressing daily concerns. Whether it be enmity, disappointment or hope, this book aims to convey something of the diverse emotions experienced by those who lived through one of Ireland's most tumultuous years.

by Darragh Gannon and Fearghal McGarry

NOTES

[1] Martin Maguire, *The civil service and the revolution in Ireland, 1912–38. 'Shaking the blood-stained hand of Mr Collins'* (Manchester, 2008), 127–8.

[2] Robert Lynch, *The partition of Ireland 1918–1925* (Cambridge, 2019), 134–6.

[3] *The Irish Times*, 7 December 1922.

[4] Michael Hopkinson (ed.), *Frank Henderson's Easter Rising. Recollections of a Dublin Volunteer* (Cork, 1998), 8.

[5] Military Archives, Bureau of Military History, witness statement 939, Ernest Blythe, 192.

[6] Lynch, *Partition*, 138.

[7] Northern Ireland, a devolved UK jurisdiction rather than a state, is described here as a state for reasons of brevity.

[8] *Dáil debates*, vol. 2, no. 3 (8 December 1922), 'Debate on Mountjoy executions'; available at: www.oireachtas.ie/en/debates/ (8 April 2021).

[9] David Hogan [Frank Gallagher], *The four glorious years* (Dublin, 1953), 2.

[10] *Irish Independent*, 26 April 1922.

[11] Quoted in Michael Hopkinson, *Green against green: the Irish Civil War* (Dublin, 1988), 52.

[12] Niall Harrington, cited in *The Ballyseedy massacre* (RTÉ, 1997).

[13] Quoted in Charles Townshend, *The Republic: the fight for Irish independence* (London, 2013), 447.

[14] Expert Advisory Group on Centenary Commemorations, *Guidance from the Expert Advisory Group on Commemorations to support the state's approach to the remembrance of significant historical events over the remainder of the decade of centenaries* (Dublin, 2019), 13.

[15] *Dáil debates*, vol. 2, no. 1 (6 December 1922), 'Statement by the president'; available at: www.oireachtas.ie/en/debates/.

[16] *Dáil debates*, vol. 2, no. 1 (6 December 1922), 'Údarás ó Sheanascal an tSaorstát'; available at: www.oireachtas.ie/en/debates/.

[17] Stephen Collins and Ciara Meehan, *Saving the state: Fine Gael from Collins to Varadkar* (Dublin, 2020).

[18] Anne Dolan, *Commemorating the Irish civil war: history and memory, 1923–2000* (Cambridge, 2003).

[19] Expert Advisory Group, *Guidance*, 11.

[20] *Seanad Éireann debate*, vol. 3, no. 13 (10 July 1924), 'Indemnity Bill (1924), Second stage; available at: www.oireachtas.ie/en/debates/.

[21] Darragh Gannon, *Proclaiming a republic. Ireland, 1916 and the National Collection* (Dublin, 2016), 1–2.

[22] David Fitzpatrick, 'Commemoration in the Irish Free State: a chronicle of embarrassment', in Ian McBride (ed.), *History and memory in modern Ireland* (Cambridge, 2001), 184–203.

[23] Richard Grayson and Fearghal McGarry (eds), *Remembering 1916: the Easter Rising, the Somme and the politics of memory in Ireland* (Cambridge, 2016).

[24] Keith Jeffery, *Ireland and the Great War* (Cambridge, 2000), 131–4. Lynch, *Partition*, 223.

[25] Lynch, *Partition*, 223.

[26] Diarmaid Ferriter, 'Birth of a Nation: the Treaty that transformed Ireland', *The Irish Times*, 3 December 2011.

[27] John McGahern, *Amongst women* (London, 1990), 5.

[28] Frank McCourt, *Angela's ashes* (New York, 1996).

[29] The first comprehensive account was Robert Lynch's *The northern IRA and the early years of partition, 1920–1922* (Dublin, 2006).

[30] Christopher Magill's *Political conflict in East Ulster, 1920–22* (Woodbridge, 2020) is the first major study to benefit from partial access to the Ulster Special Constabulary archive.

[31] Ronald McNeill, *Ulster's stand for Union* (London, 1922), 2.

[32] Lynch, *Partition*, 221.

[33] Patrick Buckland, *The factory of grievances: devolved government in Northern Ireland, 1921–1939* (Dublin, 1979).

[34] Brian Follis, *A state under siege: the establishment of Northern Ireland, 1920–25* (Oxford, 1995).

[35] Susannah Riordan, 'Politics, economy, society: Northern Ireland, 1920–1939', in Thomas Bartlett (ed.), *The Cambridge history of Ireland*. Volume iv: *1800 to the present* (Cambridge, 2018), 296–98.

[36] P.S. O'Hegarty, *The victory of Sinn Féin* (Dublin, 1924; 2015 edn), 91.

[37] Dorothy Macardle, *The Irish republic* (London, 1937).

[38] F.S.L. Lyons, *Ireland since the Famine* (London, 1971; 1973 edn), 479.

[39] Joseph M. Curran, *The birth of the Irish Free State, 1921–1923* (Alabama, 1980), 280.

[40] This literature is surveyed in Bill Kissane, *The politics of the Irish Civil War* (Oxford, 2005), 202–30, and Jason Knirck, *Afterimage of the revolution. Cumann na nGaedheal and Irish politics, 1922–1932* (Madison, WI, 2014), 6–19.

[41] Jeffrey Prager, *Building democracy in Ireland* (Cambridge, 1986).

[42] J.J. Lee, *Ireland 1912–1985. Politics and society* (Cambridge, 1989), 67.

[43] Tom Garvin, *1922: the birth of Irish democracy* (Dublin, 1996).

[44] Ronan Fanning, *Fatal path. British government and Irish revolution 1910–1922* (London, 2013), 5.

[45] John Regan, 'Southern Irish nationalism as a historical problem', *Historical Journal* 50(1) (2007), 197–223: 197.

[46] Kissane, *Irish civil war*, 177–201.

[47] Charles Townshend, 'Historiography: telling the Irish revolution', in Joost Augusteijn, *The Irish revolution, 1913–1923* (Basingstoke, 2002), 1–16: 7.

[48] R.F. Foster, *Vivid faces. The revolutionary generation in Ireland 1890–1923* (London, 2014), 117.

[49] Anne Dolan, 'Politics, economy and society in the Irish Free State, 1922–1939, in Bartlett (ed.), *Cambridge history of Ireland*, vol. iv, 323–48: 323.

[50] Dolan, 'Politics, economy and society', 330.

[51] R.F. Foster, 'Varieties of Irishness', in Maurna Crozier (ed.), *Cultural traditions in Northern Ireland* (Belfast, 1989), 5–24.

[52] Fearghal McGarry, *The Rising. Ireland: Easter 1916* (Oxford, 2010), v–xv.

[53] Oona Frawley (ed), *Women and the Decade of Commemorations* (Bloomington, IN, 2021).

[54] R.F. Foster, *Modern Ireland. 1600–1972* (London, 1988), 596.

[55] Eunan O'Halpin and Daithí Ó Corráin, *The dead of the Irish revolution* (New Haven, 2020), 12, 20, 18.

[56] Paul Bew, *Churchill and Ireland* (Oxford, 2016), 118.

[57] Patrick Mannion and Fearghal McGarry (eds), *The Irish revolution: a global history* (New York, 2022).

[58] Michael D. Higgins, 'Foreword', in John Crowley *et al.*, *Atlas of the Irish revolution* (Cork, 2017), xiii–xiv: xiv.

JANUARY

4 JANUARY 1922

THE TREATY DEBATES

THE POLITICS OF EMOTIONS

On 4 January 1922 the cool concrete façade of Earlsfort Terrace in Dublin concealed a pressure-cooker atmosphere as the debates over the ratification of the Anglo-Irish Treaty approached a conclusion. Seán O'Mahony, TD for Fermanagh and South Tyrone, made an emotional appeal to the 'youth of the Irish Republican Army' who, he declared, 'had proved themselves too straight, too true, too unselfish in their love and loyalty to the Republic to be decoyed from the path of honour, or righteousness and of duty', unlike those who, he claimed, 'live in trembling' and would 'bend the knee and sign their rights away'.[1] O'Mahony's intervention that day encapsulated key features of the Treaty debates: opening with a joke, prompting laughter, but moving swiftly to invoke strong emotions—love, loyalty, fear, betrayal—and ending with a round of applause. These debates of course have long featured as a climactic point in the history of the Irish revolution: the moment when the fraternal camaraderie of the republican movement was fractured, ushering in the bitterness and divisions of the civil war. An 'avalanche of oratory' akin to O'Mahony's was unleashed, in support of and against the proposed Treaty.[2]

The contours of the debate have attracted sustained historiographical attention, not least elsewhere in this volume, with particular attention paid to the weighing of the constitutional arguments on either side, the gendered dynamics and, latterly, the class dimensions of the Treaty split.[3] But alongside

Above and opposite: Crowds gather at Earlsfort Terrace as the Dáil debates the Anglo-Irish Treaty, January 1922.

questions of constitutional integrity and competing conceptions of republican liberty, the most oft-noted feature of the Treaty debates was the tenor of the exchanges. The mood at the lecture halls at University Buildings was frequently underlined, from the cheers of the waiting crowd outside as deputies entered, to the tension, gravity and gloom that progressively engulfed the debates themselves. These debates unfolded in a curious mixture of publicity and privacy: the public sessions were avidly reported in the national and provincial press, with particular attention paid to the tone and mood of the chamber, while even the comings and goings to the closed sessions were closely followed for hints of the debates' progress. The emotional register of the Treaty debates thus formed a significant part of how the Irish public learned about the emerging split in the republican movement.

Despite the bitterness, which was the abiding memory of the debates, the emotion most frequently expressed in the debates themselves was love—of

Ireland, and of each other. Patriotic flourishes coloured many of the contributions. Seán Mac Eoin declared:

> I say I am an extremist, but it means that I have an extreme love of my country. It was love of my country that made me and every other Irishman take up arms to defend her. It was love of my country that made me ready, and every other Irishman ready, to die for her if necessary.[4]

Mary MacSwiney affirmed, 'I love my people, every single one of them; I love the country, and I have faith in the people.' Declarations of love, friendship and admiration for each other were also evident: Arthur Griffith, anxious to minimise the depth of the impending split after the results of the vote on the Treaty were known, emphasised that 'there is scarcely a man I have ever met in my life that I have more love and respect for than President de Valera', while Collins emphasised de Valera's 'position in my heart'.

Successive speakers invoked patriots of the past—the sacred trio of Tone, Mitchel, Davis—and as the urge grew to maintain unity in the face of the rapidly deepening fissures, the *bona fides* of both sides of the divide were emphasised: Éamonn Duggan underlined that 'there is no monopoly of patriotism on either side of this house'. This rattling of the bones of the patriot dead grew more noisy as recent martyrs were invoked, largely in favour of rejecting the Treaty. Piaras Béaslaí enlisted his 'dearest friend Seán MacDiarmada [who] loved Ireland just as Michael Collins and Arthur Griffith love Ireland'. Kathleen Clarke spoke of her last visit to her husband in Kilmainham in (for her) unusually emotional terms:

> though sorrow was in my heart, I gloried in him, and I have gloried in the men who have carried on the fight since; every one of them. I believe that even if they take a wrong turn now they will be brave enough to turn back when they discover it. I have sorrow in my heart now, but I don't despair; I never shall.[5]

Margaret Pearse ventriloquised her son Patrick, admitting that 'the Black and Tans alone would not frighten me as much as if I accepted that Treaty: because I feel in my heart—and I would not say it only I feel it—that the ghosts of my sons would haunt me.'[6]

More negative emotions were also openly expressed. Daniel O'Rourke declared he would 'yield to no man in his hatred of British oppression' (before voting in favour of acceptance); Constance Markievicz 'despised' what she saw as the Treaty's attempt to entrench privilege in the so-called Free State; while Seán T. O'Kelly underlined the 'accursed union...which we shall never cease to detest and to loathe'. Fear was present too: it stalked the chamber. The prospect of a split and of sundering the political community which had been forged through the revolutionary process was uppermost in deputies' minds and was a recurrent if implicit emotion throughout the debates. Joseph McBride voiced the precedent many must have been thinking of—'the foul implications and the degradation of the Parnell split'—while another O'Rourke stressed he was 'quite prepared to do anything for unity because the curse of this country has been disunion.' Éamon de Valera, in one of several highly emotive outbursts, denounced his political opponents as 'trying to make out that I am trying to split the country...to put on me...to represent me as trying to prevent unity'. Some accused their opponents of being motivated by fear—Liam Mellows, a staunch anti-treatyite, claimed that 'it is not the will of the people but the fear of the people' that propelled the pro-treaty arguments—while others were adamant that the people in Ireland were steadfast and fearless in spite of the terror that was waged against them.

The lecture hall at Earlsfort Terrace was also a performative space: deputies used and transgressed the formalities of parliamentary procedure to reinforce the emotional weight of their arguments. In this heightened atmosphere, feelings bubbled over and passions ran high. Reading the extremely well-detailed transcript of the debates, the heated nature of the exchanges is immediately apparent, as well as the degree to which the Dáil transcribers wished to preserve the emotional tenor of the Great Debate. There were multiple bursts of applause, surprisingly frequent breaks of laughter, cheers and counter-cheers, cries of 'hear-hear' and 'No!'. This fevered emotional environment also was reflected in the tenor of many of the speeches. The bitterness and anger has been much commented upon: notably Brugha's railing against Collins, in which clearly his personal dislike bled into his political opposition, or Arthur Griffith's tetchy and bad-tempered responses throughout, encapsulated in his dismissal of Erskine Childers as a 'damned Englishman'. De Valera made lengthy statements detailing his outrage, and famously broke down in his statement to the Dáil after the Treaty was narrowly accepted. Michael Collins, de Valera's chief political opponent, is equally interesting in terms of his emotional responses to the heated and frequently highly personalised debates; as Jason Knirck has pointed out, Collins tended to favour multiple sarcastic, offhand interjections, rather than lengthy defences of his own position.

Todd Andrews, a junior IRA officer watching the final vote from the doorway of the Council chamber, noted that the result was received with a mixture of 'triumph, grief and worry'.[7] De Búrca gave more colour to the 'awful scene', with women weeping openly and men 'trying to restrain their tears'.[8] A feature of the disintegration of republican unity in the months leading up to the outbreak of civil war is the spilling over into the public sphere of the emotional tenor of these Treaty debates—recrimination, anger, accusations of bad faith, pragmatism, and hope. This complex bundle of emotions can all be charted in the public statements made by both sides as Ireland slid towards fraternal conflict. Assessing the Treaty debates as a decisive moment in the emotional history of the Irish revolution thus opens up new ways of thinking about how emotions were expressed and instrumentalised as a means to bolster or undermine political arguments throughout the revolutionary period.

by Caoimhe Nic Dháibhéid

FURTHER READING

Padraig de Búrca and John Boyle, *Free State or Republic? Pen pictures of the historic treaty session of Dáil Éireann* (Dublin, 1922)

Jason Knirck, *Imagining Ireland's independence: the debates over the Anglo-Irish Treaty of 1921* (Plymouth, 2006)

Liam Weeks and Mícheál Ó Fathartaigh (eds), *The Treaty: debating and establishing the Irish state* (Newbridge, 2018)

NOTES

[1] Unless otherwise noted, quotations are taken from the Dáil debates on the Anglo-Irish Treaty; see, *Dáil debates*, vol. T, no. 2 to vol. T, no. 14, 'Debate on Treaty' (14 December 1921 to 6 January 1922); available at: www.oireachtas.ie/en/debates/. For O'Mahony's contribution on 4 January, see vol. T, no. 11; available at: www.oireachtas.ie/en/debates/debate/dail/1922-01-04/2/ (12 April 2021).
[2] Padraig de Búrca and John Boyle, *Free State or Republic? Pen pictures of the historic Treaty session of Dáil Éireann* (Dublin, 1922), 51.
[3] See, especially Jason Knirck, *Imagining Ireland's independence: the debates over the Anglo-Irish Treaty of 1921* (Plymouth, 2006) and Liam Weeks and Mícheál Ó Fathartaigh (eds), *The Treaty: debating and establishing the Irish state* (Newbridge, 2018).
[4] *Dáil debates*, vol. T, no. 6, 'Debate on Treaty' (19 December 1921); available at: www.oireachtas.ie/en/debates/ (12 April 2021).
[5] *Dáil debates*, vol. T, no. 9, 'Debate on Treaty' (22 December 1921); available at: www.oireachtas.ie/en/debates/ (12 April 2021).
[6] *Dáil debates*, vol. T, no. 11, 'Debate on Treaty' (4 January 1922); available at: www.oireachtas.ie/en/debates/ (12 April 2021).
[7] C.S. Andrews, *Dublin made me* (Dublin, 2001 edn), 221.
[8] De Búrca and Boyle, *Free State or Republic*, 71.

7 JANUARY 1922

THE RATIFICATION OF THE ANGLO—IRISH TREATY

POLITICAL THOUGHT IN REVOLUTIONARY IRELAND

The 'Articles of Agreement for a Treaty between Great Britain and Ireland' were signed at Downing Street on 6 December 1921 by the British delegation along with five Irish representatives enjoying plenipotentiary status.[1] Before ratification, the terms of the treaty were debated in sessions of the second Dáil convened at Earlsfort Terrace in Dublin over fifteen days between 14 December 1921 and 7 January 1922. In the end, approval of the agreement passed by a margin of seven votes, though civil war rather than national concord ensued.

One of the most controversial issues—arrangements for Ulster—had at least provisionally been settled in advance of the debates by an agreement to provide for the establishment of a boundary commission that would decide on the character and viability of Ulster as partitioned following the creation of Northern Ireland in 1920. That left relations between Ireland and the empire as the principal issue in contention when delegates gathered. Most controversial was the maintenance of an oath of allegiance to the British Crown under article 4 of the Treaty, together with the retention by Britain of naval facilities in certain Irish ports as set out in the annex. Nonetheless, most contributors to the debates were agreed about one issue: the legitimacy and desirability of securing a republic. The only question was the means of achieving that objective. In entering into treaty negotiations with the British, the Irish side had implicitly conceded a measure of compromise. As Michael Collins himself put it: 'it was the acceptance of the invitation that formed the compromise'.[2] It remained to be established, however, what might have to be bargained away. After the settlement, since the immediate establishment of a republic was forlorn, the question was whether the plenipotentiaries had yielded too much.

The Dáil debates on the Treaty followed an intense period of intellectual contestation spanning over a decade in Ireland during which writers and publicists addressed a range of fundamental issues. These included the role of religion, economic relations, social structure, the character of the family, constitutional arrangements and the franchise.[3] Discussion was therefore certainly not narrowly focussed. Equally, it took many forms—from fine art and the handbill to the article and the monograph. Commentary about Ireland from outside the country resulted in some significant works, such as Louis François Alphonse Paul-Dubois's *L'Irlande contemporaine* (1907) and A.V. Dicey's *A fool's paradise* (1913). There were also notable studies by Irish thinkers: George Russell's 'Nationality and imperialism' (1901), Horace Plunkett's *Ireland in the new century* (1904), Arthur Griffith's *The resurrection of Hungary* (1904), D.P. Moran's *The philosophy of Irish Ireland* (1905), Alice Stopford Green's *Irish nationality* (1911), T.M. Kettle's *The open secret of Ireland* (1912), Erskine Childers's *The framework of home rule* (1911), Roger Casement's *The crime against Ireland* (1914), James Connolly's *Labour in Irish history* (1914), Robert Lynd's *Ireland a nation* (1919), Lyndsay Crawford's *The problem of Ulster* (1920), Stephen Gwynn's *The Irish situation* (1921) and Ronald McNeill's *Ulster's stand for union* (1922). In addition, numerous important pamphlets appeared and a considerable volume of journalism by, among others, Helena Molony, Patrick Pearse, Constance Markievicz, Hanna Sheehy Skeffington, Eoin MacNeill

THE STEPPING STONE.

DE VALERA: "You'll never do it, Mick—your costume's too tight."

and Louie Bennett. As the titles above suggest, the relationship between Britain and Ireland was a major concern. By extension, so too were constitutional structures and the question of national jurisdiction.[4]

These latter themes pervaded the fraught exchanges between TDs on the Treaty. While a large majority of the 124 protagonists in the Dáil remained faithful to the same goal, they divided on which concessions entailed defeat for their shared ambition. De Valera asserted on the opening day of proceedings that the 'honour of this nation, which is dear to us, is at stake'.[5] Indeed, the value of 'honour' was frequently invoked by TDs, suggesting that the dilemma involved fidelity to an ideal. Yet the real question was the extent to which deviation from that ideal threatened to undermine its integrity altogether. The achievement of a republic implied independence, although what this meant was subject to divergent interpretations. 'What I want, what the people of Ireland want, is not shadows but substances', remarked Seán Mac Eoin, seconding Arthur Griffith's motion in support of the Treaty.[6] But what exactly was the 'substance' of independence? Famously, for Michael Collins, it meant the freedom to achieve freedom: 'In my opinion it gives us freedom, not the ultimate freedom that all nations desire and develop to, but the freedom to achieve it.'[7]

De Valera likewise accepted that the negotiations could not have delivered 'freedom' in the sense of complete autonomy or an isolated republic. Yet, he believed, they could have brought about a form of imperial 'association' that was at least compatible with genuine self-government. De Valera spelt the details out in what was referred to as 'Document No. 2'. In it, he sketched a form of *external* association with the British Commonwealth that prioritised domestic autonomy and the right to self-defence. Erskine Childers advocated this potential set-up by urging: 'Establish that principle that authority in Ireland belongs solely to the Irish people, then make your association, and the rights of Ireland are safe.'[8] The oath of allegiance seemed to the opponents of the Treaty to undermine this basic principle.

Supporters of the Treaty had described what had been achieved as a form of 'dominion status', in accordance with article 1 of the Agreement. This was expected to place the Irish Free State on a par with Canada and Australia. Yet Childers was anxious to explode the analogy: Ireland was a small neighbour geographically bound to Britain, whereas Canada was a sizeable portion of a remote continent, amounting to an 'immense nation, absolutely unconquerable by England, and, what is even more important, attached to England by ties of blood'.[9] Two days later, in a speech that lasted over two and a half hours, Mary MacSwiney reiterated Childers's assessment, and proceeded to reaffirm what she thought of as the fundamental republican position: she, like her comrades, stood on 'principle', proclaiming an essentially 'spiritual ideal'.[10] She observed that the Treaty represented the culmination of Griffith's ambitions, although for Collins it remained only a stepping-stone. In either case, she refused to impugn her opponents' honour, although she did question their intelligence and their command of history. It had always, she claimed, been a minority who redeemed the soul of the nation, as demonstrated by the 1916 Rising. The will of that minority could never be broken, for even if England should exterminate 'the men, women and children of this generation, the blades of grass, dyed with their blood, will rise, like the dragon's teeth of old, into armed men and the fight will begin in the next generation'.[11]

Yet it transpired that the fundamental truths of republican doctrine were at the same time represented by other voices articulating divergent programmes. For Constance Markievicz, along with MacSwiney, this had been a fight against the fleshpots of temptation. Yet, while the fundamental problem for MacSwiney had been the 'rapacious and material Empire' of the British, for Markievicz it was capitalist exploitation, which called for the establishment of a 'co-operative commonwealth'.[12] Along with its establishment would come the abolition of luxury, as well as an end to the 'divorce laws of the English nation'.[13] Yet even MacSwiney's most ardent antagonists affirmed as a fact what she claimed as an aspiration: under the Treaty itself, Liam de Róiste insisted, 'The right of Ireland to national freedom is recognised'.[14]

To view the Treaty debates as driven by radically competing ideals is largely mistaken. Instead, divisions were fomented by rival strategies, whose partisans presented them as incompatible principles. '[W]e Republicans are going to carry out this fight', announced MacSwiney. '[D]eath is preferable to dishonour', Markievicz declared. The treatyites, in due course, opted to join battle.

by Richard Bourke

FURTHER READING

Frank Gallagher, *The Anglo-Irish Treaty* (London, 1965)

Nicholas Mansergh, *The unresolved question: the Anglo-Irish settlement and its undoing, 1912–1972* (New Haven, 1991)

Maurice Walsh, *Bitter freedom: Ireland in a revolutionary world, 1918–1923* (London, 2015)

NOTES

[1] Jason Knirck, *Imagining Ireland's independence: the debates over the Anglo-Irish Treaty of 1921* (Lanham, MD, 2006).

[2] *Dáil debates*, vol. T, no. 6 (19 December 1921); available at: www.oireachtas.ie/en/debates/.

[3] Richard Bourke, 'Reflections on the political thought of the Irish revolution', *Transactions of the Royal Historical Society* 27 (2017), 175–91; Richard Bourke, 'Political and religious ideas of the Irish revolution', *History of European Ideas* 46 (7) (2020), 997–1008, published online 31 March 2020, DOI: 10.1080/01916599.2020.1747227.

[4] W. Alison Philips, *The revolution in Ireland, 1906–1923* (London, 1923).

[5] *Dáil debates*, vol. T, no. 2, 'Debate on Treaty' (14 December 1921); available at: www.oireachtas.ie/en/debates/.

[6] *Dáil debates*, vol. T, no. 6, 'Debate on Treaty' (19 December 1921); available at: www.oireachtas.ie/en/debates/.

[7] *Dáil debates*, vol. T, no. 6, 'Debate on Treaty' (19 December 1921); available at: www.oireachtas.ie/en/debates/.

[8] *Dáil debates*, vol. T, no. 6, 'Debate on Treaty' (19 December 1921); available at: www.oireachtas.ie/en/debates/.

[9] *Dáil debates*, vol. T, no. 6, 'Debate on Treaty' (19 December 1921); available at: www.oireachtas.ie/en/debates/.

[10] *Dáil debates*, vol. T, no. 8, 'Debate on Treaty' (21 December 1921); available at: www.oireachtas.ie/en/debates/.

[11] *Dáil debates*, vol. T, no. 8, 'Debate on Treaty' (21 December 1921); available at: www.oireachtas.ie/en/debates/.

[12] *Dáil debates*, vol. T, no. 10, 'Debate on Treaty' (3 January 1922); available at: www.oireachtas.ie/en/debates/.

[13] *Dáil debates*, vol. T, no. 10, 'Debate on Treaty' (3 January 1922); available at: www.oireachtas.ie/en/debates/.

[14] *Dáil debates*, vol. T, no. 9, 'Debate on Treaty' (22 December 1921); available at: www.oireachtas.ie/en/debates/.

16 JANUARY 1922

THE 'SURRENDER' OF DUBLIN CASTLE

ADMINISTERING IRELAND

In the history of the Irish revolution of 1916–21 it is the IRA campaign that attracts most attention. It is arguable, however, that the decision of the Sinn Féin candidates elected in the December 1918 general election to assemble in Dublin's Mansion House in January 1919 and to declare themselves, as Dáil Éireann, the legitimate government in Ireland, was in fact the decisive revolutionary action. In a strategy originally devised by Arthur Griffith, Dáil Éireann gave a state form to the historic demands of Irish nationalism for separation. Nationalist resistance to the British state was to be expressed, not through riot and rebellion, but through the establishment of an Irish rival state. Popular support for the IRA campaign was largely unquantifiable whereas support for Dáil Éireann could be measured by the number of votes won in local and general elections. The emphasis on a state-centred revolutionary struggle necessarily focuses on the role of the civil service, rather than the soldiers, in both the British and revolutionary counter-state administrations.

On 16 January 1922 a Dáil Éireann delegation, led by Michael Collins, entered the Privy Council chamber in the upper yard of Dublin Castle and handed a signed copy of the Treaty to Viceroy FitzAlan and thus became the Provisional Government of Saorstát Éireann. The Provisional Government then returned to the Mansion House, announced it had accepted the 'surrender of Dublin Castle' and issued its first directive ordering that 'all Public Servants and functionaries hitherto under the authority of the British Government shall continue to carry out their functions unless and until otherwise ordered by us'. The Provisional Government also prohibited 'the transfer, or dismissal of any officer, servant, employee or functionary of the state or the removal of any records, documents or correspondence'. Three days later the Provisional Government took over the existing forty-eight departments and offices of the Castle administration, announcing that it had 'appointed certain members and others to direct their activities and to be responsible to that Government for their efficient conduct and maintenance'.[1] The committee charged under the 1920 Government of Ireland Act with partitioning

Michael Collins (centre) and Kevin O'Higgins (pulling on gloves), watched by (hatless) British civil servant Andy Cope, leave Dublin Castle, 16 January 1922.

the civil service was ordered to cease meeting. For the civil servants of the Irish administration, the Union had come to an end: London was no longer in charge, and they were now in the hands of a native government. While Churchill might bluster that the Provisional Government had no legal authority to act as it did, the British government had no choice but to accept Griffith's and Collins's interpretation of the Treaty.[2]

The Provisional Government had now to assimilate the inherited Castle administration into the Dáil administration while dealing with the well-organised civil servants themselves. In May 1920 Warren Fisher, permanent secretary of the Treasury, had been sent to investigate the Castle administration. His conclusion that the government of Ireland was 'woodenly stupid' justified despatching a select group of English civil servants led by John Anderson, chairman of the Board of Inland Revenue, to take over the civil administration in the Castle.[3] There was already a well-founded suspicion in London that, rather than being woodenly stupid, a group of 'die-hard' unionist senior civil servants in the Castle administration was deliberately working to create conditions in which any political settlement would become impossible, necessitating martial law.[4] The advice of the Anderson team shifted the terms of the debate that was then taking place in Cabinet away from the 'die-hards', who were prepared to impose military rule, towards those committed to maintaining civil government. It was a close-run contest, and Ireland might well have come under a military regime rather than self-government.

Immediately the Treaty was approved, representatives of the new 'Conference of All Associations of Irish Civil Servants' introduced themselves to the Provisional Government. The civil servants signalled that they were enthusiastic about serving a native government and demanded nothing more than an assurance of 'no worsening of conditions'. They hoped for a civil service that reflected the Sinn Féin ideal of a 'one-grade' administration free of sectarian discrimination and the English 'caste' system of hierarchical classes.[5]

By the time of the Treaty, in contrast with an administration in Dublin Castle that was stained with militarism, Dáil Éireann basked in the general acceptance of the Dáil courts and police, a local government department that was pushing through reforms, an energetic programme of industrial development and a thoroughly modern propaganda department. The Dáil administration, organised in functional departments under political ministers answerable to the Dáil, also looked more modern than that of the Castle's autonomous boards. The key department was Finance under Michael

Collins, controlling recruitment and payment of all the civil servants of the counter-state. As late as June 1922 the Provisional Government, regarding the inherited civil service with suspicion, was still planning a process by which the Dáil administration would take over and assimilate the Castle civil service. The outbreak of civil war in June prevented the sweeping changes that were being planned for the Irish administration.[6] From that point on the Provisional Government had to assert control not only over the Castle administration but also over the remnants of the Dáil departments. The legitimacy of the Provisional Government was challenged by some within the Dáil administration, and there were instances of insubordination and refusal to obey instructions. In contrast, whatever the private sentiments of individual civil servants, the Castle administration accepted the legitimacy of the Provisional Government. Plans to construct a completely new apparatus were abandoned and the civil service of the Dáil was assimilated into the old Castle administration; the reverse of what was originally intended.

As the Provisional Government concentrated on the growing military threat of the anti-Treaty IRA, its attention to the development of civil government wavered as the leading figures, especially Collins, donned military uniform. The survival of the new state now depended on its army rather than civil government. With the death of Griffith, and then of Collins, it lost its visionaries, but also reverted to civil control. Thoughts of building a new and national civil service were abandoned. Contemporaries believed that the handover on 16 January would be a day remembered by future generations in Ireland as 'epochal'.[7] That it is not so remembered is partly because instead of seizing the opportunity to create a civil service more suited to the revolutionary conditions, one less hierarchical and more dynamic, the government attempted to create nothing more than a frugal version of the Whitehall model. This was not the sort of administrative reform that the civil service anticipated or that the revolution had signalled, nor was it even desirable. The Castle civil service was confident of its ability to deliver on radical policies and offered enthusiastic support rather than hostility to the new state. An opportunity to engage in truly revolutionary state-building and administrative transformation was lost. In response, the civil service retreated behind Article 10 of the Treaty that conferred a constitutional guarantee of their pre-Treaty status, one that would be tenaciously defended in the courts against the government of the Irish Free State.

by Martin Maguire

FURTHER READING

Michael Hopkinson (ed.) *The last days of Dublin Castle: the Mark Sturgis diaries* (Dublin, 1999)

Martin Maguire, *The civil service and the revolution in Ireland, 1912–38. 'Shaking the blood-stained hand of Mr Collins'* (Manchester, 2008)

Arthur Mitchell, *Revolutionary government in Ireland: Dáil Éireann, 1919–22* (Dublin, 1995)

NOTES

[1] National Archives of Ireland (NAI), TSCH/3/S1A, 'Transfer of services hitherto administered by the British government in Ireland', 16 January 1922.
[2] Charles Townshend, *The Republic: the fight for Irish independence, 1918–1923* (London, 2013), 384–6.
[3] House of Lords Record Office, Lloyd George papers, F/31/1/32933, 'Dublin Castle Report', 12 May 1920.
[4] *The Times*, 'Irish peace in danger', 1 December 1919.
[5] NAI, TSCH/3/S36, 'Civil service general position', January–September 1922.
[6] NAI, TSCH/1/1/2, Provisional Government minutes, 27 June 1922.
[7] *The Irish Times*, 17 January 1922.

19 JANUARY 1922

DEDICATION OF THE JOHN NICHOLSON STATUE, LISBURN

IRELAND AND EMPIRE

On 19 January 1922 the town of Lisburn in Northern Ireland unveiled a statue to an imperial icon and one of its famous sons, the East India Company officer John Nicholson. Having been promoted to the rank of Brigadier-General during the Indian Rebellion, Nicholson was mortally wounded while leading the British assault on Delhi in September 1857. He was revered as one of the great 'Mutiny' heroes of late Victorian Britain, an 'Irish Paladin' and devout evangelical who brought order to the northwest frontier of India, where he was worshipped as a god dubbed 'Nikal Seyn'.

Viewed from the twenty-first century, Nicholson, who advocated summary executions and corporal punishment for Indian rebels, stands as an example of the pervasive violence of colonialism. Yet for the predominantly Protestant and unionist residents of Lisburn on that day, the unveiling of Nicholson's statue represented a day of civic, Ulster and imperial pride. The town came to a halt as shops and schools closed, and most factories and mills suspended business. As Northern Ireland prime

minister James Craig looked on, the statue was unveiled by another prominent Irish military officer, Field Marshal Sir Henry Wilson.

The field marshal's tales of Nicholson vanquishing 'the most savage, the most warlike and the most terrible tribes' of India received cheers from the crowd, as did his admiration for how 'this little corner of Ireland, this Ulster' had produced some of the greatest heroes of 1857.[1] The ceremony reflected not only Ireland's imperial past but its tumultuous imperial present. James Craig honoured Wilson, who in the following month would be elected as MP for North Down, with the honorary title of 'gallant Ulsterman'.[2] A member of Lisburn's Urban District Council contrasted the achievements of imperial Irishmen such as Nicholson and Wilson with nationalists' efforts 'to tear down and dismember' the British empire 'that men like Nicholson, Rhodes and others had died to build up'.

The unveiling of the John Nicholson statue thus took place not only in the midst of revolutionary upheaval in Ireland, but also at a time in which Irish men and women engaged deeply with the British empire in various ways. As the foundation of the Irish Free State ended some imperial relationships, others were transformed and new linkages between Ireland and the British empire developed.

Shortly before the ceremony in Lisburn, empire had occupied a prominent place in the first Dáil's debates on the Anglo-Irish Treaty, which accorded the Free State the status of a dominion of the British empire. The continuing connection to the empire, highlighting the failure of separatists to achieve an independent republic, drew fierce criticism from anti-Treaty members of Sinn Féin. At the same time, many viewed Ireland's independence struggle as anomalous, spurning comparisons with either African or Asian colonies or the colonies of white settlement such as Canada or Australia.

Since the end of the First World War, Irish republican representatives overseas had built strong relationships with anti-imperialist activists from the colonial world. Some members of the Dáil did express solidarity with global anti-colonial movements during the Treaty debates. Liam Mellows lamented that 'we are going into the British Empire now to participate in the Empire's shame...to participate in the shame and the crucifixion of India and the degradation of Egypt. Is that what the Irish people fought for freedom for?'[3]

While supporters of the Treaty displayed little imperial enthusiasm, they nonetheless argued that dominion status offered protection from British interference in Ireland's internal politics.[4] Members of the Cumann na nGaedheal government subsequently extended this argument, contending that Ireland's history and status within the British empire offered the possibility of anti-imperial action in the League of Nations. In September 1922 P.S. O'Hegarty contended that

> Ireland's position is unique. By virtue of our special history, our special position, we can not only lead the British Dominions in an anti-Imperial policy against the British Empire, but we can, through the League, organise the small Nations in a Small Nations League against the Empires.[5]

In spite of these anti-imperial sentiments, partition, the civil war and the continuing ties of the Irish Free State to the empire also presented a negative example for anti-colonial activists. The August 1922 issue of the Indian communist publication *Vanguard* featured an article on the 'Irish tragedy, conveying a lesson for India from the Free State fiasco and the tragic betrayal of the principle of Republicanism by its sponsors Collins and Griffith'.[6]

Nonetheless, the solidarity forged between Irish separatists and anti-colonial activists endured. Shapurji Saklatvala, the Bombay-born, communist member of parliament for Battersea, devoted his maiden speech on 20 November 1922 to a critique of the Anglo-Irish Treaty, condemning it as 'a forced freedom' that was 'the only alternative to a new invasion of Ireland by British troops'.[7] Estimating that ninety per cent of his Irish constituents in London opposed the Treaty, Saklatvala proposed an amendment to alter the Treaty four days later. 'The Constitutions for Ireland and India and Egypt and Mesopotamia', he contended, 'should be Constitutions written by the men of those countries…without interference from outside.'[8]

Irish separatists, particularly republican socialists and communists, continued to pursue these anti-colonial alliances. Roddy Connolly travelled to Hamburg in 1922 to liaise with M.N. Roy, the former revolutionary nationalist and founder of the Communist Party of India. British intelligence described Connolly as an important recruit to Roy's cause, and possibly a source of arms for Indian insurgents. Perhaps in an effort to deceive British agents, Roy advertised that his journal, *Advance Guard*, was published by the 'Emerald Press' of Dublin, when it was in reality printed in Germany.[9]

Many intelligence reports on Indian communism in 1922 were authored by a Protestant Irishman, Charles Tegart, the flamboyant police commissioner of Calcutta who at the time served in the office of Indian Political Intelligence in London. Tegart's role in the surveillance of both Indian and Irish revolutionaries demonstrates another way in which Irish imperial connections continued beyond 1922.

As with Irish anti-imperialism, the contours of Irish imperial engagement took various forms. The disbandment of most Irish regiments of the British army in July 1922 had a marked imperial dimension. Regiments such as the Royal Irish Fusiliers and Munster Fusiliers were frequently deployed for imperial garrison duty in locales such as Egypt and India in the post-war period. In June 1920 members of the Connaught Rangers in India had staged a protest against the actions of the British army in Ireland. Negotiations for the release of Rangers imprisoned for their role in the 'mutiny' continued through 1922; in December William Cosgrave wrote to Prime Minister

Andrew Bonar Law that the question of the prisoners' release was still 'occupying the public mind very considerably and also the minds of many members of our Parliament'.[10] Irish troops stationed in India at the time of disbandment were given the option of transferring to other regiments. In battalions such as the 2nd Dublin Fusiliers, virtually all officers and over one-fifth of other ranks chose to continue their imperial service.[11]

The disbandment of the Royal Irish Constabulary in 1922 similarly did not mark an end of Irish imperial relationships. A significant percentage of the more than 1,400 members of the RIC who emigrated overseas between 1919 and 1923 relocated to imperial locales.[12] The year 1922 also witnessed perhaps the largest single contribution of the RIC to imperial policing, as close to 700 former members of the force entered the initial draft of the British Palestine Gendarmerie.[13] Former Royal Irish Constabulary members, chiefly Black and Tans and auxiliaries, dominated the ranks of the gendarmerie, and close to forty per cent of the force was Irish-born.

At the close of the year, another ceremony was held at the Nicholson statue in Lisburn. This memorialised not only the centenary of Nicholson's birth but also the aforementioned Sir Henry Wilson, who had been shot dead in London on 22 June by two members of the Irish Republican Army. Wilson's assassins, who had both served in Irish regiments during the Great War, had targeted not only a staunch defender of the Union, but the most prominent Irish imperial officer of his generation.

Wilson's assassination by two former Irish soldiers illustrates in dramatic form the reconfiguration of Irish imperial relationships in 1922. While Irish engagement with empire was never as straightforward as Protestant, unionist loyalism versus Catholic, nationalist anti-imperialism, these binary divisions were given increased force by independence and partition. In terms of Irish identity, a commitment to empire was increasingly seen to reside in the 'imperial province' of Ulster. In southern Ireland, in spite of the Free State's dominion status, anti-imperial sentiments assumed a more central role, while traditions of Irish imperial service came to be increasingly remote to public debate and the process of nation-building.

by Michael Silvestri

FURTHER READING

Seán William Gannon, *The Irish imperial service: policing Palestine and administering the empire, 1922–1966* (London, 2018)

Kate O'Malley, *Ireland, India and empire: Indo-Irish radical connections, 1919–1964* (Manchester, 2008)

Michael Silvestri, *Ireland and India: nationalism, empire and memory* (Basingstoke, 2009)

NOTES

[1] *Lisburn Standard*, 20 January 1922.

[2] *Lisburn Herald*, 21 January 1922.

[3] Jason Knirck, 'The Dominion of Ireland: the Anglo-Irish Treaty in an imperial context', *Éire–Ireland* 42 (1 and 2) (2007), 229–55, 244.

[4] Knirck, 'Dominion of Ireland', 249.

[5] National Archives of Ireland (NAI), Department of the Taoiseach, S33332, P.S. O'Hegarty, 'Memorandum on Irish membership of the League of Nations', 15 September 1922; available in R. Fanning, M. Kennedy, C. Crowe, D. Keogh and E. O'Halpin (eds), *Documents on Irish Foreign Policy*, vol. 1, *1919–22*, No. 320 (Dublin, 1998).

[6] British Library, Asia, Pacific and Africa Collections [hereafter cited as BL, APAC], IOR L/P and J/12/46, 'Indian Communist Party', 22 September 1922.

[7] Cited in Kate O'Malley, *Ireland, India and empire: Indo-Irish radical connections, 1919–1964* (Manchester, 2008), 26.

[8] O'Malley, *Ireland, India and empire*, 26–7.

[9] BL, APAC, IOR L/P and J/12/46, 'Indian Communist Party', 30 September 1922 and 11 November 1922.

[10] Parliamentary Archives, London, Andrew Bonar Law papers, 114/1/10, W.T. Cosgrave to Andrew Bonar Law, 16 December 1922.

[11] Patrick McCarthy, 'The twilight years: the Irish regiments, 1919–1922', *Irish Sword* 21 (85) (1999), 314–35: 333.

[12] Kent Fedorowich, 'The problems of disbandment: the Royal Irish Constabulary and imperial migration, 1919–29', *Irish Historical Studies* 30 (117) (May 1996), 88–110: 105.

[13] Seán William Gannon, *The Irish imperial service: policing Palestine and administering the empire, 1922–1966* (London, 2018), 35–6.

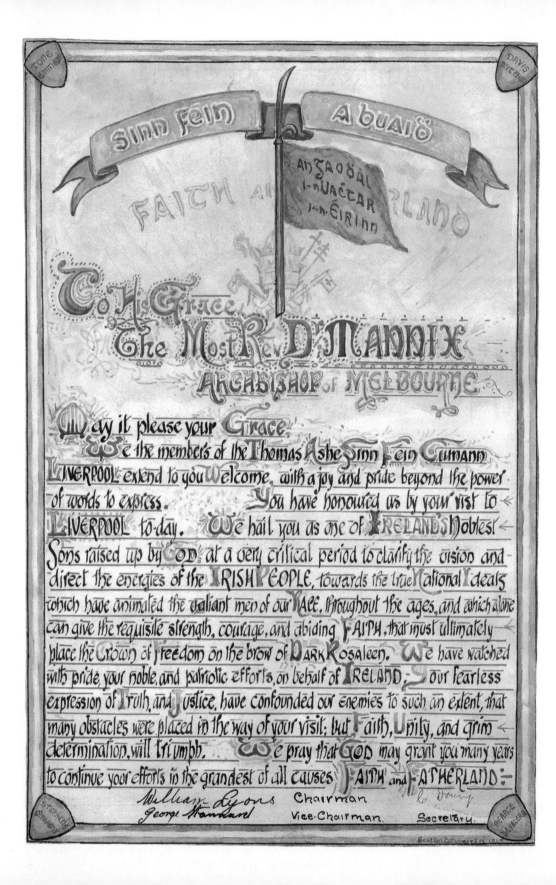

Sinn Fein **A buaiḋ**

An Ṫaoḋal
i-nUaċtar
i-n-Éirinn

**To His Grace
The Most Rev. D. Mannix
Archbishop of Melbourne**

May it please your Grace,

We the members of the Thomas Ashe Sinn Fein Cumann
LIVERPOOL extend to you Welcome, with a joy and pride beyond the power
of words to express. You have honoured us by your visit to
LIVERPOOL to-day. We hail you as one of IRELAND's Noblest
Sons raised up by GOD at a very critical period to clarify the vision and
direct the energies of the IRISH PEOPLE, towards the true National Ideals
which have animated the valiant men of our RACE, throughout the ages, and which alone
can give the requisite strength, courage, and abiding FAITH, that must ultimately
place the Crown of Freedom on the brow of DARK ROSALEEN. We have watched
with pride your noble, and patriotic efforts, on behalf of IRELAND; Your fearless
expression of Truth, and Justice, have confounded our enemies to such an extent, that
many obstacles were placed in the way of your visit; but Faith, Unity, and grim
determination, will triumph. We pray that GOD may grant you many years
to continue your efforts in the grandest of all causes FAITH and FATHERLAND.

William Lyons   Chairman   C Doury

George Stannard   Vice-Chairman.   Secretary.

21 JANUARY 1922

THE IRISH RACE CONGRESS

GLOBAL IRELAND

On 21 January 1922 John Whelan arrived from Java for the Irish Race Congress in Paris. It was held between 21 and 28 January, and was an initiative of Irish nationalists in South Africa that sought to offset the power of the British empire during the War of Independence and Anglo-Irish Treaty negotiations by mobilising the political and cultural influence of the global Irish diaspora. Over one hundred delegates from twenty-two countries would attend. Journeying over four weeks to be in attendance at the event, the single representative of the Dutch East Indies cut an isolated figure among the delegations representing Australia, Argentina and Great Britain. 'You have a representative here from Java. It is absurd', the London-based Art O'Brien commented: 'the Irish colony of Java, I understand, consists of six or seven people, and they are not organised at all'.[1] Whelan's presence at once illustrates the global scope, and great divergences, that characterised Irish nationalism during the revolution. The worldwide movement of Irish revolutionaries, transnational organisers and internationalist activists collectively signified

An illuminated address presented to Daniel Mannix, Archbishop of Melbourne, by Liverpool's Thomas Ashe Sinn Féin cumann to mark his 1920 visit to Britain.

the importance of political activism beyond Ireland's borders. To what extent did the eventful year of 1922 mark a rupture in the global order of Irish nationalism? To assess the legacy of the civil war, we must locate revolutionary Ireland in its international historical context.

Ireland was a subject of global import in the aftermath of the First World War. Reports of the first meeting of Dáil Éireann in Dublin on 21 January 1919 travelled the world: 'Irlanda y el Sinn-Feinismo' (Mexico City); 'Sinn Fein assembly, independence declared' (Mumbai); 'Demand English leave Ireland' (Tokyo).[2] Terms such as 'republic', 'self-determination', and 'small nations' were immediately recognisable in this global 'moment'. 'The High Command of Fiume…now associates itself with the analogous declaration of the Irish Republic', the Italian revolutionary Gabriele D'Annunzio informed the League of Nations.[3]

Without access to the immediate publicity offered by political representation at Westminster, securing international recognition of the republic, paradoxically, became integral to the politics of Sinn Féin. In early 1919, Versailles, not the Mansion House, was the centre of the Irish world. The Dáil's premier diplomats Seán T. O'Kelly and George Gavan Duffy lobbied the world's powers for entry to the Paris Peace Conference, while associating with internationalist activists such as Egypt's Sa'd Zaghlul and Vietnam's Ho Chi Minh beyond its halls and mirrors. Neither the Irish Republic, nor its representatives, ultimately, would be admitted at Versailles. A network of envoys, press agents and cultural influencers would, however, represent the nascent Irish Republic across the continent thereafter: in Antwerp, Geneva, Rome, Stockholm. Irish nationalist women, notably, enjoyed considerable political status and responsibility in Europe; Nancy Wyse Power and Máire Ní Bhriain assumed publicity portfolios on behalf of Dáil Éireann in Berlin and Madrid respectively. Most significantly, Patrick McCartan journeyed to Moscow with a view to establishing diplomatic relations with Soviet Russia, drafting a provisional treaty between the two governments.

The international ambitions, and internationalist connections, of Irish nationalists had put the Irish Republic on the map in Europe. In a letter to Monsignor John Hagan at the Pontifical Irish College in Rome, Seán T. O'Kelly addressed a second strand of global Ireland: the Irish diaspora (a worldwide community often denoted in Irish-Catholic terms). 'Our people would take all possible steps to have the Catholics of America, Australia,

Canada, New Zealand, and South Africa, and all the other places where the Irish have planted and maintained the Catholic Church, join them in a form of protestation to the Vatican.'[4] The outspoken archbishop of Melbourne, Daniel Mannix, meanwhile, toured the United States in 1920 campaigning against British policy in Ireland. His later arrest off the coast of Cork further focused media attention in Australia and the United States on British rule in Ireland. In a meeting at the Vatican in May 1921, Mannix convinced Pope Benedict XV to issue a call for peace in Ireland, rather than the denunciation of the IRA demanded by British diplomats.

As the dominant power in the post-war world, and the largest centre of Irish settlement, the United States presented the most auspicious political space for recognition of the republic. The America-first politics of the New York-based Friends of Irish Freedom influenced the passing of resolutions in support of Irish self-determination in the US Senate. The failure to apply self-determination to Ireland, Woodrow Wilson confided to leading Irish Americans, had proven the 'great metaphysical tragedy of today'.[5] Éamon de Valera's high-profile campaign across the United States between June 1919 and December 1920 attracted unprecedented financial support ($60 million in today's money) on behalf of the republic. His island-centric politics, however, would imbalance the equation of Irish American nationalism, prompting a public split over his comparisons between Ireland and Cuba.[6] To Daniel Cohalan, who presented the case for Irish self-determination at the Republican Party Convention, de Valera was 'woefully out of touch with the spirit of the country'.[7] While his Washington D.C.-based American Association for the Recognition of the Irish Republic failed, ultimately, to secure recognition from the US administration, de Valera's campaign secured the freedom of speech of Irish nationalists, an increasing challenge for Dáil Éireann in Dublin.

Elsewhere, Irish nationalists were to co-ordinate their efforts across the British empire as part of the 'self-determination league' movement. Successive organisations were established in Great Britain, Canada, Australia and New Zealand, forming what Dáil envoy Osmonde Grattan Esmonde described as 'the complete framework of a world-wide race organisation'.[8] Esmonde was one of many 'global connectors', individuals who propagated Ireland's cause through their movement across borders and cultural boundaries. Departing New York in December 1920, he arrived in Auckland in March 1921, with a view to organising the self-determination league in New Zealand. Arrested one month later for issuing seditious speeches on the islands of Fiji, he was deported to Canada.

Other 'global connectors' mobilised support for the republic through Ireland's diaspora communities. The Prince Edward Island-born journalist and activist Katherine Hughes successively established branches of the Self-Determination for Ireland League of Canada and Newfoundland; toured the 'Deep South' of the United States with Éamon de Valera; organised the Self-Determination League movement in Australia and New Zealand; and coordinated the arrival of Irish representatives from twenty-two countries for the Irish Race Congress in Paris. The transnational movement of individuals underpinned the political ideology of 'global Ireland'.

Over the course of the Irish revolution, Irish nationalists around the world institutionalised the idea of 'global Ireland' through the organisation of successive Irish Race Conventions. Between 1919 and 1921, these events were convened in Philadelphia (1919), Melbourne (1919) and Buenos Aires (1921). The Irish Race Congress in Paris in January 1922, most impressively, was coordinated by nationalist organisers in London, Dublin, Toronto and Pretoria. 'It is not the Ireland of four millions that we are thinking of now', the South African-based leadership explained: 'we are thinking also of the greater Ireland, the Magna Hibernia across the seas…they must not be, and they are not, wholly lost to Ireland'.[9]

Having been envisaged by its convenors as a means of invoking the global influence of the Irish diaspora during the Treaty negotiations, the Irish Race Congress would eventually descend into acrimony in the aftermath of the signing of the Anglo-Irish Treaty on 6 December 1921. Its one hundred delegates would be divided, not only on their views of the Treaty, but on their vision for a global Ireland. Differences of perspective between the Irish in South America and South Africa on issues of race, citizenship and nationality, much less the Treaty, would undermine the coherence of the projected global Ireland organisation: Fine Ghaedheal. The *New York Times* commented presciently of proceedings:

> whether in Paris or Dublin or New York, sensible Irishmen must be aware that the final test of their capacity to govern themselves is now upon them…the only Irish Race Congress which the world will note, or long remember, is not the one in Paris but the one in Dublin.[10]

The Irish civil war altered the outlook of Irish nationalism, narrowing the focus of Irish revolutionaries from a global Ireland to a more island-centred politics, and diverting attention from the scale of republican international achievements to the minutiae of intra-national differences. A century of independent statehood and historical scholarship has reinforced the 'ourselves alone' narrative of the Irish revolution. The separation of the Irish diaspora from the historiography of the Irish revolution to date speaks to the 'double marginalisation' of the Irish migrant: from Irish society and from its historical record. Fine Gael has been written into the Irish history books as the twentieth-century political successor to the pro-Treaty party; 'Fine Ghaedheal', by contrast, has been consigned to the footnotes of Irish history, and the distant scholarship of diaspora Ireland. The worldwide movement of Irish nationalists is deserving of a historical legacy to remember. A century after the Irish Race Congress in Paris, the Irish state has, significantly, returned to the idea, and influence, of 'global Ireland'.

by Darragh Gannon

FURTHER READING

Enda Delaney and Fearghal McGarry, 'Introduction: a global history of the Irish revolution', *Irish Historical Studies* 44 (165) (2020), 1–10

Gerard Keown, *First of the small nations: the beginnings of Irish foreign policy in the interwar years, 1919–1932* (Oxford, 2016)

Arthur Mitchell, *Revolutionary government in Ireland: Dáil Éireann, 1919–22* (Dublin, 1995)

NOTES

[1] Fine Ghaedheal, *Proceedings of the Irish Race Congress in Paris, January 1922* (Dublin, 1922), 175.

[2] *El Universal*, 22 January 1919; *Times of India*, 22 January 1919; *Japan Times*, 25 January 1919.

[3] European University Institute, Special Collections, League of Nations records, K 11/3039/1348, Gabriele D'Annunzio to Eric Drummond, 1 February 1920.

[4] Archives of the Pontifical Irish College, Rome, John Hagan papers, HAG1/1921/46(1), Seán T. O'Kelly to Monsignor Hagan, 1 February 1921.

[5] New York Public Library Archives and Manuscripts, Frank P. Walsh papers, box 124, Diary of the American Commission of Irish Independence, 11 June 1919.

[6] See, Darragh Gannon, 'Addressing the Irish world: Éamon de Valera's "Cuban policy" as a global case study', *Irish Historical Studies* 44 (165) (May 2020), 41–56.

[7] American Irish Historical Society Archives, Friends of Irish Freedom papers, box 4, folder 1, Daniel Cohalan to Éamon de Valera, 22 February 1920.

[8] National Archives of Ireland, Department of Foreign Affairs, DFA ES box 32, file 220, Ormonde Grattan Esmonde report, 1921.

[9] *The Republic*, 12 March 1921.

[10] *New York Times*, 23 January 1922.

25 JANUARY 1922

PREMIERE OF SWAN HENNESSY'S
SECOND STRING QUARTET, PARIS

ART MUSIC AND THE STRUGGLE
FOR INDEPENDENCE

'In my early Dublin days', the English composer (and Master of the King's
Music) Arnold Bax wrote in 1952, 'I moved in an almost wholly literary
circle. There was no talk of music whatever'.[1] I have always taken this
comment (as have many other people) as a byword for the general apathy
and indifference surrounding art music in Ireland in the years leading up
to the foundation of the state. Bax's own enchantment with Irish culture
was mediated through his profound admiration for Yeats: in the shadow of
Yeats's poetry and plays, the temple of his own art was raised. His early tone
poems are orchestral works inspired not by traditional music (he disdained
the arrangement of Irish melodies by Sir Charles Villiers Stanford, whose
music, according to Bax, 'never penetrated to within a thousand miles of
the Hidden Ireland'), but by a visionary romanticism that lay on the cusp
of political awareness.[2] Bax lived continuously in Dublin from 1911 until

the outbreak of the Great War. On one occasion he invited Patrick Pearse to his home (in Rathgar) through the agency of their mutual friends, Padraic and Molly Colum. Bax was deeply impressed with

his 'death-aspiring' guest, and recounts that when later he read the first reports of the Easter Rising (by the shore of Lake Windermere), he said to himself, 'I know that Pearse is in this!'[3] On 9 October 1916 he completed the short score of an orchestral work, entitled *In memoriam* and dedicated to the memory of Pearse; it lay unperformed until 1998. The original short score was presented to Éamon de Valera by Harriet Cohen in 1955, and subsequently deposited in the library of University College Dublin.[4]

Until the publication in 2019 of Axel Klein's *Bird of time,* a biography of the Irish American composer Swan Hennessy (1866–1929), Bax's commemoration of Pearse had stood alone in the annals of Irish musical history on two counts, one of which endures. It was and remains the first musical work of art to memorialise a leading figure in Irish revolutionary politics by a (then) contemporary composer. Thanks to Axel Klein's research, however, the solitary estate of Bax's work (to say little of its long neglect) has been significantly modified by the rediscovery of a string quartet (opus 49) by Swan Hennessy written in memory of Terence MacSwiney, shortly after MacSwiney's death on hunger strike in 1920. And whereas Bax's commemoration of Pearse was either set aside or suppressed (we cannot really be sure), Hennessy's string quartet was premiered by four Dublin-based musicians at the World Congress of the Irish Race in Paris on the evening of 25 January 1922. The audience at this first performance included de Valera, Countess Markievicz and Mary MacSwiney (sister of Terence), all prominent opponents of the Anglo-Irish Treaty.[5]

Given that a primary objective of the Irish Race Congress, organised prior to the signing of the Anglo-Irish Treaty, had been to promote support for the international recognition of the Irish Republic, it is not mistaken to argue that Hennessy's quartet was at least implicitly sympathetic to the anti-Treaty delegation (led by de Valera). But the work's immediate reception eclipsed the bitter identity politics that soon afterwards would herald the Irish civil war, in favour of its programmatic engagement with MacSwiney's life, political struggle and death. In *Bird of time,* Axel Klein cites reviews of the premiere by the Paris correspondent of the *New York Herald* and of the Dublin premiere (a week later) in *The Irish Times* in support of this reading, together with an acknowledgement

DEUXIÈME QUATUOR

à la Mémoire de Terence Mc SWINEY
Lord Mayor de Cork

Swan Hennessy

I

INTRODUCTION

Paris, E. DEMETS Editeur,
2 Rue Louvois.(IIᵉ Arrᵗ)

of the ebullient optimism of the work's finale. Hennessy's quartet mourned MacSwiney's death and yet hoped for a better outcome.

In Dublin, Paris and (shortly afterwards) Berlin, Hennessy's music was immediately intelligible as an inherently and ineluctably Irish work

of art, whatever the nationality of its composer. Klein documents twelve concert performances of the quartet between 1922 and 1939, in addition to two radio broadcasts.[6] Thereafter, it lapsed into long silence. It would not be heard again until the work was revived by the RTÉ ConTempo Quartet (at the instigation of Axel Klein) in 2016. A recording of Hennessy's complete string quartets by the same ensemble would follow in 2019.

How does one account for this mute afterlife? How can one reinscribe a work such as Hennessy's opus 49 into the cultural narrative that ensues upon the commemoration of 1922 represented by the present publication? The centenary itself prompts an answer. So too does Yeats's prestige, and that of the literary revival he fomented. If we think of works of art in relation to the upheavals of the era, we think perhaps first and foremost of 'Easter 1916' (completed within a month of Bax's *In memoriam* in September 1916, and published in 1921 within a year of the composition of Hennessy's string quartet). We may also think of 1922 as the *annus mirabilis* of European literary modernism, given that Joyce's *Ulysses* was published that year (in Paris), to say little of Eliot's *The waste land*. We are unlikely to think of Hennessy's string quartet, however, as anything other than a *pièce d'occasion*, now faded within the folds of a largely forgotten cultural history. Even if this appears to do scant justice to Hennessy, who lived in Paris from 1903 until his death in 1929 and whose work is constantly imbued with an awareness of his Irish musical heritage (his father was an Irish emigrant to the United States), it remains nevertheless true that there was little or no contextual affordance by which this work might belong to an Irish musical soundscape. As late as 1937, an Irish civil servant could characterise art music as a 'Victorian form of educational recreation', fundamentally irrelevant to the young state's artistic ambitions. To borrow a phrase from Klein, modern Ireland was 'no state for music'.[7]

Klein means 'art music', or 'contemporary classical music', a distinction that gains in importance when we consider how assiduously (by contrast) the new state sought to recuperate its ethnic musical inheritances. 'The more we foster modern music, the more we help to silence our own',

Richard Henebry, a passionate ideologue of cultural chauvinism, had written in 1903.[8] This was long in advance of the general silence and neglect that would rapidly envelop the enterprise of art music as an indigenous pre-occupation in the Ireland of the 1920s. For decades, Irish art music would remain an 'invisible art', and an inaudible one. A century after partition, this remains largely the case. Most of Bax's Irish tone poems have very rarely (if ever) been heard in live performance in Ireland, and the same is true for the greater part of Stanford's oeuvre. Almost a century after independence, the greater part of Ireland's art music estate remains shrouded in silence.[9]

And yet: as Axel Klein has shown, the implacable record of this estate suggests otherwise. There is a history of Irish musical ideas deserving of our attention, notwithstanding the complacency (and worse) of a cultural and educational matrix that regards 'classical music' as a bewildering antag-onism to the Irish story. To recover Swan Hennessy's serenely achieved meditations on Terence MacSwiney in 1920, destined as these originally were in 1922 for an audience in the throes of state formation, is an enter-prise which deepens rather than diminishes our reception of Irish history over the past century.

by Harry White

FURTHER READING

Michael Dervan (ed.), *The invisible art: a century of music in Ireland, 1916–2016* (Dublin, 2016)

Axel Klein, *Bird of time. The music of Swan Hennessy* (Mainz, 2019)

NOTES

[1] Arnold Bax, 'Foreword', in Aloys Fleischmann (ed.), *Music in Ireland. A symposium* (Cork, 1952), iii–iv: iv.

[2] Bax, 'Foreword' to *Music in Ireland*, iii.

[3] See, Lewis Foreman (ed.), *Farewell, my youth and other writings by Arnold Bax* (Farnham, 1992), 91–2.

[4] See, Graham Parlett, 'The background to "In Memoriam"' [9 March 2017], available on The Sir Arnold Bax website: arnoldbax.com/the-background-to-in-memoriam/ (accessed 26 August 2020).

[5] See, Axel Klein, *Bird of time. The music of Swan Hennessy* (Mainz, 2019), 193–4; 261–9. I am deeply indebted to Axel Klein for his generous assistance in the writing of this piece.

[6] For details of these performances see, Klein, *Bird of time*, 473–4.

[7] See, Axel Klein, 'No state for music', in Michael Dervan (ed.), *The invisible art: a century of music in Ireland, 1916-2016* (Dublin, 2016), 47–68: 50; Klein cites a memorandum from the Department of Finance to the Department of the President, dated 21 May 1937.

[8] Richard Henebry, *Irish music* (Dublin, 1903), 14.

[9] See, Harry White, 'The invisible art review—a mosaic of music brought to light', *The Irish Times*, 10 December 2016.

FEBRUARY

1 FEBRUARY 1922

FRANK WALSH'S AMERICAN IMPERIALISM

IRISH REVOLUTION AND AMERICAN EMPIRE

On 1 February 1922 the Irish American political reformer Frank P. Walsh published an article in the liberal US weekly, *The Nation*. Unlike many of his other publications over the previous few years, this short opinion piece did not concern Ireland. Walsh focused instead on the US military occupation of Haiti and the Dominican

Opposite: Irish-American lawyer, republican and anti-imperialist, Frank P. Walsh, *c.* 1915.

Republic, and the thrust of his analysis was summed up in the article's two-word title: 'American imperialism'.[1] Nonetheless, Ireland's recent history was not far from his mind. As he argued forcefully in his article, British policy in Ireland provided a near-perfect prism for understanding what was currently transpiring in the Caribbean.

Difficult as 1922 was for Ireland, it was also a challenge for American liberals like Walsh. By the end of 1921 political conservatism was ascendant. Both Democratic and Republican party leaders had abandoned the progressivism that had shaped much of the US political landscape for the previous two decades. Big business was dominant in Washington, D.C. and efforts to regulate the market on behalf of workers and consumers had been effectively blocked. Black Americans and immigrants from Asia and eastern and southern Europe faced a rising tide of racism, while trade unions had suffered defeats in a number of dramatic post-war strikes.

Over the course of 1922, however, a new kind of progressive coalition began to take shape, one that placed what the social reformer Jane Addams called 'a nascent world consciousness' at the centre of its political vision.[2] Integral to this perspective was a bracing critique of US imperialism. There were many factors shaping this critique, which would culminate in Robert La Follette's Progressive party presidential bid in 1924. The Women's International League for Peace and Freedom, which Addams had helped found five years earlier, embraced a new moral realism that subjected US foreign policy to the same scrutiny as that of other great powers. Black leaders like W.E.B. Du Bois grew increasingly critical of both American and European colonialism, and labour radicals began to explore new forms of international working-class solidarity. But equally important was a small group of liberal and left-wing Irish Americans who had worked assiduously to build US support for the Irish revolution. Frank Walsh was one of these.

Born to a working-class family in St Louis's immigrant 'Kerry Patch' in 1864, Walsh had come of age politically as a labour lawyer and reform Democrat in turn-of-the-century Kansas City. He went on to serve prominently in both of Woodrow Wilson's administrations, first as chair of the US Commission on Industrial Relations (1913–16), which drew public attention to the abusive power exercised by the nation's largest corporations, and later as co-chair of the National War Labor Board (1918), which consistently ruled in favour of workers and helped prepare the ground for the pro-labour policies of the later New Deal era. An exponent of a Catholic-based vision of social justice, Walsh remained a passionate advocate for working people, arguing in April 1922 that the case for a 'living wage' was 'one far above the law and went down into the deepest moral questions, the structure of society, and even into fundamental religion'.[3]

Walsh was also a major figure in transatlantic Irish republicanism. At the February 1919 Irish Race Convention, he was picked to chair the American Commission on Irish Independence, a group of three prominent US citizens who travelled to the Paris Peace Conference with the goal of winning an international commitment to Ireland's independence. Their mission failed, but Walsh subsequently advised Éamon de Valera during his American tour of 1919–20 and took the lead in organising the US sale of Irish bond-certificates, which raised over $5 million for Ireland's revolutionary government. In 1922 he cast his lot with anti-Treaty forces and played a critical role in the New York legal battles to keep those funds out of the hands of the Irish Free State government. When Walsh died in 1939 de Valera hailed him as 'one of Ireland's truest friends' and dispatched Robert Brennan, Ireland's minister in Washington, to attend his Kansas City funeral.[4]

Walsh was no narrow Irish nationalist, however, but rather a committed opponent of imperialism in general. In a December 1918 speech in New York, he lashed out at the British empire, emphasising not Ireland, but Egypt, where 'for 50 years England has continued its grievous assaults'.[5] While in Paris the following spring, he reached out to Sa'd Zaghlul, who was working to put the Egyptian independence case before the Peace Conference and who asked Walsh to serve as 'Egyptian Counsel' in the United States. An arrangement worked out by Seán T. Ó Ceallaigh (who was also in Paris, representing the Irish Republic) provided Walsh with $90,000 in expenses and fees. Once back in New York, he used some of this money to found an organisation called the League of Oppressed Peoples, whose ambitious goals were 'to defeat militaristic aggression and to secure self-determination for all peoples'. With representatives from Ireland, India, Korea, and sub-Saharan Africa, the league presented the Irish cause as an integral part of a movement of all those oppressed by imperialism.[6]

In 1922 Walsh extended his critique to include American conduct in the Caribbean. Though justified by a rhetoric of 'benevolence' that administrators of the British empire would have understood, the US military occupation of Haiti (1915–34) and the Dominican Republic (1916–24) was motivated mainly by a desire to cement American control of those two neighbours' economies and to protect the new and strategically important Panama Canal. US marines soon found themselves fighting local rebels (known in Haiti as Cacos) and, in response, burned entire villages and brutally executed those they believed to be rebels. These were the events that prompted Walsh's angry *Nation* article.

'The American Foreign Office is in Wall Street. Its agents are the Imperial General Staff in Washington', he began, observing sadly that 'the imperialism which our ancestors resisted our present rulers have condoned and practiced to our national disgrace'. Especially troubling to Walsh were the parallels with British policy in Ireland:

In the story of these subjugated [Caribbean] republics American atrocities take the place of British atrocities. Padraic Pearse, Connolly, and Kevin Barry have French and Spanish names; and the 'murder gang' are called Cacos and bandits instead of Sinn Feiners; otherwise Haiti and Santo Domingo might be Ireland.

Walsh ended his piece with a call to action. Just as Irish men and women had struggled to force 'British Imperial Forces' from the soil of Ireland, so now 'all true Americans and all true Irishmen' should work to drive 'the Imperial United States Forces from the republics of Haiti and Santo Domingo'. Over and over again through the nineteenth and early twentieth century, Irish nationalists had stressed the sharp distinction between 'republican' America and 'imperial' Britain. Walsh emphasised the similarities.

Walsh's views were not widely held among Irish Americans. But they were not totally out of the mainstream. Many Irish nationalists had opposed the US acquisition of Puerto Rico and the Philippines as colonies after the Spanish–American War (1898), and even the moderate Friends of Irish Freedom provided financial support for the League of Oppressed Peoples. 'When one understood British imperialism, it was an open window to all imperialism', the famous Irish American radical, Elizabeth Gurley Flynn, once observed.[7] Frank Walsh would have agreed.

by David Brundage

FURTHER READING

David Brundage, *Irish nationalists in America: the politics of exile, 1798–1998* (New York, 2016)

Alan Dawley, *Changing the world: American progressives in war and revolution* (Princeton, NJ, 2003)

Laurent Dubois, *Haiti: the aftershocks of history* (New York, 2012)

NOTES

[1] Frank P. Walsh, 'American imperialism', *The Nation*, 1 February 1922, 115–16.

[2] Jane Addams, *The second twenty years at Hull-House* (New York, 1930), 7.

[3] Frank P. Walsh, 'Catholic economics', *The Nation*, 8 February 1922, 170; 'Frank P. Walsh pleads for living wage for rail workers', *New York Times*, 14 April 1922.

[4] Francis M. Carroll, *Money for Ireland: finance, diplomacy, politics, and the First Dáil Éireann loans, 1919–1936* (Westport, CT, 2002), 16–20, 38–39, 50–51, 57–62, 69–75; University College Dublin Archives, Éamon de Valera papers, P150/971, de Valera to Mrs Kate Walsh, 2 May 1939; 'President mourns Walsh', *New York Times*, 6 May 1939.

[5] New York Public Library Archives and Manuscripts (hereafter NYPL), Frank P. Walsh papers, Mss Col 3211/ 7, William P. Harvey, untitled typescript, December 1918.

[6] NYPL, Maloney Collection of Irish historical papers, Mss Col 1854/9, memorandum by W.J. Maloney of conversation with Frank Walsh, 30 December 1921; National Library of Ireland, Seán T. O Ceallaigh papers, MS 27,690, typescript 'Recollections of Zaghloul Pasha' [193?]; David Brundage, 'The Easter Rising and New York's anticolonial nationalists', in Miriam Nyhan Grey (ed.), *Ireland's allies: America and the 1916 Easter Rising* (Dublin, 2016), 347–59: 355–57.

[7] Elizabeth Gurley Flynn, *The rebel girl: an autobiography* (New York, 1973; reprint of 1955 edn), 35.

2 FEBRUARY 1922

THE PUBLICATION OF *ULYSSES*

'IRISH BLACK BOTTOM BLUES': RACE, MODERNITY AND THE CITY

James Joyce's *Ulysses* was published on his 40th birthday, 2 February 1922. In the Circe episode, it captures Leopold Bloom's spinning thoughts on the American blackface entertainer Eugene Stratton. Bloom's crude racial characterisation of minstrels in 'white duck suits' and hands that 'jingle the twingtwang wires' is woven into his stroll through the modern city. Stratton also appears in The Wandering Rocks episode, when Father John Conmee glimpses a billboard advertising his appearance that evening at the Theatre Royal.

Although published in 1922 *Ulysses* was set in 1904, so Joyce's rich details on the social and material culture of city life evoke the Edwardian, rather than the Irish Free State, era. Among other things, *Ulysses* offers a narrative of Irish urban life and puts the city at the heart of experience in a way that is unusual in Irish literary writing of the early twentieth century. For the most part within Irish literary discourses, narratives of the city, and particularly the urban middle classes, take second place to the importance of rural life.

The dominance of the agrarian, posited as the most 'authentic' landscape, resulted in its representation (notably by Synge, Gregory and Yeats) in city theatres 'showcasing the rural in the urban centre'.[1] The tendency in political discourse in presenting rural Ireland (particularly a bucolic version) as a synecdoche for the nation as whole persisted during the early years of the Free State.[2] As a reading of *Ulysses* shows, city spaces are complex, with poverty and wealth within a few streets of each other, and theatres, cinemas, parks and shops are open to all people. The importance of the city as a socio-political agent of change, of industry, technology and leisure means that analyses of urban experiences are crucial to understanding how different cultural representations are circulated, seen and understood.

The presence of Eugene Stratton in *Ulysses* demonstrates the types of popular entertainment available in Dublin in 1904, and by 1922 there was still a demand for American-style minstrel shows. *The Irish Times* of 16 September 1922 advertised a blackface double act, Chick Harlem and Joan Bronx, at the Tivoli theatre on Burgh Quay. Harlem & Bronx appeared with 'Rastus and Banks, the coloured American Entertainers'. Chick Harlem became Bud Flanagan, singer of 'Underneath the Arches', with the duo Flanagan and Allen. All that summer, blackface acts performed on Dublin stages: G.H. Elliott, a British act described as 'the chocolate coloured coon', appeared at the Theatre Royal in June, while the 'black and white' comedian act, Dene & Dixon performed the following week.

From the late nineteenth century, American minstrel shows had been popular sources for cheap sheet music. The music was easily sight-read making it suitable for piano lessons, and its vocal range suited the amateur singer. Consequently, songs from the minstrel repertoire were widely known, creating a demand for music hall shows featuring touring American black musicians. As early as 1903 an American troupe, Uncle Sam's Pickaninny Minstrels and Creole Singers, had played Waterford, Clonmel and Cork, and the renowned minstrel group Mohawk, Moore and Burgess played the Dublin circuit in 1916.[3]

The popularity of minstrel shows, and the shortage of black entertainers, meant that home-grown British blackface acts appeared on the bill in the larger theatres. For example, Stewart Morton, reviewed as the 'present day Eugene Stratton' (Stratton died in 1918), performed Stratton's popular repertoire of 'coon songs' in The Tivoli, Dublin and The Palace, Cork in spring 1922. The show, 'direct from the London Palladium', was 'a pleasing delineation of coon character studies'.[4]

Yours Right
D J Banks
London 11-12-22.

Recording blackface events and song titles is painful, as the terms casually used to describe minstrels and other black entertainers are offensive to us now, but at the time they did not attract censure

from lobby groups such as the National Association for the Advancement of Coloured People (NAACP) in the United States.[5] The presentation of these shows, however, featuring songs about plantation life, skits about foolish farmhands, and extolling lazy afternoons, suggests that the experience of slavery was nothing more harsh than a boarding school. Moreover, the infantilising representation of blackness is evident in how blackness as costume is associated with children and entertainment at this time. In March 1922 young Donald Lewin won a fancy-dress competition dressed as a golliwog at a children's hospital benefit. That summer, a troupe of children performed 'a pickanniny dance' at an Eye and Ear Hospital fundraiser, and the Leggett-Byrne School of Dancing staged a show at the Theatre Royal featuring 'a coon dance' alongside minuets and 'other picturesque examples'.[6]

By the early 1920s the popularity of the pre-war minstrel songs and their sentimental delivery was waning in favour of syncopated dancing, ragtime and jazz orchestral music circulated through radio broadcasts from the London Palladium and the availability of gramophone records. Dances featuring syncopated orchestral music were advertised all over Ireland.[7] Ragtime and jazz had been popular with select audiences since the late teens, but there was now a marked shift away from British minstrel acts towards authentic African American acts such as the Southern Syncopated Orchestra. In truth, this was more about the growing hegemony of American culture, but it also indicates the emergence of a distinctly modern sound, generated and performed by black bodies and voices. Blackface shows, plantation melodies and soft-shoe shuffles rendered black experience safe and harmless and as an object of comic regard, even fondness, by Irish audiences. By contrast, the syncopated rhythms, energetic vocals and complicated choreography of the new shows was undeniably contemporary. An October 1921 review of the Southern Syncopated Orchestra in Dublin, identifies this difference, noting the quality of the company compared with the usual 'negro mistrelry' and its performers 'flanked by bones and banjos'.[8] This particular performance was exceptional, as shortly before, the SS Rowan—a passenger ship taking the troupe from Glasgow to Dublin—sank, drowning 36 people including nine members of the orchestra. British Pathé footage shows the remaining members landing in Dublin.[9]

Some of the difference in taste was generational; younger audiences were keen to learn American dance steps and styles such as the *Charleston* and the *Black Bottom*. Dance schools and exhibition dancers offered instruction on the latest dance crazes. The *Black Bottom* was 'a combination of the hula-hula, the *Charleston*, and the shuffle'.[10] Both dances suited the unrestricted, shorter skirt lengths favoured by women at the time; pleated skirts were perfect for 'kicking up your heels' and knee bumps. The *Black Bottom* dance originated in the Harlem show *Dinah*, but another version, 'Irish Black Bottom Blues', was performed and sung by Louis Armstrong. He sings: 'all the ladies and the cooies/laid aside their Irish reels' and laughs 'now Ireland's gone Black Bottom crazy/you ought to see them dance'. Harlem's cultural renaissance, nightlife and popular culture was not unknown to Irish people and there are many connections to be drawn between the Irish cultural revival and the Harlem renaissance.[11] Indeed, in a 1922 anthology of negro poetry, James Weldon Johnson acknowledges that black music, dancing and performance are important cultural expressions, but what black literature needed was to find a vernacular: 'to do…what Synge did for the Irish'.[12] Bridging the urban and rural divide, Synge's idiomatic rural language resonates through urban theatres in Irish cities and, travelling across the Atlantic, is refracted back via Harlem within articulations of black experience.

by Elaine Sisson

FURTHER READING

Tracy Mishkin, *The Harlem and Irish renaissances: language, identity and representation* (Gainesville, FL, 1998)

Michael Pickering, *Blackface minstrelsy in Britain* (Hampshire, 2008)

NOTES

[1] Marilyn Reizbaum, 'Urban legends', *Éire-Ireland* 45 (1 and 2) (Spring/Summer 2010), 242–65: 256.

[2] Joseph Valente, 'Editor's introduction', *Éire-Ireland* 45 (1 and 2) (Spring/Summer 2010), 5–10: 6.

[3] Uncle Sam's pickaninny minstrels and Creole singers, Theatre Royal Waterford, 25–9 May 1903; the Palace Cork, Assembly Rooms, 14 May 1903; the Theatrical Town Hall/Murphy's Theatre Clonmel, 1–2 June 1903. Mohawk, Moore and Burgess were a combined minstrel group (Eugene Stratton had been an early member) who played the Queen's Theatre in October 1916, followed by a week at the Theatre Royal in Waterford.

[4] *Evening Herald*, 14 March 1922.

[5] Tim Brooks, 'The minstrel show on records', *The Blackface minstrel show in mass media: 20th century performances on radio, records, film and television* (Jefferson, NC, 2020), 1–5: 2.

[6] Donald Lewin in fancy dress, *Irish Life*, 3 March 1922; Royal Victoria benefit, *Irish Life*, 12 May 1922; Theatre Royal show, *Irish Life*, 26 May 1922.

[7] For example, on 7 January 1922, the *Sligo Champion* advertised a weekly dance in Sligo Town Hall to the music of the Grafton Syncopated Orchestra. Dublin had a regular dance night with 'jazz and syncopated orchestra' at Mills Hall on Merrion Row. *Dublin Evening Telegraph*, 10 November 1922.

[8] 'Modern Minstrels: features of the Syncopated Orchestra', *Freeman's Journal*, 18 October 1921.

[9] British Pathé, '*SS Rowan* survivors land in Dublin', October 1921; available at: www.britishpathe.com/video/s-s-ss-rowan-survivors (14 April 2021).

[10] Thomas Brothers, *Louis Armstrong, master of modernism* (New York, 2014), 236.

[11] Tracy Mishkin, *The Harlem and Irish renaissances: language, identity and representation* (Gainesville, FL, 1998).

[12] James Weldon Johnson, 'Preface', *The book of American Negro poetry* (New York, 1922), vii–xxxvii: xxxiv.

5 FEBRUARY 1922

CUMANN NA MBAN OPPOSES THE ANGLO−IRISH TREATY

WOMEN ACTIVISTS DURING THE CIVIL WAR

On Sunday, 5 February 1922, Cumann na mBan held a special convention in the Round Room of Dublin's Mansion House to discuss the Anglo-Irish Treaty. A majority of those present (419 of 482, or 87 per cent) voted in favour of the motion by Mary MacSwiney (Sinn Féin TD for Cork Borough in the second Dáil) to reaffirm allegiance to the Irish Republic and reject the Treaty. Jenny Wyse Power's counter-proposal that the organisation remain neutral was defeated.[1] Thus, Cumann na mBan became the first republican organisation to reject the Treaty.

During the Dáil debate on the Treaty in December 1921, MacSwiney had delivered one of the longest and most vehement speeches against it. Over the course of two hours and forty minutes she denounced it as a rejection of the republic 'proclaimed and established by the men of Easter Week, 1916', making particular reference to the opposition of the 'women of Ireland' to 'the men that want to surrender'.[2] This illustrated a gendered division on the Treaty; MacSwiney was one of the six women TDs in the second Dáil, all of whom voted to reject the Treaty.

Among the reasons cited for the unanimity of the female TDs in voting against the Treaty was their close familial relationships to men who had died in the cause of Irish independence. Four of the six had lost close male relatives to violent or traumatic deaths.[3] MacSwiney's brother, Terence, died in October 1920 after a prolonged hunger strike. Two of Margaret Pearse's sons, Patrick and William, and Kathleen Clarke's husband, Thomas, were executed for their roles in the Easter Rising. Kate O'Callaghan's husband, Michael, a former Sinn Féin mayor of Limerick, was shot dead in her presence in their home by Crown forces in March 1921.

To suggest that female political opposition to the Treaty was predicated on the importance in the republican pantheon of these women's husbands, brothers and sons, negates the significance of their own political ideology. Their activities to that point, and their subsequent political careers, illustrate their own personal commitments to republicanism. Kathleen Clarke belonged to a family of noted republicans with links to the Fenians, and during her terms of office as the first female lord mayor of Dublin (1939–41) she refused to wear the mayoral chain because of its links to William of Orange. Although a close friend of Éamon de Valera, Mary MacSwiney was never reconciled to his new Fianna Fáil party or to the legitimacy of the independent Irish state. Two of the six women TDs—Dr Ada English and Constance Markievicz—did not have any males relatives fighting for Irish independence, further undermining the notion of female political opposition to the Treaty being based on such personal relationships.[4] The minority of women who supported the Treaty re-convened under a new organisation named Cumann na Saoirse. Though lasting only until 1923 and not as active as Cumann na mBan during the civil war, Cumann na Saoirse demonstrated 'that not all Irishwomen rejected the Treaty'.[5]

The activities of Cumann na mBan during the civil war largely mirrored those the organisation had engaged in during the War of Independence. Applications for military service pensions detail how women secured and transported arms and ammunition for the IRA and catered, provisioned and offered safe houses for men on the run. Although not involved in actual direct combat, the military-related activities of women exposed them to serious danger; in November 1922 Margueritte (Fleming) Sinnott travelled

about a mile across country while under fire from the National Army in order to re-supply the local IRA unit with ammunition for an ambush.[6]

Opposite: Depiction of Countess Markievicz by artist and anti-Treaty republican activist Grace Gifford Plunkett, 1927.

Most of these women were active where IRA resistance to the Irish Free State was strongest, including Dublin, Munster and the west. A small number were active in Northern Ireland, assisting the cross-border campaign of Frank Aiken's division. Annie (Keelan) Maguire used her Dundalk base to transmit despatches from Dublin to the northern IRA, hid arms in the Sperrin mountains, raised funds for prisoners' dependants and oversaw intelligence operations that resulted in the rescue of republican prisoners from Dundalk prison, prior to her arrest in Northern Ireland and deportation back to the Free State.[7]

Cumann na mBan's former comrades-turned-adversaries had few illusions about the significance of their role in the republican campaign and as a result a significant number were arrested and imprisoned; at least five hundred women and girls were incarcerated, most of them in Dublin's Mountjoy and Kilmainham jails and the hastily re-purposed North Dublin Union workhouse, where sanitary conditions and facilities were primitive.[8]

A valuable insight into the Kilmainham female prisoners' political ideology and derisive attitudes towards their captors exists in the extant graffiti on the jail's (now museum) walls and in surviving autograph books, a topic explored further in the following essay.[9] The poor conditions experienced by women prisoners and the experience of some in undertaking life-threatening activities, such as hunger strikes, often impaired their subsequent health. Following her release from prison in May 1923 Eilish McNamara continued to suffer from bronchial problems for a further two years; while in 1951 Nora Gavin was diagnosed as being in 'an advanced state of nervous exhaustion' arising from the trauma she experienced during the revolutionary years.[10]

Many women faced challenges in convincing pension assessors of the validity of their claims for military service and disability pensions. This attitude arose in part from hostility within the Free State to the strength of Cumann na mBan's anti-Treaty stance and was most obvious in the initial refusal of a pension to Margaret Skinnider, ostensibly on the grounds that as a woman she did not adhere to the legislative definition of a 'soldier', but also because she was 'a prominent irregular'.[11] The predominance of women on the republican side resulted in fewer women TDs in the Dáil in its early years because of the refusal of republicans to take their seats, and a misogynistic backlash from treatyite commentators such as P.S. O'Hegarty, who dismissed the women TDs who voted against the Treaty as 'furies'.[12] This negative attitude towards women infused the restrictive role envisaged for women in public life in the new state after 1922.

by Marie Coleman

FURTHER READING

Jason Knirck, *Women of the Dáil: gender, republicanism and the Anglo-Irish Treaty* (Dublin, 2006)

Cal McCarthy, *Cumann na mBan and the Irish revolution* (Cork, 2014 edn)

Sinéad McCoole, *No ordinary women: Irish female activists in the revolutionary years, 1900–1923* (Dublin, 2003)

NOTES

[1] *Irish Independent*, 6 February 1922.
[2] Jason Knirck, *Women of the Dáil: gender, republicanism and the Anglo-Irish Treaty* (Dublin, 2006), 76.
[3] Knirck, *Women of the Dáil*, 96.
[4] Kathleen Clarke (Helen Litton ed.), *Revolutionary woman: my fight for Irish freedom* (Dublin, 1991); Charlotte H. Fallon, *Soul of fire: a biography of Mary MacSwiney* (Cork, 1986); Brendan Kelly, *Ada English: patriot and psychiatrist* (Dublin, 2014).
[5] Mary McAuliffe, '"An idea has gone abroad that all women are against the Treaty": Cumann na Saoirse and pro-Treaty Women, 1922–3', in Mícheál Ó Fathartaigh and Liam Weeks (eds), *The Treaty: debating and establishing the Irish state* (Newbridge, 2018), 160–82.
[6] Military Archives (MA), Military Service Pensions Collection (MSPC), MSP34REF50888 Margueritte Sinnott.
[7] MA, MSPC, MSP34REF56373 Annie (Keelan) Maguire.
[8] Sinead McCoole, *No ordinary women: Irish female activists in the revolutionary years, 1900–1923* (Dublin, 2003), 218–39.
[9] Laura McAtackney 'Kilmainham Gaol graffiti: exploring female experiences of imprisonment during the Irish civil war, 1922–1923', available at: www.kilmainhamgaolgraffiti.com (6 August 2020).
[10] MA, MSPC, MSP34REF60762 Eilish McNamara; MSP34REF55990 Nora Gavin.
[11] Mary McAuliffe, *Margaret Skinnider* (Dublin, 2020), 82–6.
[12] P.S. O'Hegarty, *The victory of Sinn Féin* (Dublin, 1924), 103.

6 FEBRUARY 1922

PIUS XI ASCENDS TO THE PAPACY

RELIGION, GRAFFITI AND POLITICAL IMPRISONMENT

Pius XI's papal reign (1922–39) officially began on 6 February 1922. It may seem an unlikely event to tie into Irish history, but there are a number of compelling reasons as to why it is a date of symbolic and material value. The role of religion in the so-called revolutionary period has been explored in a number of ways by historians. In recent years there have been contentious debates about the role of religious sectarianism in the targeting of people and places in the south of Ireland during the War of Independence and the civil war.[1] In the north of Ireland, the 'Belfast pogroms' (1920–22) and associated civil disturbances, riots and orchestrated attacks demonstrably had a sectarian motive, with religion functioning primarily as an identifier. There have also been thoughtful reflections on the role of rank-and-file priests, as well as the policies of the Catholic hierarchy, in their active support or rejection of the various sides during the conflict.[2]

From the perspective of combatants, Michael McCabe has argued that the anti-Treaty forces made claim to the moral high ground in their

rejection of the Anglo-Irish Treaty.[3] Eventually, this claim was categorically contradicted by the hierarchy of the Catholic Church in Ireland through the bishops' pastoral letter of 22 October 1922, which unambiguously condemned the violence of the anti-Treaty forces. In response to spiritual sanctions against them, ranging from refusal to provide communion or absolution to excommunication, the anti-Treaty forces looked outside of Ireland, specifically to the Vatican, for moral and institutional support. By the end of 1922, the figure of Pope Pius XI did not simply represent the highest level of the Roman Catholic Church, he was also the ultimate court of spiritual appeal to both sides. Arthur Clery and Conn Murphy made a direct appeal against the October pastoral to Pope Pius XI, and as a result Monsignor Salvatore Luzio arrived as papal envoy in March 1923. His mandate was to investigate the situation in Ireland, much to the hostility of the Irish bishops.

The desperate nature of republican appeals to the new pope became materially manifest in what is now itself almost a holy relic of the revolutionary period—Kilmainham Gaol. During an extensive survey of historic graffiti in the building (initially funded by the Irish Research Council in 2012–14 on the West Wing of the gaol; extended by the Office of Public Works to the East Wing and Courthouse in 2015), a portrait of Pope Pius XI was located. This is not entirely unusual—religious iconography dating from the civil war period was common throughout the prison cells—but

no portrait or other depiction of any other identifiable member of the Roman Catholic Church was discovered during the entire survey.[4] The location of the portrait of the pope was also unusual. It was only during a supplementary phase of recording that a long-locked room on the top floor of the Administrative area was opened to reveal an extant assemblage of various forms of graffiti—text, portraits and shapes, mainly in pencil—spread across all of the room's walls. While the assemblage was not numerically extensive—65 separate pieces of graffiti were recorded—the contents of the room were unusual, and featured examples not recorded elsewhere in the building. Most of the graffiti remaining in the room appear to have been created contemporaneously, and the most prominent examples were strategically located: two framed portraits were located beside the door and one was above the fireplace.

Opposite and above (l–r): Located in Debtors' Room 1, this portrait of Pope Pius XI replicated details from photographs of his February 1922 inauguration, including his glasses and robe.

Depiction of the Sacred Heart, inscribed with 'IHS' and 'Thy Kingdom Come', located on the West Wing's middle floor.

The classical title of this image, located in a cell on the West Wing's middle floor, refers to the goddess Aphrodite / Venus.

The title of this image, located on the West Wing's top floor, depicting a ball-gown-wearing socialite (presumed to be Countess Markievicz), appears to have been expunged.

The portrait of Pope Pius XI was the centre-piece of the room, situated above the fireplace and drawn with an elaborate *trompe l'oeil* oval frame. There is no signature associated with the portrait so it is impossible to know for sure who created this image, but there are some clues. First, this graffito was not located in the cell blocks, where the majority of the thousands of examples of civil war graffiti remain. It was inscribed on the wall in what is known as 'Debtors Room 1', which is a large, rectangular room with sash windows and a fireplace, far away from the prisoners' wings and cells. This room would not have been used to hold 'ordinary' prisoners during the revolutionary period, but probably to isolate exceptional individuals, particularly leaders and/or hunger strikers. The portrait of Pope Pius XI is not the only portrait in the room—there are five extant portraits; two have been whitewashed and another is partially hidden under the pope's portrait— but it is the only datable piece of graffiti by virtue of having a *terminus post quem* of 6 February 1922.

The surviving graffiti at Kilmainham Gaol are an important source for revealing lived experiences of the civil war.[5] This is especially the case for women who were interned in the gaol for periods from November 1922 to April 1923, and who left many marks,[6] but are less prominently recalled in public memory.[7] Most of the gaol's extant pieces of graffiti are contained in the West Wing, but their survival does not simply correlate to where graffiti were originally created; rather, it reflects decisions made by the Kilmainham Jail Restoration Society. Meeting notes from 1958 reveal that the old IRA committee would only support the restoration of the prison if 'nothing of or relating to the period after 1921 would be identified with the Kilmainham project'.[8] While the restoration committee focused on the East Wing, they removed most of the plastered walls and with them the majority of the post-1921 graffiti (only seven cells have even partial walls intact). The relative neglect of the West Wing to early restoration efforts ensures its graffiti survive better. There is evidence of targeted whitewashing of graffiti (including in Debtors Room 1), often because of references to sensitive matters relating to the civil war (mainly partition and executions), but this is minimal.

While depictions of Pope Pius XI have not been found elsewhere in the prison, there are textual and pictorial references to religion in every corridor in the West Wing. The most common forms of religious graffiti are crosses or crucifixes, from simple, engraved, hatched crosses through to elaborate, stepped, cruciform monuments. The most well-known piece of religious graffiti in the prison, the mural of Mary and Child created by Grace Gifford Plunkett in the East Wing, survives (although extensively 'restored'); the large altar mural she created has, however, long disappeared. There are ornate and intricate religious graffiti that persist in the West Wing, but nothing that matches the scale or extent of Grace Gifford's murals. Rather, a range of small crosses, monuments, prayers and even an ornate Sacred Heart with the words 'Thy Kingdom Come', remain as material indicators of the religious sentiments of the anti-Treaty prisoners.

by Laura McAtackney

FURTHER READING

Laura McAtackney, 'Material and intangible interventions as future-making heritage at Kilmainham Gaol, Dublin', *Journal of Contemporary Archaeology* 6 (1) (2019), 120–35

Rory O'Dwyer, *The Bastille of Ireland: Kilmainham Gaol: from ruin to restoration* (Dublin, 2010)

Niamh O'Sullivan, *Written in stone: the graffiti in Kilmainham Jail* (Dublin, 2014)

NOTES

[1] Andy Bielenberg, 'Exodus: the emigration of southern Irish Protestants during the Irish War of Independence and the civil war', *Past & Present* 218 (1) (February 2013), 199–233.
[2] M.P. McCabe, *For God and Ireland: the fight for moral superiority in Ireland, 1922–1932* (Dublin, 2013).
[3] McCabe, *For God and Ireland*.
[4] Laura McAtackney, 'Kilmainham Gaol graffiti: exploring female experiences of imprisonment during the Irish Civil War, 1922–1923'; available at: www.kilmainhamgaolgraffiti.com (14 April 2021).
[5] Niamh O'Sullivan, *Written in stone: the graffiti in Kilmainham Jail* (Dublin, 2014).
[6] Laura McAtackney, 'Material and intangible interventions as future-making heritage at Kilmainham Gaol, Dublin', *Journal of Contemporary Archaeology* 6 (1) (2019), 120–35.
[7] Margaret Ward, *Unmanageable revolutionaries: women and Irish nationalism* (Dublin, 1995).
[8] Rory O'Dwyer, *The Bastille of Ireland: Kilmainham Gaol: from ruin to restoration* (Dublin, 2010).

12 FEBRUARY 1922

THE NICHOLSON REVIVAL

'DIVINE DYNAMITE': POPULAR PROTESTANTISM IN BELFAST

Against the backdrop of sectarian violence, economic depression and attempts to consolidate the new state of Northern Ireland, an evangelistic mission began in the Shankill Road area of west Belfast on 12 February 1922. At the end of the first week, *The Witness*, the Presbyterian newspaper of record, reported overcrowded venues and that 'Large numbers' had 'entered definitely into a new relationship with God'. The lively meetings were a welcome challenge to 'the dull, prosaic, ordinary services' that were said to have deterred the working classes from attending church. The success of the mission led to rejoicing among 'the people in Ulster who love the Lord' and who were 'looking with wistful longing to a similar visitation in the districts where they live'. *The Witness* concluded that the gospel was

> still the Divine dynamite to change men and women, and to bring in the brighter and the better day which multitudes of hungry hearts are longing...It would be a terrible thing if our

want of faith or our prayer should hinder the rising tide of God's boundless grace from visiting the stricken land of Ireland.[1]

The individual who had sparked this outbreak of religious fervour was William Patteson Nicholson. Nicholson was born near Bangor, Co. Down, in April 1876. After a spell as a hard-living merchant seaman and a railway construction worker in South Africa, his life was transformed by a personal religious conversion on 22 May 1899 and another spiritual experience soon afterwards. He undertook religious training in Glasgow and worked as an evangelist in Lanarkshire from July 1903 until September 1908. He then joined the American revivalists, J. Wilbur Chapman and Charles M. Alexander, and preached extensively in Australia and the United States. While in America, he was ordained in April 1914 as an evangelist by one of the many Presbyterian denominations, and during the Great War was employed by the Bible Institute of Los Angeles. He returned to his homeland from Glasgow in January 1921 and began a series of missions that swept Protestant Ulster until June 1923.

Nicholson defined himself as an evangelist whose sole responsibility was to call individuals to turn from their sin and to undergo the personal religious experiences that had transformed his own life. Nicholson worked with, not against, the Churches, though he was a constant critic of religious formalism or 'churchianity'. He described his role as 'quarry work', blasting the rock of sin and indifference and allowing the Churches to shape the rough-hewn converts into useful church members. Preaching a demanding code of personal devotion and morality that offered certainty in uncertain times, Nicholson attracted thousands, not least because this so-called vulgar evangelist spoke in the idiom of Protestant Ulster. 'There are many things which make Mr Nicholson's presentation of the truth pleasing to an Ulster audience; but nothing more surely than that he speaks in the common tongue.'[2] Nicholson spoke exclusively to Protestants and was a unionist, yet, apart from his advocacy of a form of prohibition, he never discussed politics. He was, first and foremost, an evangelist:

> Ye must be born again. There is no substitute for this...You may be a minister, or an elder, or a deacon, or a Sunday School teacher, or an evangelist, or a missionary; but ye must be born again. If you are rich, you must be born again; if you are poor, you must be born again; if you are learned, you must

be born again; if you are a Presbyterian, or a Methodist, or an Episcopalian, you must be born again; if you are a Sinn Feiner or an Orangeman, you must be born again. There are not 50 ways to heaven; there is only one. You must be born again.[3]

The Shankill Road Mission where Presbyterian preacher W.P. Nicholson (1876–1959) conducted meetings in early 1922.

Many lives were transformed under Nicholson's influence, and he especially appealed to working-class men, a social group that the Protestant Churches struggled to engage. But he also divided opinion. For instance, the *Belfast Telegraph* published a letter from an inhabitant of the Shankill Road who claimed that 'it is abundantly clear that that outspoken evangelist has succeeded in loosening quite a number of agents of the devil in Belfast and district'; on the same page, another correspondent declared, 'Mr Nicholson is preaching a creed of hatred, of cursedness, and vulgarity, which, if allowed to continue, will do more harm than good.' An editorial note informed readers that the paper had 'received a very large number of letters dealing with this controversy, but the limitations on our space preclude us from continuing the correspondence'.[4]

In November 1922, Archibald Irwin, an evangelist connected with the Presbyterian Church, sought to answer the question, 'Is there a revival in Ulster?' He calculated that 12,409 individuals had undergone spiritual counselling, most of whom were adults, and that there had been 'large and unprecedented' numbers of new communicants in local churches. Nicholson had reenergised religious activism and piety, and this resurgence was perpetuated by Christian Workers' Unions for the benefit of local churches. Irwin's conclusion was circumspect, but hopeful:

> That in the places where the missions have been held there are many signs of a general revival of religion, but that this revival is not of such a widespread character as to enable me to say that it has touched much of Ulster yet. However, the signs are distinctly hopeful that it will ultimately do so.[5]

At a farewell meeting in June 1923, Nicholson attributed his success to a steadfast commitment to gospel truth; he had made no compromise with either 'unworldliness in the church or unbelief in the pulpit and pews'.[6] To underline the broader significance of Nicholson's campaign, a commemorative pamphlet was produced, *From civil war to revival victory*, in which leading Irish Protestants sang Nicholson's praise.[7]

Nicholson returned to Northern Ireland in July 1924, this time conducting missions in provincial towns, and held his first mission in Dublin in November 1925. Yet by that stage, patience with Nicholson was wearing thin amongst many of the leaders of the Protestant Churches. He was now identified as a troublemaker, associated with unsuccessful efforts within the Presbyterian Church to stamp out so-called theological 'modernism'. This impression was subsequently reinforced by Ian Paisley, who sought Nicholson's approval.[8] Though both shared a populist appeal and bitterly opposed theological liberalism, Nicholson did not advocate separation from Churches that tolerated error, and he ignored politics. Nicholson may have been sincerely wrong in his analysis and blind to the constraints of his culture, but his claim to be an evangelist committed to saving souls needs to be taken seriously. There has always been more to popular Protestant religiosity in Northern Ireland than simple opposition to 'Rome Rule'.

by Andrew R. Holmes

FURTHER READING

Mavis Heaney (ed.), *To God be the glory. The personal memoirs of Rev. William P. Nicholson* (Belfast, 2004)

Andrew R. Holmes, 'Revivalism and fundamentalism in Ulster: W.P. Nicholson in context', in D.W. Bebbington and David Ceri Jones (eds), *Evangelicalism and fundamentalism: the experience of the United Kingdom during the twentieth century* (Oxford, 2013), 253–72

R.A. Wells, 'Transatlantic revivalism and Ulster identity: the career of W.P. Nicholson', in Patrick Fitzgerald and Steve Ickringill (eds), *Atlantic crossroads: historical connections between Scotland, Ulster and North America* (Newtownards, 2001), 99–113

NOTES

[1] 'The Nicholson united mission', *The Witness*, 24 February 1922, 8.
[2] 'Nicholson united mission', *The Witness*, 31 March 1922, 8.
[3] 'Nicholson Mission', *Newtownards Chronicle*, 5 November 1921, 5.
[4] 'Nicholson Letters', *Belfast Telegraph*, 26 October 1922, 6.
[5] Archibald Irwin, 'Is there a revival in Ulster?', *The Witness*, 24 November 1922, 5.
[6] 'The revival movement', *The Witness*, 15 June 1923, 8.
[7] *From civil war to revival victory: a souvenir of the remarkable evangelistic campaigns in Ulster, from 1921 till December, 1925*, conducted by Rev. W.P. Nicholson (n.p., 1926).
[8] Steve Bruce, *Paisley: religion and politics in Northern Ireland* (Oxford, 2007), 28–9.

The author gratefully acknowledges that the research for this article was funded by a Research Project Grant from the Leverhulme Trust (RPG-2018-062).

25 FEBRUARY 1922

PUBLICATION OF THE *FREE STATE* NEWSPAPER

THE PROPAGANDA WAR OVER THE ANGLO-IRISH TREATY

Before the physical fighting of the civil war began, a propaganda war was fought by those divided over the Anglo-Irish Treaty. Both sides turned to newspaper publishing to make their case. *An Saorstát: the Free State*, referred to simply as *Free State* by contemporaries, first appeared on 25 February 1922. It served as a voice for those who endorsed the agreement before an official pro-Treaty party, which would become Cumann na nGaedheal, was formed. Appearing weekly, thirty-nine issues of the eight-page newspaper were published. It was filled with lengthy articles, interspersed with satire. Although official circulation figures are not available, other evidence suggests that the paper did not have a great reach. Nonetheless, *Free State* offers the historian further insight into how the pro-treatyites sought to present their case in the weeks and months after the Dáil voted to accept the agreement.

As the Dáil debates drew to a conclusion, the anti-Treaty side moved quickly to disseminate its case to the broader public. The newspaper

Poblacht na hÉireann: the Republic of Ireland, or *Republic*, was launched at the start of January 1922. From February, Erskine Childers directed a vigorous propaganda campaign in its pages, seeking to emphasise that the Dáil was powerless to function as a parliament.

This was intended to undermine the process of transferring power, including the civil service structure, from the British government to the new Irish Free State.[1]

Free State was conceived in late January amidst concerns about the influence of *Republic*. It sold for two pence, but free bundles were also dispersed around the country for distribution at public meetings. Though the majority of articles did not carry a by-line, Ernest Blythe, Darrell Figgis, Eoin MacNeill, Kevin O'Higgins and Kevin O'Shiel were among those who signed their names to their occasional contributions. When read consecutively, the columns start to feel like repackaged versions of earlier editions. The 'sameness' of the content can be explained by the recorded difficulties in securing copy.[2] Advertisements broke up some of the text, but the revenue generated from them made only a minimal contribution to the coffers. That they were mainly for luxury goods was an early sign that the pro-Treaty organisation would have little appeal for the working class.

A lengthy discussion of the Treaty occupied the front page of the inaugural edition. Echoing the Dáil debates, the choice was presented as one between accepting the terms of the agreement or the 'resumption of war or political chaos'. The latter, readers were told, would leave them further than ever from the realisation of their hopes—an inverted version of Michael Collins's claim that the Treaty would provide the freedom to achieve full freedom. Another article in the same issue positioned the Treaty in the longer republican tradition. Summoning Robert Emmet, it claimed that 'Ireland again takes her place amongst the recognised Nations'.[3]

'Legitimacy' was a recurring feature of the political lexicon in the months that followed the vote on the Treaty.[4] De Valera's 'Document No. 2' was repeatedly scrutinised in *Free State*, and its perceived shortcomings, relative to the Treaty, were highlighted. As the threat of violence hung in the air, there was occasional scaremongering, mostly in the shape of vague warnings that discontent could lead to the return of British rule. On 15 April, the day after anti-Treaty forces led by Rory O'Connor occupied the Four Courts, a satirical 'proclamation of lawlessness', signed by 'Roderick (or Gory) O'Connor. Dictator', appeared on the front page. Much of that

DOCUMENT
No. 2

MR. DE VALERA SAID AT THE ARD FHEIS:

"FORGET DOCUMENT No. 2 !"

WHY?

Because **HE NOW PRETENDS** that a **REPUBLIC** can be obtained by **KILLING THE TREATY!**

He has to pretend that it is easier to obtain **A REPUBLIC** now than it was in July last **WHEN HE DROPPED THE REPUBLIC FOR DOCUMENT** No. 2.

DOCUMENT No. 2 is the evidence that he realised that **A REPUBLIC** was not practicable!

WE CANNOT FORGET THAT!

WE DO NOT MEAN TO FORGET THAT!

WE DO NOT MEAN TO LET MR. DE VALERA FORGET THAT!

SUPPORT THE TREATY CANDIDATES

issue was taken up with discussions of despotism—a dominant theme in the newspaper from its inception, though earlier references tended to relate to Éamon de Valera.

When Collins and de Valera agreed a pact for the 1922 election intended to avert civil war, a pro-Treaty sub-committee agreed that all propaganda would be suspended from 23 May.[5] While subsequent *Free State* articles were more muted, elements of the pro-Treaty narrative lingered. A recurring advertisement for the Treaty fund asked, 'Where does your interest lie? In good government or in gun-law?'[6]

In the aftermath of the election, and the failure of the pact, the Provisional Government issued an ultimatum to the anti-Treaty forces to withdraw from the Four Courts. After they refused to do so, the Free State army bombarded the complex on 28 June and the civil war began. The next nine issues of *Free State* were branded 'special war numbers'. They justified the attack and further vilified those who opposed the Treaty.

These special editions were disrupted by the killing of Michael Collins, resulting in the publication of a 'memorial number' on 30 August. The newspaper then reverted to its usual format. Although the civil war continued, references to war were dropped from the banner. As the newspaper went to print at the start of September, the third Dáil was days away from convening for the first time. The purpose then was to add legitimacy to the new parliament. By the time *Free State* ceased production in November, the Dáil had been convened; W.T. Cosgrave was elected president of the Executive Council; and the new constitution was adopted. The process of implementing the Treaty was nearing its conclusion. Discussions were also underway about the formation of a pro-Treaty party.[7] These developments alone, however, do not explain the newspaper's demise.

Minutes of the *Free State* sub-committee repeatedly record maladministration by its manager, Lyons. While the precise identity of the manager is not clear, it is likely that the Lyons in question was George A. Lyons, a friend of Arthur Griffith's who was active in the independence movement. Among his failings were incomplete financial records for the paper and an absence of any details about circulation figures—an essential piece of information if one of the expectations was that the newspaper would counteract its rival. A decision had been taken at the start of April that, if his performance did not improve, 'drastic action would be taken'.[8]

Lyons ultimately resigned, but the newspaper's future remained uncertain. Its continued existence was championed in June by Arthur Griffith, whose long career as editor of various newspapers demonstrated his belief in the power of that medium. His intervention gave *Free State* only a temporary stay, however, and the 11 November edition was its last. By then circulation had dropped so substantially that the newspaper was deemed to have lost all propaganda value.[9] Although the pro-Treaty side saw the usefulness of a newspaper, Cumann na nGaedheal did not launch a new publication after its creation (as Fianna Fáil later would with the *Irish Press*). That the national newspapers and the majority of the provincial press were sympathetic to W.T. Cosgrave's government negated the need.

by Ciara Meehan

FURTHER READING

Michael Laffan, *The resurrection of Ireland: the Sinn Féin party, 1916–1923* (Cambridge, 1999)

Owen McGee, *Arthur Griffith* (Sallins, 2015)

Ciara Meehan, *The Cosgrave party: a history of Cumann na nGaedheal, 1923–1933* (Dublin, 2010)

NOTES

[1] Owen McGee, *Arthur Griffith* (Sallins, 2015), 305.
[2] University College Dublin Archives (UCDA), Cumann na nGaedheal and Fine Gael Party Minute Books, P39/Min/1, meeting of the *Free State* paper sub-committee, 19 June 1922.
[3] *Free State*, 25 February 1922.
[4] McGee, *Arthur Griffith*, 305.
[5] UCDA, P39/Min/1, meeting of the propaganda sub-committee, 23 May 1922.
[6] *Free State*, 27 May, 10, 17 and 24 June 1922.
[7] See, Ciara Meehan, *The Cosgrave party: a history of Cumann na nGaedheal, 1923–1933* (Dublin, 2010), 6–10.
[8] UCDA, P39/Min/1, meeting of the *Free State* paper sub-committee, 3 April 1922.
[9] UCDA, P39/Min/1, meeting of the *Free State* paper sub-committee, 30 October 1922.

MARCH

2 MARCH 1922

COUNTESS MARKIEVICZ DEFENDS FEMALE CITIZENSHIP

'FREE STATE FREAKS':
THE POLITICS OF MASCULINITY

On 2 March 1922 Constance Markievicz, by then a strongly anti-Treaty member of the Dáil, addressed her fellow TDs and, in a short but oddly bipartisan speech, urged them to support female suffrage in the new Ireland. Responding to an earlier statement by the Cumann na nGaedheal TD Joseph McGrath, who had condemned female anti-treatyites as 'women in men's clothing', Markievicz offered an ample defence of women's voting rights. Women, she said, had fully fought for national liberation and so had proven their right to be full citizens, or as she stated at the end of her brief remarks: 'these young women and young girls...took a man's part' in the Anglo-Irish War.[1] This debate about voting rights slipped into a deeper debate about gender norms and the porous divide between 'male' and 'female' identities. This was, in fact, a recurring debate both in 1922 and later.

In 1924, two years after Markievicz's speech, Patrick Sarsfield O'Hegarty published his seminal contemporary history, *The victory of Sinn Féin*. Intemperate and readable, the book ranged across the tumult of post-1916

FREE STATE FREAKS.
Nº II

DESMOND FITSGERALD

LIAR IN CHIEF
TO PUBLICITY DEPARTMENT.
SLAVE STATE.

Ireland with an unsurprisingly nationalistic tone and content. And when it came to discussing the civil war, O'Hegarty proffered an interesting theory as to the root causes of the split between treatyites and anti-treatyites. In a chapter entitled simply 'Furies', he argued that the wartime conditions prevailing in Ireland since 1914 had irreparably damaged the women of Ireland, 'cutting [them] loose from everything which their sex contributes to civilisation and social order'. Nationalist women, members of Cumann na mBan most of all, had supposedly violated the gendered division of labour of Irish nationalist politics; these were the 'Furies' of O'Hegarty's imagination. And he laid the blame for the civil war at the feet of the 'Furies' whose 'hysterical' dedication to republicanism served to fatally undermine the bond of brotherhood previously uniting the nationalist men of Ireland. 'Left to himself, man is comparatively harmless', O'Hegarty observed, but

> it is woman...with her implacability, her bitterness, her hysteria, that makes a devil of him. The Suffragettes used to tell us that with women in political power there would be no more war. We know better now. We know that with women in political power there would be no more peace.[2]

Writing from the vantage point of 1924, O'Hegarty was channelling the soft-authoritarianism and hostility to feminism that were already coming to characterise the Free State. But his arguments also drew on a well-established strand of Irish nationalist thought (and of nationalism more generally around the world): the notion that the national project was a masculine project, that the nation was defined by its fraternal unity, and that the nation-state would and should be led by men. Such predilections not only denied women's right to an equal role in nationalist politics, but also meant that male political opponents were accused of being the 'wrong' kind of men; this was certainly the case in the political debates surrounding the Treaty and the outset of the civil war.

Constance Markievicz was one of the paradigmatic of these civil war-era 'furies'. In furious style, she produced an evocative series of hand-drawn posters, now preserved at the National Library of Ireland, which caricatured the treatyites as 'Free State Freaks'. She portrayed the newly elected president of the Executive Council, W.T. Cosgrave, as a Union-Jack-waving

'Jester in Chief to the Freak State'. The minister for defence, Richard Mulcahy, was a gruesome Macbeth-like character, haunted by the dreams of the Irish men he had executed. The minister for

Opposite: Handbill depicting anti-Treaty republicans as cowardly.

posts and telegraphs, J.J. Walsh, was a dissolute figure, whilst Minister for External Affairs Desmond FitzGerald was presented as a preening liar of seemingly indeterminate gender, a servile functionary of the 'slave state'. Anti-treatyite propaganda from 1922 also described Free State supporters as 'Seoinins', 'Spineless worms', 'Slave Staters', 'recreant Irishmen', and 'Unnatural enemies'. In general, the Irish Free State was depicted as a 'craven state' and the embodiment of 'Rotten Means and Men'. A contemporary open letter to members of the Free State army raised some pointed questions about where the pro-Treaty side fitted into the schema of nationalist time:

> Have you ever read Irish History? If you have. Pause! Think! Let your conscience answer. Why are you fighting for England? Who are your Historical Comrades in the centuries old persecution of Ireland? The Priest-Hunters of the penal days. The Yeoman Pitch-Cap Brigade of '98. The Proselytisers and Soup Providers of the Famine Days. The Police and Militia of '67. The R.I.C. and the Black and Tans of 1916–'21. England equipped and armed these degraded allies in all her needs, and sent them to do her dirty work. To torture, maim and murder the true men whom Ireland honours...Do not carry on a war for England that will make your kinsmen in the present and your posterity in the future generations hang their heads with shame. Come over while ye may to the side of Ireland—your motherland. Let England find others degraded enough to do the devilish work. Line up with Tone, Emmet, Mitchell, Pearse, Connolly, MacSwiney, and Brugha.[3]

Anti-treatyite propaganda set up a claim that 'the true men' of Ireland were on their side and that 'true men' from the nation's past, if they were alive, would never support the Treaty.

Such gendered rhetoric was certainly not the sole preserve of the anti-treatyites. Free Staters regularly portrayed their republican opponents as men unable to take control of the freedom now presenting itself, unable to take responsibility for their actions. Anti-treatyites were often

THIS IS WHERE HE WAS IN

1921

THEN THE TREATY CAME

AND THE WIND OF LIBERTY BLEW HIM OUT

UP THE REPUBLIC

1922

NOW THUS IS HE !

dismissed as 'trucileers', dastardly men too cowardly to fight the English in the War of Independence, but who now attacked their fellow Irishmen and adhered to an irrational (that is, hysterical and feminised) republicanism. Batt O'Connor, soon to be a member of Cumann na nGaedheal, remarked at the outset of the civil war:

> the strangest thing of all is the number of weaklings who now are talking big, but who were very mute and done [sic] damn little when the reign of terror was sweeping over the land...I know men who resigned even from our local Sinn Féin club through sheer cowardice of the Black and Tans and now they say they stand for a Republic and 'will not let down de Valera'[.] These same fellows did not visit my house for 9 months when I could not sleep at home fearing they would be marked men if they were seen friendly with O'Connor or visiting his house.[4]

Kevin O'Higgins, rapidly emerging as a dominant treatyite figure, was aghast at the changes he saw in de Valera, accusing him in March 1922 of becoming a deeply irrational 'fury-ridden partisan of the wild words and bitter taunts, the leader of men whose methods are rapidly degenerating into emulation of the "Black-and-Tans"'. O'Higgins would later claim that centuries of English rule had left Irish men without 'political faculties' and with little in the way of 'civic sense'. Thus, anti-treatyite republicans were ignorant that 'man is a social being and not a wild animal'.[5]

Many nationalist movements around the world have followed this pattern, with male interests generally being to the fore and political divisions understood via masculine lenses, with women's concerns relegated to a secondary status if not ignored completely.[6] P.S. O'Hegarty's accusations were representative of a broad swathe of treatyite and anti-treatyite politics and pointed to a bigger debate in Irish nationalism about women's equality and the role women should play in a future Irish state. Ultimately, this was to be a debate that feminists lost. W.T. Cosgrave, newly installed as president of the Executive Council of the Irish Free State, pined for a gendered public–private split. He felt that rather than being involved in anti-Treaty politics, women 'should have rosaries in their hands or be at home with knitting needles'.[7] Éamon de Valera, who a decade later would take power, backed away from fully supporting the radical anti-treatyites: 'I must be the heir to generations of conservatism', he informed Mary MacSwiney in a letter in September 1922. 'Every instinct of mine would indicate that I was meant to be a dyed-in-the-wool Tory or even a Bishop, rather than the leader of a Revolution'.[8] Whether or not 1922 marked the final year of a political revolution, it was not the final year of a sexual revolution!

by Aidan Beatty

FURTHER READING

Sikata Banerjee, *Muscular nationalism: gender, violence and empire in India and Ireland, 1914-2004* (New York, 2012)

Rebecca Mytton, Revolutionary masculinities in the IRA, 1916–1923. Unpublished Ph.D. thesis, University of Sheffield (2020)

Joseph Valente, *The myth of manliness in Irish nationalist culture, 1880–1922* (Urbana-Champaign, IL, 2010)

NOTES

[1] *Dáil debates*, vol. S2, no. 3, 'Irishwomen and the franchise' (2 March 1922); available at: www.oireachtas.ie/en/debates/ (accessed 15 April 2021).

[2] P.S. O'Hegarty, *The victory of Sinn Féin: how it won it and how it used it* (Dublin, 1924).

[3] National Library of Ireland (NLI), uncatalogued political ephemera, box 2, 'To the Free State Forces', anti-Treaty handbill, n.d.

[4] Quoted in John M. Regan, *The Irish counter-revolution, 1921–1936: treatyite politics and settlement in independent Ireland* (Dublin, 1999), 54.

[5] NLI, IR 94109 P70, item 13, Kevin O'Higgins, 'The new de Valera: a contrast and some disclosures', March 1922; Kevin O'Higgins, *The Catholic layman in public life* (Dublin, 1923).

[6] Anne McClintock, 'Family feuds: gender, nationalism and the family', *Feminist Review* 44 (Summer 1993), 61–80.

[7] Louise Ryan, *Gender, identity and the Irish Press, 1922–1937: embodying the nation* (New York, 2002), 213.

[8] Unless otherwise noted, sources quoted in this chapter can be found in Aidan Beatty, *Masculinity and power in Irish nationalism, 1884–1938* (London, 2016).

3 MARCH 1922

FRICTION ON THE FRONTIER

At 11 p.m. on Friday, 3 March 1922, a party of B-Specials (a section of the Ulster Special Constabulary) opened a trench across the road at Gortineddan—a townland between Derrylin in County Fermanagh and Ballyconnell, County Cavan—severing motor access between Northern Ireland and the south. It was 'filled' the following day by local people but was reopened by A-Specials that night.[1] This was only the beginning. Over the course of that weekend, and in the weeks that followed, numerous attempts to seal the border were reported. Saturday saw three roads 'cut' near Clones, County Monaghan, blocking off the market town and important railway junction, both from Newtownbutler in Fermanagh and from access to the Cavan villages of Redhills and Belturbet, via routes that passed through Northern Ireland on the way. On Monday, 6 March two bridges near Swanlinbar, County Cavan—one leading to Derrylin, the other to Enniskillen—were destroyed by a combined force of A and B Specials. When the latter bridge was partially repaired by local farmers 'to get their stock and goods across', a group of A-Specials tore it down again.

On Wednesday two more trenches were dug 'in certain districts in Fermanagh, adjoining Clones, while in other instances existing trenches cut across the roads were even widened.'[2] Elsewhere, more rudimentary barriers—using stones and felled trees—were erected. A fortnight later, on Tuesday, 21 March, 'a large force of special constabulary (principally "B" men)…commandeered picks, shovels, crowbars, and barrows' from the stores of the Derry Corporation 'for which they gave a receipt'. These 'articles were then placed in Crossley tenders' and driven to the Donegal border where trenches were dug across the thoroughfares of 'numerous by-roads at points where the counties meet'.[3] 'Road contractors near the County Cavan border who went to fill in opened trenches were warned by specials not to do so, otherwise they would be shot.'[4]

Barricaded roads were not at all unusual in early 1920s-Ireland as rival parties of combatants sought to curtail the movements of their enemies or facilitate an ambush. What set these border blockages apart was that they reified political partition. In some areas—notably around Clones and Swanlinbar—efforts to keep the border closed would continue for more than a year, even after the customs barrier was in place. As such, March 1922 was a significant step towards the imposition of a new, bounded, spatiality upon the older landscape of conflict and division, and the closure of these crossings one of the first ways in which partition was experienced.

Theretofore the frontier had been blurry on the ground. Political and martial mobilisations throughout the region traditionally drew on connections and concentrations of communal strength that were scattered across county lines. In Cavan, Donegal and Monaghan, enrolment in the pre-First-World-War Ulster Volunteers had been greater, relative to the Protestant population, than it had been in more solidly-unionist Antrim or Down.[5] When the Ulster Special Constabulary (with its full-time A, part-time B, and reserve C-Special classes) was formed, from November 1920 onwards, it attracted men from both sides of the border. A year before the roads were closed, in March 1921, a substantial group of militant Monaghan loyalists had even gone so far as to invade Northern Ireland, helping to sack the nationalist village of Roslea, County Fermanagh; in August the same year, Reverend Burns, rector of Drum, also in County Monaghan, predicted confidently that 'the six counties which excluded them would yet invite them back'.[6]

Despite the signing of the Treaty in December 2021, the future status of the border still seemed uncertain in the first months of 1922. On the

one hand, the agreement itself introduced fresh doubt owing to its Article 12 provision for a boundary commission that could potentially redraw the frontier line. On the other hand, conflict escalated on and around the border. Responding to the imprisonment of republicans in the north, the night of 7 February saw 44 prominent unionists—among them Orange activists and security personnel—kidnapped by the IRA and

Northern Irish forces pose on a south Fermanagh border road that has been trenched and barricaded by felled trees, March 1922.

taken across the border. Even this, however, was overshadowed a few
days later by the 'Clones Affray', a chance encounter on 11 February 1922
between IRA members and an armed party of nineteen uniformed Special
Constabulary who were travelling by train from Belfast to Enniskillen, a
journey that required them to change trains at Clones. The ensuing gun-
fight claimed the lives of four Special Constabulary members and the local
IRA commandant, with many others wounded.[7] Supported by the British
government, the northern authorities flooded the border region with what

Winston Churchill described as 'overwhelming forces', and reports of Catholic families fleeing the north and Protestants likewise abandoning the south increased.[8]

Nevertheless, the road closures came as a surprise and produced confusion. In the week following the first wave of trenching, the nationalist *Fermanagh Herald* reported that it was 'stated in some quarters that the trenching of the border roads...was not authorised'. Similarly, the unionist *Belfast News-Letter* cast doubt upon the claims of the 'Dublin Nationalist papers...that the barricades were erected by order of the Northern Government' but later suggested that the 'Loyalists of the Border districts' had trenched additional roads 'to prevent further raids on Northern territory'. To the *Irish Independent*'s 'special representative at Clones', it appeared that 'the directors of Belfast policy' had begun 'to attach great importance to a definite line about the Six Counties'.[9]

Social life and trade on both sides was affected. According to the *Freeman's Journal*, by early March 'Roslea fair was completely shunned by both buyers and sellers' because of 'the timidity of people to go there as well as the fact that no person could travel on account of torn or blown up bridges and gaping trenches'. Clones market too was 'practically boycotted by all Unionists', who had set up a rival market 'within the Northern area'.[10] As time went on, merchants at Swanlinbar, in the habit of trading via the railway line at Florencecourt, switched to using the narrow-gauge train at Bawnboy Road in Cavan despite less favourable rates.

As with later periods of conflict, however, the border was not completely blockaded. In June 1922 the Northern Ireland Cabinet considered but did not implement a proposal from extremist military advisor Major-General Sir Arthur Solly-Flood 'to prohibit all ingress and egress', even though in practice this was already happening 'to a considerable extent'.[11] In addition to repeated attempts to physically reopen the crossings, creative efforts were made to circumvent the barriers. Goods from Enniskillen and Fermanagh milk bound for the separating station at Swanlinbar came by lorry as far as the broken bridge, where they were 'transhipped' to awaiting vehicles on the other side. At some places alternative back roads were used for a time and, at the Annie Bridge, a ford was built to bring turf across the river until it too was blocked with barbed wire.[12]

For a century the Irish border has been contested, not merely in the realms of politics and ideology, but also in the everyday struggles of many within border communities and beyond them to preserve its permeability when faced with diverse attempts to impose it as a barrier. In significant ways, that to and fro began in March 1922 with trenches dug in country roads and with local people filling them in.

by Peter Leary

FURTHER READING

Catherine Nash, Bryonie Reid and Brian Graham, *Partitioned lives: the Irish borderlands* (Farnham, 2013)

Cormac Moore, *Birth of the border: the impact of partition in Ireland* (Newbridge, 2019)

Robert Lynch, *The partition of Ireland, 1918–25* (Cambridge, 2019)

NOTES

[1] *Sligo Champion*, 25 March 1922.
[2] *Donegal News*, 25 March 1922. *Evening Echo*, 10 March 1922.
[3] *Belfast News-Letter*, 22 March 1922. *Freeman's Journal*, 22 March 1922.
[4] *Evening Echo*, 10 March 1922.
[5] David Fitzpatrick, 'The Orange Order and the border', *Irish Historical Studies* 33 (129) (May 2002), 52–67.
[6] Tim Wilson, 'The strange death of loyalist Monaghan, 1912–21', in Senia Pašeta (ed.), *Uncertain futures: essays about the Irish past for Roy Foster* (Oxford, 2016), 174–87.
[7] Robert Lynch, 'The Clones affray, 1922: massacre or invasion?', *History Ireland* 12 (3) (Autumn 2004), 33–7; available at: www.historyireland.com/20th-century-contemporary-history/the-clones-affray-1922-massacre-or-invasion/ (accessed 15 April 2021).
[8] *Nenagh Guardian*, 25 March 1922. *Irish Independent*, 22 March 1922. *Sligo Champion*, 25 March 1922.
[9] *Fermanagh Herald*, 11 March 1922. *Belfast News-Letter*, 8 March 1922. *Belfast News-Letter*, 23 March 1922. *Irish Independent*, 24 March 1922.
[10] *Freeman's Journal*, 10 March 1922. *Anglo-Celt*, 18 March 1922.
[11] Public Record Office of Northern Ireland, Cabinet Secretariat, CAB/4/47, Cabinet conference minutes, 2 June 1922 (Conference held: topic discussed: general security situation. [proposed to close the border]). On another occasion Solly-Flood proposed the internment of nationalist children. See, Robert Lynch, *The partition of Ireland, 1918–25* (Cambridge, 2019), 144.
[12] National Archives of Ireland, TSCH/3/S3161, Joseph Johnston report on visit to Swanlinbar and Clones, 6 July 1923.

4 MARCH 1922

THE WIFE OF A PLASTERER TELLS
THE ARCHBISHOP OF DUBLIN A SECRET

GENDER AND POVERTY
IN THE NEW 'FREE STATE'

> Dear Archbishop
> I humbly ask pardon for the liberty I take of writing to you +
> also hope you will excuse me as I don't know how to address
> you I am the wife of a plasterer + we have 7 children the eldest
> only 14 years old.[1]

On the 4 March 1922 Mrs Anna Lalor* was heartbroken. Little had changed
in the previous two years for her family of nine; if anything, things had got
worse. Indeed, on this morning she felt compelled to sit down in her overcrowded two-roomed house in Dún Laoghaire, County Dublin, to write
to one of the most powerful men in her universe—the Roman Catholic
archbishop of Dublin, Edward Byrne (1921–40). Her letter is but one
among thousands the archbishop received: these letters represent an extensive archive of the experience of poverty in the first two decades of Irish
independence.

According to the 1901 census, prior to marriage Mrs Lalor had been a domestic servant, an occupation she shared with one in three single women: domestic service remained the biggest single employer of women in Ireland until the 1950s. In 1907 she left the formal workplace to marry, thereby entering a period in her life when little was within her control, not her fertility nor the waxing and waning of her husband's earning capacity. The meaning of this impotence must have become apparent quite quickly to her: within four years she had birthed three children, almost one a year. By 1922 Anna had seven children; the maths of seven children in fifteen years indicates that some of the gaps were miscarriages or infant deaths. Infant mortality was still disturbingly high in 1920s Ireland, and it was a clear barometer of social inequality mapping closely to the geography of class. The 1926 census revealed that Dublin city had an infant mortality rate of 170 per 1,000 births, compared to 79 per 1,000 in the affluent, seaside Dublin village of Howth.[2] Despite the knowledge that multiple pregnancies increased infant mortality and maternal morbidity, birth control was criminalised in 1935.

The spacing in Mrs Lalor's brood also reflected the geography of her husband's work-life, as she explained:

> last October twelve months, there was a strike declared in the Building Trades in Dublin and at the very time I was in Bed seriously ill my husband was forced to go to England to get Bread for his children leaving me heartbroken as I was so ill, he got work in England + was allowed to join the English Trades Union for the sum of 8[d] with a lot more Irish men.

The unemployment rate in the building sector was 34 per cent, with 32 per cent of workdays lost through strikes.[3] She was referring to the bricklayers' strike in Dublin that had lasted between October 1920 and June 1921. The strike had only secured the workers a temporary increase of 1d per hour, while 'keeping the city's modest slum clearance programme on hold'.[4] That outcome was indicative of the false promise of political independence for the new Ireland's poorest citizens. While the president of the Executive Council, William T. Cosgrave, oversaw welfare cuts, including to the Old Age Pension, he drew an annual salary of £2,500.[5] The average industrial wage was £126 per annum.

The new state promoted with vigour the stay-at-home mother as the bedrock of society; women like Mrs Lalor, however, could rarely afford such

to persuade my husband to remain
with me & the children. he told me he
would but the Dublin Plasterers had put
a penalty of £3— entrance fee on the
plasters who did not come home when
the Strike was Settled in Dublin. my
husband told me he had promised the
English Builder to remain on till the
work was finished as he explained
that we were glad of him when the
Strike was on. my husband is
planning to go again as he thinks
he is being Victimised. he is
paying this £3: at 10/- out of his
wages. my husband is the only Support
of 7 young children leaving 9 in all
depending on him. while they are
taking this 10/- my children are in
want. they are taking the Bread from
my children. Most Rev Archbishop.
I will tell you a secret— my husband
has not been to the Sacraments for
2 years being away when we had our
last retreat. England did not improve
him I heard from him that the people
go nowhere no church no mass
I am praying to the Sacred Heart for
him. we want him here,
I feel I am doing a terrible thing in
writing to Your Grace. but also I feel
Sure that you will try to do Something

idealism. The poor continued to survive through seasonal migration and emigration, largely to England. Mrs Lalor articulated the emotional cost of that strategy, deftly connecting it with a sense that political freedom was a ruse that would not feed her children:

Opposite: An excerpt from the letter of Mrs A.L., Desmond Avenue, Dún Laoghaire (Co. Dublin), to Archbishop Byrne, 4 March 1922.

> my husband Keeps saying this is free Ireland the Englishman can give the Irishman liberty to earn Bread for his family for 8^d per week while the Irishman who is supposed to be good roman catholic christians demand £5 to get liberty to work in their own country.

She was referring to a £5 penalty her husband's union had imposed on workers who had not returned to Ireland upon the resolution of the strike. This occurred, she explained, even though her husband had regularly sent 'strike money' to the 'Dublin Trade Union'. To her the trade unions were just another source 'taking the Bread from my children' with their fees and penalties. She was also appealing to her Church's dread of socialism, while placing those 'supposed to be good' Catholics at the centre of a narrative of social injustice and hypocrisy. By contrast, she portrayed her faith as central to her ability to cope:

> I was unhappy all the time being separated from my husband while he was also in the beginning, but later he seemed not to mind while my children + myself were praying hard for God to send him home. I wrote to the poor Clares + told them my trouble + asked them to pray also last christmas my husband came home + I prayed + tryed to [--------] persuade my husband to remain with me + the children

With a hint of where her husband's growing acceptance of separation might lead, she proceeded to tap into deep contemporary anxieties regarding the faith of Irish emigrants in England:

> Most Rev. Archbishop I will tell you a secret my husband has not been to the Sacraments for 2 years being away when we had our last retreat. England did not improve him, I heard

from him that the people go nowhere no church no mass I am praying to the Sacred Heart for him we want him here.

The *en passant* mention of 'our last retreat' underscore her spiritual dominion over the seven little souls she was sheltering.

Faithful Place, off Lower Tyrone Street, inner-city Dublin, *c.* 1913.

Mrs Lalor's letter provides barely a hint of the violence and uncertainty swirling around her country, for she represents the continuity of human experience, which does not always beat to the rhythm of historical periodisation. The challenge of feeding a family changed little for women like her. Despite her mention of ill health, Mrs Lalor outlived her husband by 23 years, dying in December 1974. During her lifetime the structure and trajectory of social inequality remained largely unchanged: the children of the poor continued to be the parents of the disadvantaged. In the intimate relationship Mrs Lalor conjured in her letter, the Catholic archbishop became both her confidante and trusted friend: 'my husband Knows nothing about me writing …

Most Rev. Father again excuse me I could not trust anyone else'. While she feared she was 'doing a Terrible thing in writing', she was also 'sure that you will try to do something'. She wanted him to use his influence to change a system that condemned people like her to live as she did. In asking for nothing specific, she asked for everything in spirit. She already knew what, a year prior to her death, the 1973 report of the *Commission on the Status of Women in Ireland* laid bare: power is always measured in pounds and pence.

by Lindsey Earner-Byrne

FURTHER READING:

Mel Cousins, *The birth of Irish social welfare in Ireland, 1922–1952* (Dublin, 2013)

Mary E. Daly, 'Marriage, fertility and women's lives in twentieth-century Ireland', *Women's History Review* 15 (2006), 571–85

T.J. Morrissey, *Edward J. Byrne 1872–1941: the forgotten archbishop of Dublin* (Dublin, 2010)

NOTES

* The name of the author of this letter has been changed but her initials have been maintained. No changes have been made to the original spelling, capitalisation or punctuation in her letter, to retain the authenticity of the source material.

[1] Dublin Diocesan Archives, Byrne papers, Charity cases, box 1: 1921–26, Mrs A.L., X Desmond Avenue, Dún Laoghaire, (Co. Dublin) to Archbishop Byrne, 4 March 1922. See, Lindsey Earner-Byrne, *Letters of the Catholic poor: poverty in independent Ireland, 1920–1940* (Cambridge, 2017).

[2] Saorstát Éireann, Census of population, general report, volume x, 1926, Chapter 5: 'Housing', 70; available at: www.cso.ie/en/media/csoie/census/census1926results/volume10/C_1926_V10.pdf (accessed 15 Aprl 2021).

[3] David Fitzpatrick, 'Strikes in Ireland', *Saothar* 6 (1980), 26–39: 34 and 36.

[4] Padraig Yeates, *A city in turmoil: Dublin 1919–1921* (Dublin, 2012), 222.

[5] Tony Farmar, *Privileged lives: a social history of middle-class Ireland, 1888–1989* (Dublin, 2010), 172.

17 MARCH 1922

THE 'SCATTERED CHILDREN OF ÉIRE': THE GLOBAL DIASPORA AND IRISH IDENTITY

On 17 March 1922 over 50,000 people marched in the New York St Patrick's Day parade, sending a strong message to the Irish at home. The Anglo-Irish Treaty as negotiated with the British government fell short of the expectations of the American Irish, as the Grand Marshal Edward J. Gavegan outlined in a telegram to Michael Collins, the head of the Provisional Government, to mark the occasion. Collins had a message of his own, sending St Patrick's Day greetings and conveying the 'Irish Nation's gratitude for the generous support given by America through the long years of its struggle for freedom'.[1]

Two years earlier it was very different, when unity was the theme. The parade then was addressed by the president of the Irish Republic, Éamon de Valera. De Valera urged that his Irish American audience take an active role in securing Irish freedom for the motherland:

St Patrick's
Day parade,
New York
City, 1919.

Sons and daughters of the Gael! Wherever you be
today, in the name of the motherland Greetings.
Whatever flag be the flag you guard and cherish,
it is consistent with your highest duty to link your-
selves together to use your united strength to break
the chains that bind our sweet sad mother and never before
have the scattered children of Eire had such an opportunity
for noble service. Today you can serve not only Ireland but
the world.[2]

Across the world, St Patrick's Day provided an opportunity for the
exiled children of Éire to celebrate their Irishness, and more pointedly
to consider what they could do to further the cause of Irish politics. This

tradition began in the later nineteenth century and was the pivotal moment in the calendar for the Irish in the United States, Canada, Australia, New Zealand, Britain and many other places around the world.

When the new Irish state became independent in December 1922 it was distinctive in one critical respect. Not that a small revolutionary movement had managed to overthrow British rule, although that was a major achievement given the asymmetry of both military might and resources; not in the experience of the unity of the revolutionary movement fracturing and descending into civil war and fraternal conflict, as that happened in many independence movements; but in the existence of a large diasporic population estimated to number 1.76 million people scattered across the world.[3] That figure did not include the children and grandchildren of those emigrants who had left Ireland, and could therefore be multiplied by a factor of at least two to calculate the number who would identify as being of Irish descent. This represented an enormous well of goodwill and practical support.

Between 1800 and 1921 over eight million people left Ireland. It was a land that, as the historian David Fitzpatrick memorably put it, 'most people wanted to leave'.[4] After the Great Famine of the 1840s somewhere between a half and two-thirds of those born in Ireland ended up emigrating (with some returning at a later date).

For many of these migrants, displacement and exile from Ireland did not result in a disconnection with the vexed politics of the homeland. From the 1798 rebellion onwards, prominent nationalist exiles became a vital source of inspiration for the diasporic Irish. The 1848 Young Ireland rising created important communities of radical nationalists in the United States, Canada and Australia, including leaders such as John Mitchel. The Fenian movement of the 1860s was largely, but not exclusively, a diasporic revolutionary organisation, as was its successor, Clan na Gael, in the later nineteenth and early twentieth century. The origins of the Fenian movement lay in Paris in the 1850s, where one of the leaders, James Stephens, took refuge after 1848.

Organisations such as Clan na Gael and its associated group, the Friends of Irish Freedom, mobilised Irish American support for the Irish republican movement between 1916 and 1922. Finance and fundraising were key activities, and to a large degree the Irish revolution was made possible by the money generated by diasporic nationalism, much to the irritation of the British authorities who closely monitored the activities of the exiled sons and daughters of Éireann.

But that is only part of the story. Historians now recognise that diasporic nationalism was a crucial feature in explaining the ultimate success of the Irish revolutionary movement and realising Irish independence. Leaders such as Michael Collins and Éamon de Valera recognised this, and Collins in particular was closely involved in the direction of the activities of the IRA in Britain. De Valera's famous American tour of 1919–20 underlined the significance that Sinn Féin attached to the support of Irish Americans.

Support was about more than money. Irish nationalist organisations in North America, Britain and Australasia played another vital role—acting as conduits for information and publicity about events in Ireland, something that was especially important during the attempts by the British state to suppress Irish revolutionary violence in 1920 and 1921, using equally violent methods. British repression and atrocities committed by the Crown forces in Ireland were publicised by republican propagandists abroad to undermine British attempts to present events in Ireland as an 'internal' matter. International pressure initiated by Irish communities living abroad served to counter this partial presentation of events.

While the activities of diasporic nationalists in the United States are well known, new research has led historians to think beyond an exclusive focus on the United States and to consider how the Irish in Britain, Canada, Australia and even further afield in places such as Argentina were mobilised during the Irish revolution.

Why did Irish exiles respond with such enthusiasm, and in such large numbers, to calls to help the homeland in its time of dire need? Shared collective memory about the effects of British misrule, not least during the Great Famine when over one million people died, was a principal motivation. More so than other migratory groups, the Irish kept in close contact with events at home through letters and, by the end of the nineteenth century, repeated return visits home. So news about the late nineteenth-century Land War or the Easter Rising, or the effects of imposition of martial law by the British authorities in 1920–21, was more likely to fuel nationalist sentiment. Irish emigrant newspapers such as *Irish World* and the *Boston Pilot* carried extensive sections on events 'at home'. Being distant in physical terms may have made revolutionaries of people who, in other circumstances, would not have got involved.

After 1922 the political role of the Irish diaspora remained important. Many defeated republicans left Ireland for the United States in 1923 and

1924, putting in place a bedrock for Irish diasporic republicanism in the twentieth century, to be reactivated in the late 1960s when the 'Troubles' broke out in Northern Ireland. Beyond activism, the diaspora has served as a source of political influence across the twentieth and twentieth-first century, especially so during the peace process in Northern Ireland and up to and including the present day.

by Enda Delaney

FURTHER READING

David Brundage, *Irish nationalists in America: the politics of exile, 1798–1998* (New York, 2016)

Patrick Mannion and Fearghal McGarry (eds), *The Irish revolution: a global history* (New York, 2022)

NOTES

[1] Mike Cronin and Daryl Adair, *The wearing of the green: a history of St Patrick's Day* (New York, 2002), 109–10.
[2] Library of Congress, Éamon de Valera, Saint Patrick's Day message, 1920; available at: https://loc.gov/item/2004650654/ (accessed 15 April 2021).
[3] Commission on emigration and other population problems, *Reports* (Dublin, 1955), table 95, 126.
[4] David Fitzpatrick, *Irish emigration, 1801–1921* (Dublin, 1984), 1.

17 MARCH 1922

ÉAMON DE VALERA'S CIVIL WAR

> If the Volunteers of the future tried to complete the work the
> Volunteers of the last four years had been attempting, they
> would have to complete it, not over the bodies of foreign sol-
> diers, but over the dead bodies of their own countrymen. They
> would have to wade through Irish blood, through the blood of
> the soldiers of the Irish Government, and through, perhaps,
> the blood of some of the members of the Government in order
> to get Irish freedom.[1]

Was it a warning, or was it a threat? Éamon de Valera always insisted his
speech in Thurles on St Patrick's Day 1922 merely highlighted the dangers
of the situation; his opponents accused him of inciting violence and raising
the tension, which led to civil war.

The speech should not be seen in isolation—it was one of a series made
during a tour of the south of the country, all delivering much the same
message. De Valera told a crowd in Dungarvan that 'it was only by civil

war after this that they could get their independence'. In Waterford he claimed 'the only choice left now was acceptance of the so-called Treaty or civil war'. In Killarney, the day after Thurles, he said that the Volunteers would have 'to march over the dead bodies of their own brothers' if they continued to seek full independence, adding, significantly, 'and I hope they will continue'.[2]

Newspaper reaction was uniformly negative. His speeches were described as 'amazing' by the *Freeman's Journal* and 'wild' by *The Irish Times*, while the *Irish Independent* accused him of using 'the language of incitement'. De Valera dismissed the suggestion that he was inciting civil war as 'villainous'. But Michael Collins was unconvinced: 'They are incitements whatever may be his personal intention. Can he not strive to create a good atmosphere instead of seeking to create a bad one?'[3]

De Valera's message was that political action would be incapable of removing the barriers he believed the Treaty placed in the way of an Irish republic. And if politics was doomed to failure, the inevitable result would be armed conflict.

His disillusionment with politics was understandable as he—up to then the unchallenged leader of Irish nationalism—had suffered a series of political defeats since the previous December. His attempt to control from Dublin the plenipotentiaries negotiating with the British had failed. He had been shocked to lose a vote in Cabinet on the resultant Treaty. And he had been rejected by the Dáil, first in a vote on the Treaty itself, and then again, more narrowly, in an effort to be re-elected president.

Moreover, his loss of control was accelerating. Not only was he now in the minority in the splintered national movement, but he was in danger of losing control even of the anti-Treaty side, as more militant and extreme voices sought to assert leadership. A few days after Thurles, Rory O'Connor, chair of the anti-Treaty IRA's Acting Military Council, rejected the authority of the Dáil. 'If a government goes wrong it must take the consequences...If the Dáil is the government of the country we are in revolt against it.'[4]

De Valera later admitted that his decision to support O'Connor in his 'unfortunate repudiation of the Dáil' had been 'foolish'.[5] He did so in an effort to avoid a split in republican ranks, which would further weaken the chances of defeating the Treaty (and, of course, further weaken his own position). That strategy meant, however, that he was no longer in a position to lead, but was instead handcuffed to the most extreme of the doctrinaire republicans.

The only way for him to regain control was to reassert the primacy of politics. He appeared to have done that when he agreed an electoral pact with Collins. Sinn Féin would put forward a panel of candidates representing both sides of the Treaty divide, with the promise of a coalition government to come.

'He believed his true value to the cause lay in his political stature.' De Valera surrounded by supporters.

The pact looked like a victory for de Valera, but by allowing an election to proceed in relative peace, it actually became a defeat, because it meant 'acceptance of the people's decision as the final court'.[6] He was under no illusion that the people favoured the Treaty, as they demonstrated in the election. The pact, and the political defeat to which it led, further undermined de Valera's position with the radicals, who now had even more cause to ignore both his leadership and the verdict of the voters. The final eclipse of politics came with the shelling of the Four Courts on 28 June.

For a time, de Valera was eclipsed as well. While he served in various IRA staff positions, he came to believe that his true value to the cause lay in his political stature, which could be enhanced by establishing a republican government. Anti-Treaty chief of staff Liam Lynch at first rejected such a move, and became increasingly irritated by de Valera, particularly his calls for an end to the conflict. As early as August 1922, Lynch complained, de Valera 'was most pessimistic and regarded our position as hopeless'.[7]

De Valera hinted at this divergence of views when he secretly met Richard Mulcahy shortly after the death of Michael Collins. He said that while he was led by reason, others were led by faith, and as long as there were men of faith like Rory O'Connor setting the course, he would be 'a humble soldier following after'.[8] But he was following in what he believed to be the wrong direction.

The IRA Executive eventually agreed to the formation of a republican government under de Valera in October 1922, but there were strings attached. Recognition would depend on the new government sticking to the republican line, while the Executive retained final say on any peace deal that might be reached with the Free State.[9] Trust in politics, and in de Valera, remained in short supply, and he remained very much second fiddle to Lynch in the republican band.

De Valera continued to argue unsuccessfully that continued resistance was futile. 'To me our duty seems plain—to end the conflict without delay ...The hope of success alone would justify our continuing the fight, and, frankly, I see no such hope...'[10] But, the day after he wrote that letter, the situation was transformed by Lynch's death in action. Six weeks later, on 24 May 1923, republicans were ordered to dump arms. Militarism had failed, and politics—and, therefore, de Valera—would in time regain primacy.

The civil war was the most miserable time of de Valera's life; he was swept along by the course of events, deprived of the power to shape his own and the country's destiny. He later complained: 'I have been condemned to view the tragedy here for the last year as through a wall of glass, powerless to intervene effectively.'[11] He was in this position, of course, largely because of his own loss of belief in the political path, which left him a captive of extremists.

He had been proved right in his warning—or threat—of bloodshed in his Thurles speech. But his later career demonstrated that his underlying assumption was wrong. Politics could work, and could remove the restrictions to independence within the Treaty. Unfortunately, this demonstration came too late to prevent civil war.

by David McCullagh

FURTHER READING

Michael Laffan, *The resurrection of Ireland* (Cambridge, 2005)

David McCullagh, *Éamon de Valera, I: rise, 1882–1932* (Dublin, 2017)

Meda Ryan, *Liam Lynch: the real chief* (Cork, 2012)

NOTES

[1] *Irish Independent*, 18 March 1922.
[2] *Irish Independent*, 17 March 1922; *The Irish Times*, 18 March 1922; *The Irish Times*, 20 March 1922.
[3] *Freeman's Journal*, 18 March 1922; *The Irish Times*, 21 March 1922; *Irish Independent*, 18 March 1922; *Irish Independent*, 23 March 1922; *Freeman's Journal*, 10 April 1922.
[4] *The Irish Times*, 23 March 1922.
[5] De Valera to Charles Murphy, 13 August 1922, quoted in Michael Laffan, *The resurrection of Ireland* (Cambridge, 2005), 375.
[6] De Valera to Joseph McGarrity, 10 September 1922, in Seán Cronin, *The McGarrity papers* (Kerry, 1972), 124–5.
[7] Con Moloney (adjutant-general), on behalf of Lynch, to Ernie O'Malley, 5 September 1922, in Cormac K.H. O'Malley and Anne Dolan (eds), *'No surrender here!'. The civil war papers of Ernie O'Malley* (Dublin, 2007), 157.
[8] UCD Archives (UCDA), Richard Mulcahy papers, P7/3, Mulcahy note on conversation with Commandant Vincent Byrne, 7 January 1964.
[9] UCDA, Moss Twomey papers, P69/179(6), Executive Meeting minutes, 17 October 1922.
[10] UCDA, Éamon de Valera papers, P150/1710, de Valera to P.J. Ruttledge, 9 April 1923.
[11] UCDA, Máire Comerford papers, LA18/45, de Valera to Miss Ellis, 26 February 1923.

24 MARCH 1922

THE McMAHON MURDERS

CLASS AND KILLING IN BELFAST

Despite the truce between Crown forces and the IRA in July 1921, violence intensified in Belfast that summer, the brunt of it borne by the local Catholic community, which constituted 25 per cent of the city's population. Belfast now served as the capital of the new Northern Ireland polity, which had been established (with an in-built Protestant majority) in order to settle historically freighted Ulster unionist fears of Irish independence. In the immediate aftermath of partition, these fears remained heightened. The middle-class leaders of constitutional nationalism in Belfast harboured a hope that the adoption of a policy of 'recognition' of the Northern parliament and its government would result in an end 'to the present campaign of persecution'.[1] But, given events on the ground, this view was entirely out of step with the experiences of Catholics in working-class, ghettoised areas of the city. Of all the attacks on the Catholic community in this period, the one

Religious picture damaged by gunfire during the murder of members of the McMahon family, north Belfast, 24 March 1922.

that shocked contemporaries most, however, was the murder of the prosperous Catholic publican Owen McMahon, together with four of his sons (aged between 15 and 26 years) and a barman who was present during the attack at the family's home in north Belfast in the early hours of 24 March 1922. News of the killings reverberated throughout Ireland and beyond.

Only weeks earlier, on 16 February, Winston Churchill had stood in the House of Commons in London and lamented the divisions that continued to beset Ireland in the aftermath of the First World War. Yet the conflict to which he alluded, including its ugly sectarian manifestations, was fundamentally an Anglo-Irish conflict, with centuries of history. Indeed, as secretary of state for war in July 1920, Churchill himself had urged the arming of Protestants in Ulster as a means of defeating the IRA, the result of which—with added pressure from the then soon-to-be prime minister of Northern Ireland, James Craig—was the formation of the state-sponsored Ulster Special Constabulary, the most notorious section of which was the B-Specials. What was unleashed by this strategy was concerted attacks on republicans and Catholics generally, much of it directed in Belfast by Royal Irish Constabulary (RIC) District Inspector John Nixon, whose men operated out of police barracks at Brown Square, near the city centre. It is generally accepted that it was this unit that planned and executed the McMahon attack.[2]

For some time, Joe Devlin, MP for West Belfast and the leading nationalist politician in the north, had been protesting about Crown force involvement in the killing of Catholics. In his view, only one conclusion could be drawn from the free movement of assassins in a city under curfew. In the House of Commons on 14 June 1921 he raised the matter yet again, following the separate abduction and killing of three young men in the city only two days previously: Alexander McBride, William Kerr and Malachy Halfpenny. In addressing the Commons, Devlin paid particular attention to the sacrifice made by the youngest, Halfpenny, a 22-year-old postman who had served with the Royal Field Artillery in the First World War.[3] In fact, Halfpenny and his three older brothers had all served; the eldest, Jack, dying at the Battle of Messines in June 1917. For Rosamund Stephen, an English-born Church of Ireland lay missionary who was active among the working class in Belfast, and who had had contact with the Halfpenny family for some years, blame for the killing rested firmly with the Specials. In a letter to her sister, Katharine, she matter-of-factly referred to the Specials as 'the men[,] you know[,] who k . . . . d Malachy'.[4]

Even though Halfpenny was effectively described as a 'Sinn Féiner' in the unionist press, there is nothing to indicate that he had been anything other than a Devlinite, as Devlin himself attested. In explaining the Halfpenny murder, it has been suggested that, unlike McBride and Kerr, who appear to have had some connection with the IRA, Halfpenny may simply have been a victim of mistaken identity.[5] Yet Rosamund Stephen's 'Journal' reveals that, four months before the killing, the Halfpenny home, in the working-class Catholic enclave of Ardoyne, had been raided by Crown forces in what appears to have been an intelligence-gathering exercise.[6] This may lend some support to claims made in the nationalist press around that time, and later stated in a memo composed for the Free State Department of Defence in Dublin, that elements of the city's police were targeting constitutional nationalists, like Halfpenny, in the summer of 1921. If true, this tactic was in place well before the McMahon killings.

Yet, the attack on the McMahons does stand out in one hugely important respect. There seems to be little doubt that it was principally designed to send out the unambiguous message that even a Catholic of Owen McMahon's social standing was not off limits. To be sure, McMahon was one of the wealthiest Catholics in Belfast, where he had business and leisure ties with middle-class Protestants. His home was situated in the predominantly Protestant neighbourhood of Thorndale, an affluent section of the city. The message attached to the killing was certainly not lost on the Catholic community, especially not on Devlin, who was outraged.

However shocking the McMahon attack was in terms of scale, it is worth noting that there was no sign that the victims' bodies had been mutilated, as was the case with some others who had been killed during this intensely violent period. The victims in the McMahon case had all been shot in a clinical execution. By contrast, Halfpenny's corpse bore not only the marks of multiple gunshot wounds, but also, apparently, signs of torture and mutilation.[7] This puts into context the observation of one Catholic contemporary who recalled that 'we didn't think [the McMahon killings] especially brutal'.[8] Yet it was the class dimension that gave the attack its real significance, and the rationale for those who planned it. Speaking in the House of Commons on 28 March, two days after the burial of most of the victims, Devlin felt it appropriate to declare that the assassinations had 'shocked almost the entire world'. He even read from a leading unionist paper, the *Belfast Telegraph*, which described the deed as 'the most terrible assassination that has yet stained the name of Belfast'.[9]

The funeral of McMahon and his sons attracted at least ten thousand mourners, among whom were members of the Catholic political and clerical elite. Protestants, particularly from the business community, were also in attendance.[10] The event served as a rallying point for a Catholic community that was now more alarmed than ever. The number and the range of mourners bore witness to Owen McMahon's social status in the community. In his Commons speech, Devlin would protest that this 'leading merchant in the City of Belfast' was beyond reproach, 'the most unoffending citizen'. But therein lay the issue. In this part of the United Kingdom, where the minority status of Catholics derived from the crude demographic arithmetic of partition, McMahon's rights of citizenship were not assured, nor, as Devlin knew well, protected by political leaders in London. Though they were social worlds apart, Owen McMahon and Malachy Halfpenny had that in common, at least.

by Laurence Marley

FURTHER READING

Michael Farrell, *Arming the Protestants: the formation of the Ulster Special Constabulary and the Royal Ulster Constabulary, 1920–27* (Cork, 1983)

Eamon Phoenix, *Northern nationalism: nationalist politics, partition and the Catholic minority in Northern Ireland, 1890–1940* (Belfast, 1994)

Tim Wilson, '"The most terrible assassination that has yet stained the name of Belfast": the McMahon murders in context', *Irish Historical Studies* 37 (145) (May 2010), 83–106

NOTES

[1] Eamon Phoenix, *Northern nationalism: nationalist politics, partition and the Catholic minority in Northern Ireland, 1890–1940* (Belfast, 1994), 192–3.

[2] Tim Wilson, '"The most terrible assassination that has yet stained the name of Belfast": the McMahon murders in context', *Irish Historical Studies* 37 (145) (May 2010), 83–106: 93.

[3] House of Commons debate, *Hansard*, vol. 143, cols 340–45 (14 June 1921).

[4] Representative Church Library, Dublin, Rosamund Stephen papers, box 4, 253/4 (years 1917–22), Rosamund Stephen to her sister, Katharine, 10 January 1922.

[5] Wilson, 'The most terrible assassination', 95.

[6] Representative Church Library, Dublin, Rosamund Stephen papers, box 3, 253/4 (years 1917–22), Rosamund Stephen's 'Journal', 7 February 1921.

[7] Kieran Glennon, *From pogrom to civil war: Tom Glennon and the Belfast IRA* (Cork, 2013), 69.

[8] Wilson, 'The most terrible assassination', 92.

[9] House of Commons debate, *Hansard*, vol. 152, cols 1281–84 (28 March 1922).

[10] Wilson, 'The most terrible assassination', 85.

30 MARCH 1922

THE CRAIG—COLLINS PACT

'PEACE IS TODAY DECLARED': CONCILIATION COMMITTEES AND THE 1920S TROUBLES

'Peace is today declared.' Rising in the House of Commons late on the evening of 30 March 1922, Winston Churchill thus dramatically announced the reaching of an agreement between Sir James Craig (as prime minister of Northern Ireland) and Michael Collins (on behalf of the Irish Free State).[1] Under the circumstances, his optimism was—to put it mildly—striking. An earlier, similar, deal (of 21 January) had sunk without trace. Killing rates in Belfast were at their twentieth-century peak.[2] Yet Churchill's ebullient showmanship distracted from these brutal realities to promise 'a reformed, non-sectarian Northern Ireland so far as security and employment policy were concerned, in exchange for an end to IRA violence... and Dublin recognition'.[3]

Given that it was announced with dazzling fanfare in London, it is easy to overlook how far the Craig–Collins pact was actually a peace settlement designed in Belfast. Its substance 'derived not from Collins or the Provisional Government but from the leader of the Irish Parliamentary Party in the North, Joseph Devlin, and from a group of Belfast Catholic businessmen who favoured an accommodation with the Northern government'.[4] These were the prime movers behind the pact's commitments to create mixed police forces in Belfast as well as a Conciliation Committee 'of equal numbers (Roman) Catholic and Protestant…to hear and investigate complaints as to intimidation, outrage, etc'.[5] In fact, the thinking behind the deal was not new. After the shipyard expulsions of July 1920, in which over five thousand Catholics, and some two thousand left-wing Protestants, were forced from their jobs by loyalist groups, there had been similar public calls by the Irish Parliamentary Party for a conciliation committee.[6]

Examined closely, then, the Craig–Collins pact draws attention to wider experiments in conflict reduction that deserve to be better remembered. Self-styled conciliation or peace committees first emerged right across north-east Ulster during the troubled summer of 1920.[7] IRA activity was their direct stimulus.[8] Such peace movements were an elite, rather than a mass, phenomenon. Indeed, they were emphatically bourgeois. Politically, they usually represented a loose conservative alliance of rival 'moderates': unionists and Devlinite nationalists. Socially, they were drawn from alliances of clergy and business elites. Institutionally, they remained both under-developed and transitory. Women seem to have played no role in them.

Although widely dispersed, such committees tended to remain strongly localist in focus. But the sheer speed of their appearance across a wide region suggests the adoption of ready-made templates. Non-aggression pacts had indeed been a marked feature of the long Third Home Rule crisis of 1912–14. By their very nature, though, these agreements tended to be cold bargains inspired by 'a shared vision of catastrophe'.[9]

Such dismal visions offered unstable vehicles for cooperation—as the example of Dungannon testifies. On Friday, 3 September 1920, a peace meeting was held at the Ranfurly Arms Hotel. Chaired by Robert Leith, leader of Dungannon Urban Council, it attracted around fifty 'business and professional representatives': an impressive showing for a small town with a population under 4,000.[10] Reading between the lines of the press reports, though, one can sense the tension in the room. When Canon McEndoo proffered some guarded remarks on the dynamics of violence

('he would say nothing as to the merits or demerits of Sinn Féin, but as long as there was provocation, so long and so sure would there be a strong temptation towards reprisal'), he was sharply rebuked by a local priest ('he... was not a Sinn Féiner himself, but at the same time he thought to attribute offences to any organisation, either Sinn Féin or Orange, at a meeting such as that, might hurt the feelings of some of those present').[11] A resolution to request military protection for the town was narrowly rejected (by 29 to 21 votes).[12] In a coordinated move, clergy exhorted their congregations 'to abstain from giving offence either by word or action and to avoid crowds'.[13]

A group, mainly children, outside terraced houses, possibly in the Marrowbone, north Belfast; members of the Ulster Special Constabulary stand nearby.

Terraced houses in Saunderson Street, the Marrowbone, burned by loyalists, 17 April 1922.

Although agreeing on improving street lighting, the Dungannon Peace Committee that emerged from this public meeting clearly struggled to agree more forceful measures. Four of its members who were magistrates 'requested that the council should form patrols in the various wards', which in a 'mixed' town surely risked the possibility of sectarian composition.[14] We do not know the outcome. Attempts to reorganise the Ulster Volunteer Force in Dungannon were already underway at the time—as the Royal Irish Constabulary had noted warily.[15] It is also worth noting that 'peace pickets' had emerged that summer during the rioting in East Belfast, under the aegis of a Church of Ireland minister, John Redmond. These were highly praised.[16] But such freelance efforts arguably also risked evolving into Orange vigilantism.

Peace committees were not just precautionary. Indeed, they often emerged in the aftermath of serious blood-letting. Thus, the military crackdown on Derry (late June 1920) was accompanied by the formation of a Conciliation Committee: 'a delightful thing' in the words of the judge who opened the July Assizes.[17] By November 1920 it was attempting to calm tensions by disavowing 'rogue' death threats against both loyalists and republicans.[18] When cycles of violence petered out into fragile stand-offs, local peace conferences attempted to consolidate these: this was the pattern in both the Clones/Roslea area (April 1921) and at Desertmartin (May 1922).[19] Of course, it is often impossible to demonstrate why such violence did not then re-ignite.[20] But the investment in these efforts is nonetheless striking. At Strabane in June 1922, the Conciliation Committee brokered a cessation of sniping across the new frontier.[21]

By that time, hopes aroused by the Craig–Collins pact had long evaporated. Its Conciliation Committee was dead. Two of its Catholic members had been arrested. Another three were on the run.[22] Given the wider context, the abject failure of the pact was always its most likely outcome. But that is no reason to continue to ignore the less ambitious—but perhaps more consequential—peace movements that arose across Northern Ireland between 1920 and 1922. However ineffectively institutionalised, they bear witness to the resilience of informal mechanisms of conflict de-escalation at local levels: 'what can never be quantified is what evils may have been prevented'.[23]

by Tim Wilson

FURTHER READING

Pearse Lawlor, *The outrages 1920–1922* (Cork, 2011)

Alan F. Parkinson, *Belfast's unholy war* (Dublin, 2004)

Christopher Magill, *Political conflict in East Ulster, 1920–22. Revolution and reprisal* (Woodbridge, 2020)

NOTES

[1] Michael Farrell, *Arming the Protestants: the formation of the Ulster Special Constabulary and the Royal Ulster Constabulary, 1920–27* (London, 1983), 104.

[2] In the first six months of 1922, 285 were killed; 298 were killed in 1972: Niall Cunningham, '"The doctrine of vicarious punishment": space, religion and the Belfast Troubles of 1920–22', *Journal of Historical Geography* 40 (2013), 52–66: 52.

[3] Summary by Paul Bew, *Churchill and Ireland* (Oxford, 2016), 121.

[4] Christopher Norton, 'An earnest endeavour for peace: unionist opinion and the Craig/Collins peace pact of 30 March 1922', *Études Irlandais* 32 (1) (2007), 91–108: 94.

[5] *Belfast News-Letter*, 31 March 1922.

[6] *Belfast News-Letter*, 2 August 1920.

[7] *Anglo-Celt*, 3 July 1920 [Derry]; *Belfast News-Letter*, 30 July 1920 [Garvagh]; *Dungannon Democrat*, 11 August 1920 [Moy]; *Freeman's Journal*, 23 August 1920 [Kilrea]; *Irish Independent*, 6 September 1920 [Dungannon].

[8] *Ulster Herald*, 14 August 1920 [Moy].

[9] Brendan O'Leary, 'Foreword', in Michael Kerr, *Imposing power-sharing: conflict and coexistence in Northern Ireland and Lebanon* (Dublin, 2006), xvii–xxxv: xxii.

[10] *Dungannon Democrat*, 8 September 1920; see also the Census information available at: www.census. nationalarchives.ie/pages/1911/Tyrone/Dungannon/ (accessed 15 April 2021).

[11] *Irish Independent*, 6 September 1920; *Irish News*, 6 September 1920.

[12] *Belfast News-Letter*, 6 September 1920.

[13] *Belfast News-Letter*, 7 September 1920.

[14] *Belfast News-Letter*, 9 September 1920.

[15] The National Archives of the United Kingdom, Records of the Colonial Office, CO 904/112 (August 1920).

[16] John Redmond, *Church, state and industry in East Belfast, 1827–1929* (Belfast, 1960), 12–20; *Belfast News-Letter*, 26 July 1920; Brian Walker, 'Voices opposing violence', *The Irish Times*, 9 June 2020.

[17] *Irish Independent*, 19 July 1920. Also: *Belfast News-Letter*, 26 June 1920; *Irish Independent*, 28 June 1920.

[18] *Belfast News-Letter*, 15 November 1920; *Freeman's Journal*, 15 November 1920.

[19] T.K. Wilson, 'The strange death of loyalist Monaghan, 1912–1921', in Senia Pašeta (ed.), *Uncertain futures: essays about the Irish past for Roy Foster* (Oxford, 2016), 174–87: 184–5; *Mid-Ulster Mail*, 27 May 1922.

[20] In the case of Desertmartin, one IRA source stresses internal disarray: Military Archives, Bureau of Military History, witness statement 1741, Michael O'Donoghue.

[21] *Belfast News-Letter*, 5 June 1922; *Strabane Chronicle*, 10 June 1922.

[22] *Irish Independent*, 15 June 1922.

[23] Frank Wright, *Northern Ireland: a comparative analysis* (Dublin, 1987, 1992), 243.

31 MARCH 1922

W.B. YEATS IN THOOR BALLYLEE

MEDITATING IN TIME OF CIVIL WAR

Reflecting on the terrible events of 1922, the poet Austin Clarke wrote:

> It seems to me that a self-destructive period is beyond the expression of verse...If one were purely a dramatist and sufficiently aloof one might be able to study the amazing maelstrom of revengeful passions, cupidity and...falsehood that has swept the people of every shade of opinion and transformed quiet citizens into bloody-minded disciples of force. But silence seems best.[1]

Creative literature inspired by the civil war is not silent but remains scanty; even the literary reverberations of the preceding revolution tend towards evasion, ambiguity and disillusionment, as Frances Flanagan has incisively shown.[2] The signal exception, as so often, is W.B. Yeats. Late in his life he described himself as 'a man of my time, through my poetical faculty living its history'.[3] This is true even of his very early 'Celtic Twilight' work, for all its fey decoration. And it is powerfully demonstrated by the sequence he wrote recording the events and atmosphere of the civil war as he observed it from his tower house in east county Galway from the spring of 1922 to the end of that violent and eventful year.

When Yeats, his wife and their two small children began to occupy Thoor Ballylee in the summers from 1919, it was still being renovated, and they periodically retreated to Augusta Gregory's adjacent Coole Park, or the Dublin house they leased in Merrion Square from February 1922. At the end of March 1922, however, they could move into Ballylee and stay there till September. This was an intensely creative time for him. The tower, its architecture, its contested history and the memories which had accumulated around it, dominated Yeats's imagination.[4] Significantly, he was working on Book 1 of his occult philosophy, *A vision*, which is inscribed 'Finished at Thoor Ballylee, 1922, in a time of Civil War'. That war helped crystallise his view of history as cycles of primary and antithetical conflict, rather than as a Hegelian or Marxian dialectic moving progressively forward.

This world-view also pervades the volume of memoirs published as *The trembling of the veil* completed in 1922 and published at the end of that year. This dealt with the trauma of the Parnell split in 1890–91, and the ensuing conflicts and disillusionments in Irish political and cultural life. Out of such upheavals, he suggested, came what he later called the 'long gestation' of the revolution announced in the Rising of Easter 1916. Yeats's emphasis on the politics of division, accusations of betrayal, and the inheritance of hatred was clearly inflected by the civil war raging around him as he wrote.

Nor was his poetic attention entirely confined to the state of affairs in Ireland. His responses to the international disruptions set in motion by the First World War returned again and again to ideas about cycles of anarchy and internecine violence, expressed in poems such as 'The Second Coming' and ominous essays like 'If I were Four and Twenty', and echoed in many of his contemporary letters. Though a strong supporter of the Treaty settlement, even before the civil war sparked into life early in 1922, his mind was running on themes of violence, change, historical inheritance and—perhaps above all—'bitterness'.

This is the word which recurs in the sequence of poems, mostly written in the summer of 1922 and linked together as 'Meditations in time of civil war'. This was first published simultaneously on both sides of the Atlantic, in Marianne Moore's *The Dial* and R.A. Scott-James's *The London Mercury*, in January 1923.[5] When it was reprinted in *The tower* (1928) he was, he told friends, 'astonished at its bitterness'.[6] That word closes the first poem in

'Meditations', 'Ancestral Houses', which moves from a beautifully accomplished evocation of country-house civilisation to the chilling suggestion that these evanescent achievements are founded on violence and bitterness—and as that inheritance is diluted, the 'greatness' of an assured civilization crumbles away.

> What if the glory of escutcheoned doors,
> And buildings that a haughtier age designed,
> The pacing to and fro on polished floors
> Amid great chamber and long galleries, lined
> With famous portraits of our ancestors;
> What if those things the greatest of mankind
> Consider most to magnify, or to bless,
> But take our greatness with our bitterness?

When he began this poem (probably the year before) he had an English house in mind, Ottoline Morrell's Garsington; but as the houses of the Irish Ascendancy were being burned around him in 1922, it carried a powerful local resonance, and the classical form as well as the imagery of the stanzas invoked the Anglo-Irish inheritance he was already beginning to re-imagine. By deliberate contrast, the next poem in the sequence, 'My House', conjured up the massive tower he had converted for a summer home, and its violent history as a fortress for warring Elizabethan condottieri, as well as the once-powerful Anglo-Norman de Burgo clan. Even its poetic form suggests the craggy, obdurate shape of the building—as well as invoking an image from his by now canonical 'Easter 1916', when a 'stilted water-hen' swims with her chicks by the ancient bridge and 'more ancient tower'. Above all, the tower has seen a violent history:

> Two men have founded here. A man-at-arms
> Gathered a score of horse and spent his days
> In this tumultuous spot,
> Where through long wars and sudden night alarms
> His dwindling score and he seemed castaways
> Forgetting and forgot;
> And I, that after me

My bodily heirs may find,
To exalt a lonely mind,
Befitting emblems of adversity.

Themes of violence and continuity are further explored in the next poems—'My Table', 'My Descendants'—but in 'The Road at my Door', a sudden swerve brings the political into the personal:

An affable Irregular,
A heavily-built Falstaffian man,
Comes cracking jokes of civil war
As though to die by gunshot were
The finest play under the sun.

A brown Lieutenant and his men,
Half dressed in national uniform,
Stand at my door and I complain
Of the foul weather, hail and rain,
A pear-tree broken by the storm.

I count those feathered balls of soot
The moor-hen guides upon the stream,
To silence the envy in my thought;
And turn towards my chamber, caught
In the cold snows of a dream.

Yeats was firmly on the side of the Free State (though his friend Gregory inclined to the republicans and much admired de Valera). But he also told Gregory that 'both sides are responsible for this whirlpool of hate'[7] and the politics of this poem are committed to neither side: the representatives of dissident republicanism and Free State forces are given equal billing, and the poet engages them in deliberately non-political chat—symbolic though the 'foul weather' and broken pear-tree may be, not to mention the moor-hen, suggesting (again, as in 'Easter 1916') the consolations of quietude and family love. What strikes the reader powerfully is the admission of 'envy' of those fully committed to the conflict, a feeling repeated in the last poem of the series. This invokes visions seen from the top of the tower: 'Phantoms of hatred', the 'coming emptiness', 'rage-hungry' troops pitted against each other, and violent disputations recalled from bloody episodes of medieval history, while flocks of crazed harpie-like birds extinguish the light of the moon. Finally, the poet descends his winding stair, wondering what he has lost by not committing himself to a part in the violent confrontations that preoccupy him: 'in something that all others understand and share'. But he opts, in the end, for the world of thought and study.

> The abstract joy,
> The half-read wisdom of daemonic images,
> Suffice the ageing man as once the growing boy.

That vaguely discontented retreat to the scholar's chamber, as the world ignites around him, is not, however, the only conclusion offered. In between 'The Road at My Door; and 'I see Phantoms of Hatred...' comes the key poem of the sequence, and the most famous: a direct evocation of the state of Ireland in 1922 and a prayer for peace: 'The Stare's Nest by My Window'. Yeats would add it to the published version of his speech accepting the Nobel Prize in 1923, supplying a vivid and sharply-etched vignette of life in the terrible summer of 1922.

> I was in my Galway house during the first months of the civil war, the railway bridges blown up and the roads blocked with stones and trees. For the first week there were no newspapers, no reliable news, we did not know who had won nor who had lost, and even after news-papers came, one never knew what was happening on the other side of the hill or of the line of trees. Ford cars passed the house from time to time with coffins standing upon and between the seats, and sometimes at night we heard an explosion, and once by day saw the smoke made by the burning of a great neighboring house. Men must have lived so through many tumultuous centuries. One felt an overmastering desire not to grow unhappy or embittered, not to lose all sense of the beauty of nature. A stare (our West of Ireland name for a starling) had built in a hole beside my window and I made these verses out of the feeling of the moment:

> The bees build in the crevices
> Of loosening masonry, and there
> The mother birds bring grubs and flies.

My wall is loosening; honey-bees,
Come build in the empty house of the stare.
We are closed in, and the key is turned
On our uncertainty; somewhere
A man is killed, or a house burned.
Yet no clear fact to be discerned:
Come build in the empty house of the stare.

A barricade of stone or of wood;
Some fourteen days of civil war:
Last night they trundled down the road
That dead young soldier in his blood:
Come build in the empty house of the stare.

We had fed the heart on fantasies,
The heart's grown brutal from the fare,
More substance in our enmities
Than in our love; O honey-bees,
Come build in the empty house of the stare.[8]

Once more, the poetic voice refuses to take a stance on either side; even the dead soldier's commitment is undefined. (The victim was in fact from the National Army, and we know from Gregory's journal that Yeats interposed this powerful verse after the poem's initial composition, when he heard of the incident.) There is a refusal to embrace bitterness, and a plangent call for reconciliation and the need to build a new polity. Though the succeeding poem returns to 'Phantoms of hatred' and the historical inheritance of violence, it does not negate the message of 'The Stare's Nest by My Window': the need to begin building again. At the end of 1922 Yeats would try to play his part, by accepting nomination to the Irish Senate, where he took a notable if sometimes controversial role; he remained closely involved in Irish politics, not always wisely. In general, though, he adhered to his belief, confided to a friend, that 'nothing great comes out of violence and bitterness'—thus implicitly contradicting the conclusion of 'Ancestral Houses'.[9]

In December 1995, receiving his own Nobel Prize, Seamus Heaney would invoke 'The Stare's Nest by My Window', and his great predecessor's plea for peace at a time of internecine violence. Yeats, as Heaney pointed out, incorporated in his world-view not only the nurturing mother-love of the birds, but also the massacre by the roadside. The continuing relevance of the pleas based on this double vision is sobering as well as powerful—as is Heaney's conclusion that poetry can 'touch the base of our sympathetic nature while taking in at the same time the unsympathetic reality of the world to which that nature is constantly exposed'.[10] 'Meditations in time of civil war' remains the great literary reflection of a tragic moment in Irish history, distilled through a consummate poet's extrasensory perception of a world in crisis.

by R.F. Foster

FURTHER READING

Frances Flanagan, *Remembering the revolution: dissent, culture and nationalism in the Irish Free State* (Oxford, 2015)

R.F. Foster, *W.B. Yeats, A Life: volume II, the arch-poet, 1915–1939* (Oxford, 2003)

Joseph Hassett, *Yeats and the poetics of hate* (New York, 1986)

NOTES

[1] Quoted in Terence Brown, *The life of W.B. Yeats: a critical biography* (Dublin, 2001), 287.

[2] Frances Flanagan, *Remembering the revolution: dissent, culture and nationalism in the Irish Free State* (Oxford, 2015).

[3] 'Introduction', in W.B. Yeats (ed.), *The Oxford book of modern verse* (Oxford, 1936), xxxiii.

[4] See, R.F. Foster, '"When all is ruin once again": Yeats and Thoor Ballylee', in Hermione Lee and Kate Kennedy (eds), *Lives of houses* (Oxford, 2019), 217–31.

[5] W.B. Yeats, 'Meditations in time of civil war', *The London Mercury* (7) (January 1923), 232–38 and *The Dial* (74) (1) (January 1923), 50–56. The complete text of the work is available through the Corpus of Electronic Texts database, at: celt.ucc.ie//published/E910001-055.html (accessed 16 April 2021).

[6] He makes this observation in letters to Olivia Shakespear, 23 April 1928, and to Augusta Gregory, 24 February 1928; see, Allan Wade, *The letters of W.B. Yeats* (London, 1954), 738. W.B. Yeats, *The tower* (London, 1928).

[7] Elizabeth Cullingford, *Yeats, Ireland and fascism* (London, 1981), 112.

[8] W.B. Yeats, 'The Irish dramatic movement: Nobel Lecture, 15 December 1923', in *The bounty of Sweden* (Dublin 1925); available at: www.nobelprize.org/prizes/literature/1923/yeats/lecture/ (accessed 16 April 2021).

[9] Yeats's remark is recorded in Edith Lyttelton's recollection of a visit to Dublin in Churchill College, Chandos papers, CHAN 1, 6/4.

[10] Seamus Heaney, *Crediting poetry: the Nobel lecture 1995* (Oldcastle, 1995).

MAY

1 MAY 1922

KEEPING HOLLYWOOD'S 'MONKEY HOUSE' MORALITY OUT OF IRELAND

On 1 May 1922 the motion that 'Dáil Éireann be asked to appoint a Board of Censors for all Ireland' was passed unanimously by Dublin Corporation.[1] This request came twenty months after Dáil Éireann had considered the introduction of national film censorship,[2] while a conference of anti-cinema activists held in Dublin in December 1921 had demanded that an independent Irish government introduce such a film censorship regime.[3] These events were the culmination of campaigns by cultural, political and religious activists that had their roots in the late nineteenth-century agitation against what was perceived as immoral and anglicising imported popular culture and media. These campaigns acquired a new frisson with the increasing popularity of American cinema by the early 1910s.

For the decade prior to 1922, two competing worldviews—one embodied in Irish-Irelander nationalist, Gaelic culture, the other originating in

Hollywood's 'dream factories'—had been accelerating towards collision. Notwithstanding the former's longstanding anxiety regarding 'the anglicisation of Ireland', it was American cinema in the 1910s, with its increasingly transgressive elements (such as references to extra-marital affairs and divorce), that proved central in unifying Irish opinion—across religious and political divides, from cultural and political nationalists to unionists—to seek tighter controls over cinema.

The first legal mechanism through which censorship came to be imposed was the Cinematograph Act (1909), even though it had been designed as a public safety measure only. The courts began interpreting the 1909 act as allowing local authorities to regulate film content, such that in September 1916 a film censorship panel was set up by Dublin Corporation following pressure from the Catholic activist body the Irish Vigilance Association. In addition to the elected members of the corporation, this panel included appointees of both the Catholic and Protestant archbishops of Dublin.[4] Given that the panel only viewed films *after* their release, considerably reducing its effectiveness, and that relatively few films were banned—76 films in the period 1917–21—calls for a more rigorous national approach followed. This led to Dublin Corporation's motion on 1 May 1922.

The corporation's motion had been proposed by alderman Joseph MacDonagh, TD, brother not only to 1916 leader Thomas, but also to John, whose feature-film adaptation of William Carleton's anti-sectarian novel *Willy Reilly and his Colleen Bawn*, a key Irish film text, had been released on the Rising's fourth anniversary.[5] The motion was seconded by the long-time social and political activist, Jenny Wyse Power, chair of the Public Health Committee, which regulated cinemas.

Exactly a year later, in May 1923, the Censorship of Films Act was passed by the Dáil. Minister for Home Affairs Kevin O'Higgins introduced the bill following a meeting with an inter-denominational delegation of anti-cinema activists. The consensus against cinema also found expression in the Oireachtas. While reservations were voiced by the Labour party leader Thomas Johnson, TD, concerned that some provisions might restrict certain political views, and poet and senator W.B. Yeats, who argued for personal choice rather than state censorship, the repressive impulses of the new state was expressed most forcibly by William Magennis, TD, Professor of Metaphysics at University College Dublin, who suggested that people repeatedly found in breach of the act ought to have their citizenship revoked!

The Censorship of Films Act (1923) states that a film cannot be shown in public unless the film censor is satisfied it does not contain elements deemed indecent, obscene or blasphemous, or if it is determined that its public screening would 'inculcate principles contrary to public morality or would be otherwise subversive of public morality'; the latter an all-embracing subjective provision that came to be widely used by censors.[6] These criteria remain the reference points for present-day censors, as the act, albeit with amendments, remains on the statute book. The 1923 act also lays down the provision that an Official Film Censor be appointed, and that the censor's decision can be appealed to the Censorship of Films Appeal Board, a voluntary nine-person committee, which can confirm, alter or amend the censor's decisions.

While the first Official Film Censor James Montgomery (1923–40) boasted he knew nothing of film, but took the Ten Commandments as his guide, the members of the appeal board, who included Yeats, who resigned after ten months, and Wyse Power, who remained for over a decade (1924–38), tended in the main to reflect conservative Catholic and anti-modern views. From the outset, appointments, made by the Department of Justice, which still administers the office, included a representative from each of the two archbishops of Dublin, and excluded film distributors and exhibitors, and culturally liberal or internationalist voices.

Informed by the thesis that the family was the primary social unit of the state, and his belief that the laws of the land were sacrosanct, Montgomery set about his task with gusto: banning 100 films in his first year, the average for each of the seventeen years of his tenure. (The appeal board only occasionally reversed or modified his decisions.) With no differentiation made between representation and reality, all representations that contravened Irish law or were deemed deviant (including images of, or references to, marital infidelity, divorce, homosexuality, abortion and sexual assault), or that were contrary to Victorian morality (such as Jazz Age depictions of women in revealing clothes, in night-club chorus lines, smoking or drinking alcohol), were cause for a film to be banned or the objectionable scenes removed.

In February 1924 distributors, shaken by the severity of the new regime, withdrew their films from the Irish market. In a riposte, the censors declared they would rather have no films than the ones being submitted. Supported by the government, the censors resisted the distributors' pressure and within four months the boycott was lifted.[7] Thereafter, the censors had a free run, such that from the 1920s to the 1980s about 2,500 films were banned and another 10,000 to 12,000 cut. There was little or no public debate regarding the censorship process, as all censor files were hidden from public scrutiny until 1998, when they were deposited in the National Archives of Ireland.

A ROBERT VIGNOLA
PRODUCTION

PAULINE
FREDERICK

MAE
BUSCH

HUNTLY
GORDON

CONRAD
NAGEL

"Love me! Love me! You cannot leave me now"

MARRIED FLIRTS

A Metro Goldwyn Picture

A number of 1922 films came before the censor in 1923 and 1924. Among those banned were 'the very ugly picture' *The woman who walked alone*, which had 'most objectionable' scenes featuring a farmer's wife infatuated with another man; *The ordeal*, similarly described as 'an ugly story'; *A woman's woman*, 'a sordid story of conjugal infidelity, suggested seduction, attempted suicide, murder [and] divorce'; the 'morbid and unhealthy' *Queen of the Moulin Rouge*, featuring a dancer at the Parisian nightclub; and the Jazz Age *Nice people* dismissed as the 'usual picture of this type—wade through nastiness to a "moral end"'.[8]

Montgomery's motivation is most clear in his report on the 1924 film *My husband's wives* which he also banned: 'the remarriage of divorced people is illegal in Saorstát Éireann [and] I consider it "subversive of public morality" to allow exhibition of it', because 'the monkey house morality begotten of such a social condition is apparent'.[9] As for the same year's *Married flirts*,

Lobby card for the censored American silent drama, *Married flirts* (Robert Vignola, 1924).

in which 'the "morality" of the cave and the monkey-house is the ruling code', it contained 'all the unhealthy materials which made censorship necessary',[10] a comment validating the need for Dublin Corporation's motion of 1 May 1922.

Notwithstanding the censors' culling, what is perhaps surprising is that cinema-going in Ireland remained central to people's lives throughout this period; a cause of concern for those same censors, some of whom would have preferred its total prohibition. Though Ireland's cinema screens may have been sanitised, it seems the private fantasy lives of the people excited by film, and indeed by the cinema space, could not be fully suppressed.

by Kevin Rockett

FURTHER READING

Kevin Rockett with Emer Rockett, *Irish film censorship: a cultural journey from silent cinema to internet pornography* (Dublin, 2004)

NOTES

[1] *Minutes of the municipal council of the city of Dublin*, no. 328, 1922, 250–1; *Reports and printed documents of the Corporation of Dublin*, vol.1, no. 124, 739.

[2] *Dáil Éireann: the minutes of proceedings 1919–1921*, vol. F, no. 17, *Reports Department of Home Affairs*, 17 September 1920 (Dublin, 1921), 215.

[3] *Reports and printed documents of the Corporation of Dublin*, vol. 1, no. 124, 739.

[4] For an extended discussion of the issues outlined here see, Kevin Rockett with Emer Rockett, *Irish film censorship: a cultural journey from silent cinema to internet pornography* (Dublin, 2004).

[5] Kevin Rockett, 'The silent period', in Kevin Rockett, Luke Gibbons and John Hill, *Cinema and Ireland* (London, 1987; reprint, 2014), 23–29.

[6] Clause 7.2, Censorship of Films Act (1923).

[7] National Archives of Ireland, Office of the Official Film Censor, James Montgomery (NAI, James Montgomery), 'Report of the Official Film Censor to the Minister for Justice for the period 1 November 1923 to 31 October 1924', 13 November 1924. See, also, Irish Film and TV Research Online (at: www.tcd.ie/Irishfilm; accessed 16 April 2021), which includes 6,000 of the film censors' records from 1923 to 1938.

[8] NAI, James Montgomery, Reject book 98/29/1, 11 December 1923; 6 December 1923; 14 July 1924; 21 February 1924; 3 December 1923.

[9] NAI, James Montgomery, 10 February 1925.

[10] NAI, James Montgomery, 3 March 1925.

22 MAY 1922

THE FORCIBLE HAIR CUTTING OF THE CULLEN SISTERS OF KEENAGHAN, CO. TYRONE

GENDERED VIOLENCE AGAINST WOMEN

In June 1922 a brutal outrage that occurred in the townland of Keenaghan, in the parish of Killyman, near Dungannon, Co. Tyrone, was reported in several newspapers. Late on the night of Saturday, 22 May 1922, about twenty armed and masked men forced their way into the Cullen family home. Mrs Mary Cullen was brutally assaulted, as was her son (Peter) who was beaten unconscious. Also present in the house were two of Mrs Cullen's daughters, Mary and Teresa. The newspapers record that the 'cowardly ruffians' produced scissors they had brought with them, and proceeded to attack the sisters, cutting their hair off so roughly that their 'scalp [was] cut in each instance in several places'.[1] Some reports indicate that Mrs Cullen also had her hair sheared off. Before the raiders left, they smashed furniture and broke in the doors and windows.

Three nights later, on 25 May, in the townland of Laghey, also in Killyman, another woman was attacked and had her hair forcibly cut. The wife of an RIC constable, Sergeant Dennison, was attacked in her home by several men who gained entrance by pretending to be members of the

B-Specials section of the Ulster Special Constabulary. When Mrs Dennison opened the door, the assailants threatened her with a revolver, dragged her outside and cut off her hair. It was, the men said, punishment for flying the Union Jack over the house on Empire Day (May 24).[2] A third attack occurred in Killyman on 13 July 1922, when Meta Evangeline Cooke was attacked, in her home, by two men. They threatened her with a revolver, produced a penknife and cut off her hair. It was later reported that she had been targeted for giving information to the police.[3]

The policeman who investigated the Cullen 'outrage' said it was the most 'revolting sight he had ever seen', while the judge opined that 'the attacks on defenceless women illustrated the depths of cowardice and degradation to which the miserable warfare had descended...he had heard of such cases before but never had he found them accompanied by such violence and barbarity'.[4] These attacks, in the same parish, within a few weeks of each other, encapsulate the issue of gendered violence against women during outbreaks of violence in the northern countries in 1922, and indeed throughout Ireland from the outbreak of the War of Independence in 1919. In particular, the attack on the Cullen household illustrates the nature of gendered punishments meted out in revolutionary Ireland. All members of the household were attacked by the 'ruffians', but it was the women who were targeted for forcible hair cutting.

While the judge and the investigating policeman were horrified, the outrages cannot have been much of a surprise to them. Newspaper reports, military pension applications, Bureau of Military History witness statements, reports to the several commissions on conditions in Ireland (many by women), propaganda materials, diaries, memoirs, military, police and government records all indicate that forcible hair cutting was a gendered tactic of disciplinary violence during 1919–23. Women suspected of supporting or working with the IRA were targeted by the Crown forces, while women and girls suspected of 'company keeping' with members of the police or military were targeted by the IRA. During the reprisal and counter-reprisal of guerrilla war, as well as during the violence that accompanied partition and, later, the civil war, women were deliberately targeted. By late 1920, as Lil Conlon, a member of Cumann na mBan in Cork, stated:

> the going was tough on the female sex...[to] intensify the reign of terror, swoops were made at night, entries forced into their homes, and the women's hair cut off in a brutal fashion as well as suffering other indignities and insults.[5]

Although forcible hair cutting is often mentioned in the sources, evidence of 'other indignities and insults', particularly of sexual violence and rape, is much more difficult to uncover. Historians have claimed that there was a low incidence of sexual violence during this period, and the paucity of evidence in the archives would seem to support this claim. It has to be noted, however, that most women were reluctant to talk about or report sexual attacks, which could account for the lack of archival material. The British Labour Commission to Ireland (1921), surprised to find little evidence of sexual assaults, reasoned that this was because the women of Ireland were 'reticent on such subjects'.[6] Nevertheless, reticent as they undoubtedly were, evidence of wartime rape and sexual assault by both sides does exist. In 1922 several brutal rapes and sexual assaults were recorded. On 14 June 1922 the McGuill home in Dromintee, Co Armagh, was attacked by B-Specials.

Still from a Pathé news report, Limerick, 1920. The intertitle recorded: 'May Connelly—who was kicked and had her hair shorn for the "crime" of speaking to Black and Tans.'

Mrs McGuill was gang-raped and a female servant sexually assaulted; a provocation that likely contributed to the exceptionally brutal Altnaveigh reprisal, which resulted in the killing of six Protestant civilians three days later.[7] Further south, on 22 June, Harriet Biggs was gang-raped at her home in Dromineer, Co. Tipperary, by members of the IRA, while another IRA gang raided Sopwell Hall in Cloughjordan, Co. Tipperary, in July 1922 and sexually assaulted two of the maids.[8]

Wartime rapes and sexual assaults are infrequent in the records. However the deliberate and gendered violence of forcible hair cutting nevertheless constituted a significant trauma. The reporting of these assaults was often dry and emotionless, but there can be no doubt of the real violence—physical, psychological and possibly sexual—inflicted. Women endured extreme bodily violation, degrading treatment and possibly sexual assault during forcible hair cutting, for reasons of social and moral control. For the Crown forces, women who were suspected of republican leanings had to be controlled and contained, while the IRA used gendered violence as a way of disciplining 'its' women, especially those girls and women considered deviant because of their associations with the enemy. For decades, the voices, experiences and traumas of women during the Irish revolution have been absent; historians are now providing a corrective to those omissions, which will serve to broaden our understanding of the nature and extent of gendered violence against women during this period of conflict.[9]

by Mary McAuliffe

FURTHER READING

Gemma Clark, 'Violence against women in the Irish civil war, 1922–3: gender-based harm in global perspective', *Irish Historical Studies* 44 (165) (May 2020), 75–90

Lindsey Earner-Byrne, 'The rape of Mary M: a microhistory of sexual violence and moral redemption in 1920s Ireland', *Journal of the History of Sexuality* 24 (1) (January 2015), 75–98

Louise Ryan, '"Drunken Tans": representations of sex and violence in the Anglo-Irish War (1919–21)', *Feminist Review* 66 (2000), 73–94

NOTES

[1] *Fermanagh Herald,* 3 June 1922, 7. *Belfast News-Letter,* 9 October 1922, 9. The attack was also reported in the *Freeman's Journal,* the *Donegal News* and the *Donegal Democrat.* Bobbing, shearing, or cutting are terms most often used in contemporary reports for this type of forcible hair cutting.

[2] *Belfast News-Letter,* 26 May 1922, 9.

[3] *Belfast News-Letter,* 9 October 1922, 9.

[4] *The Irish Times,* 14 October 1922, 6. The judge awarded Mrs Cullen and Mrs Dennison £25 each, Mary and Teresa Cullen £15 each, and £15 to Miss Cooke.

[5] Lil Conlon, *Cumann na mBan and the women of Ireland, 1913–25* (Kilkenny, 1969), 224. Forcible hair cutting declines somewhat into 1921, but there are several incidents reported in local and national newspapers as violence escalated in border areas, particularly during the months of May to August 1922.

[6] Report of the Labour Commission to Ireland (1921), 29.

[7] See, Robert Lynch, 'Explaining the Altnaveigh massacre', *Éire-Ireland* 45 (Winter, 2010), 184–210, for details of this case.

[8] At the Sopwell Hall incident, the gang separated the Protestant maids from the Catholic maid and assaulted the two Protestant women. There are several known cases of rape and sexual assault during 1920–23. These were carried out by members of the Crown forces, IRA, B-Specials, and National Army. The evidence so far, however, does not indicate that rape and sexual assault was a common weapon of war.

[9] Recent studies include those by Susan Byrne, '"Keeping company with the enemy": gender and sexual violence against women during the Irish War of Independence and civil war, 1919–1923', *Women's History Review* (2020), 108–25; Linda Connolly, 'Sexual violence in the Irish civil war: a forgotten war crime?', *Women's History Review* (2020), 126–43; Marie Coleman, 'Violence against women during the Irish War of Independence, 1919–21', in Diarmaid Ferriter and Susannah Riordan (eds), *Years of turbulence: the Irish revolution and its aftermath* (Dublin, 2015), 137–56; Justin Dolan Stover, 'Families, vulnerability and sexual violence during the Irish revolution', in Jennifer Evans and Ciara Meehan (eds), *Perceptions of pregnancy from the seventeenth to the twentieth century* (London, 2017), 57–75; and Mary McAuliffe, 'The homefront as battlefront: women, violence and the domestic space during war in Ireland, 1919–1921', in Linda Connolly (ed.), *Women and the Irish revolution: feminism, activism, violence* (Dublin, 2020), 164–82.

25 MAY 1922

THE FIRST ANNIVERSARY OF THE BURNING OF THE CUSTOM HOUSE

WEARING THE GREEN: UNIFORMS, COLLECTIVITY, AND AUTHORITY

On Thursday, 25 May 1922 the first anniversary of the IRA's 'taking' of the Custom House was marked in Dublin. As the headquarters of the Local Government Board of Ireland, it had been of vital importance to the British administration

Overleaf: National Army recruits receive uniforms at Beggars Bush barracks, Dublin, early 1922.

before being attacked and burned by more than 100 young republicans dressed in civilian clothing; the necessary disguise to launch a surprise assault. The ensuing skirmish resulted in the deaths of five combatants and three civilians and the almost total destruction of James Gandon's 'jewel of Irish architecture'.[1] One year later, *An t-Óglách* reported the commemoration by 'thousands of Irish soldiers' who attended Requiem Masses with full military honours 'for those of their comrades who lost their lives in this, the last big engagement of the Liberation War'.

Headed by a kilted pipers' band, uniformed soldiers with rifles and fixed bayonets paraded through the streets to St Agatha's church in North William Street, where a large tricolour, accompanied by a list of the names of some of the fallen, was carried to the altar. At the Consecration, military drum-rolls were sounded, and the royal salute was made to the Host. After the Last Post was played at St Agatha's, the soldiers, joined by others, marched to the Pro-Cathedral for a second

Opposite: an illustration from *An tÓglach* ('official organ of the Irish Volunteers') associating the uniformed soldier with discipline and training.

Mass, and then in procession to the ruined Custom House. The day's ceremonies culminated there in a recitation of the Rosary in Irish for the repose of the dead. It was asserted in *An t-Óglách* that, except for Irish Volunteers' attendance at Mass on the St Patrick's Day before the Easter Rising, 'this was the first occasion upon which the soldiers of an Irish Army were present at a Church function in Dublin'.[2] Of course, the majority of those soldiers had been present at countless church functions before. What the author meant was that this was the first time Irish soldiers attended a religious event together as soldiers. That is to say they were at Mass *en masse* in uniform, in formation, carrying weapons, sounding pipes and drums. But most importantly, they were in uniform.

The public collation of religious and military ceremony was one aspect of the statecraft of the Provisional Government. This was not actually the first time the army had attended a religious function: in March 1922 troops from Beggars Bush barracks paraded to a special Mass in the Pro-Cathedral, initiating a tradition of troops parading to Mass every Sunday.[3] On St Patrick's Day that year, the flag of the Irish army was publicly blessed at a special ceremony, with that fusion of Church and state represented in Sir John Lavery's 1922 painting 'Blessing of the colours', which depicts the archbishop of Dublin blessing a tricolour held aloft by a kneeling soldier in Irish Free State uniform. Indeed, religious ceremonies, and in particular the Requiem Mass, became a key commemorative mode in the early years of the Free State, with the potentially divisive commemoration of Easter 1916 taking the official form of an invitation-only Mass at Arbour Hill under the Cumann na nGaedheal government and presided over by the National Army, whose members were described at the ceremony in 1923 as 'clad in the uniform the men they honoured had sanctified with their blood'.[4]

The issue of uniform and combatant clothing throughout this period in Irish history is complex and intriguing, reflecting the presence of many

DISCIPLINE   TRAINING

different armed factions and forces, the claims to identity conferred by a formal uniform, and the exigen-
cies of guerrilla warfare that concealed civilian-clad
rebels in a Dublin crowd, or clothed others on the
run in trench-coats and broad hats. Those soldiers at
the Custom House commemoration were in the new
National Army uniform, first worn on the streets in
early 1922 in limited edition by the Dublin Guard on a
photogenic cross-city parade to receive Beggars Bush
barracks from the departing British troops, and then
issued unevenly in subsequent months. Its design was

broadly based on the official dress of the Irish Volunteers, but in a green
whipcord (for officers) or scratchy dark green serge (other ranks) rather
than the grey-green described by Éamonn Ceannt in the *Irish Volunteer* in
1914 as appropriate in 'a land where the prevailing tints vary from the grey
of morning and evening twilight to the verdant green of midday'.[5] Long-
established national symbols were retained from the Volunteers for the new
uniforms, and still appear on those of the Irish Defence Forces a century
later. The buttons were cast with a harp and 'IV' for Irish Volunteers; a
cap badge, designed by Eoin MacNeill, featured 'FF' for Fianna Fáil (generally translated as 'soldiers of destiny', but a literal reference to the legendary Fianna band of warriors) within an eight-pointed star set against a
sunburst, described in later regulations as the *Gal Gréine* derived from the
Fianna banner. By means of such elements, the authority of the force on
show in May 1922 was invoked through their connection with the historical
Volunteers, and beyond them to a mythic Irish past.

As well as protecting the body, uniform functions to 'promote internal
discipline, convey hierarchy and status, legitimise violence and demonstrate the access the military force has to the means of production'.[6] Most
fundamentally, uniform visualises and shapes collectivity. In May 1922 such
ideals might have been signalled by the sight of uniformed soldiers marching in formation, attending Mass and remembering 'their' heroic dead. The
reality, however, was less comfortable. There was disquiet about the perception that the army lacked discipline, with post-truce recruits (or 'trucileers') being particularly disdained; there was internal squabbling about
rank; and the supply of uniform remained difficult. This would come to the
fore in subsequent months, when the National Army expanded rapidly to
contest the civil war and acquired ex-British army uniforms to dye green.

Adding further complexity, when asked to respond to rumours about the source of the uniforms in November 1922, the Quartermaster General's office confirmed that 'an order for 10,000 uniforms, greatcoats and slacks had been placed in England with Messers The Briscoe Importing Co.',[7] a Jewish-owned Dublin firm run by the brother of Robert Briscoe. An IRA member who was involved in importing arms for the anti-Treaty IRA, Robert was suspected of profiteering due to those family connections.[8]

Above all, of course, the split over the Treaty meant division rather than collectivity was to the fore, undermining the idea of a seamless continuity between the fallen comrades and those who publicly mourned them. The de Valera–Collins pact of 20 May, enabling the pro- and anti-Treaty sides in Sinn Féin to contest the June general election jointly, had led to reports expressing hope that the different factions might be reconciled, but for now many of the pre-Treaty combatants rejected the Irish Free State and its uniform. Reporting from the Four Courts a few weeks later, the journalist Clare Sheridan noted that the occupants 'had no uniforms, but were heavily armed. Cartridge belts over serge suits seemed the dominant note'.[9] Fractured allegiances, as well as different forms of combat, could mean rapid sartorial change, from Volunteer uniform in 1916, trench coats and hats during the War of Independence, Irish Free State army uniform in early 1922, 'and then back again into trench coats and "broad black brimmers" when the Civil War broke out'.[10] Just one month after the ceremonies at the Custom House, National Army troops would start the bombardment of the Four Courts, and Gandon's other riverine jewel would be ablaze.

by Lisa Godson

FURTHER READING

Gavin Foster, *The Irish civil war and society: politics, class, and conflict* (London, 2015)

Jane Tynan and Lisa Godson (eds), *Understanding uniform: clothing and discipline in the modern world* (London, 2019)

NOTES

[1] *Irish Builder*, 4 June 1921, 393.

[2] 'Notes', *An t-Óglách*, 3 June 1922, 1.

[3] See, *The Irish Catholic directory and almanac* (Dublin, 1923).

[4] 'The Dead of 1916', *Irish Independent*, 4 May 1923, 5.

[5] 'The Volunteer Uniform. What should it be: Mr Eamonn Ceannt's views', *Irish Volunteer*, 21 February 1914, 4.

[6] Jane Tynan, 'The unmilitary appearance of the 1916 rebels', in Lisa Godson and Joanna Brück (eds), *Making 1916: material and visual culture of the Easter Rising* (Liverpool, 2015), 25–33: 28.

[7] Military Archives (MA), DOD-A-07535 Quartermaster General department to Commander-in-Chief's Office, 1 November 1922.

[8] MA, Military Service Pensions Collection, WMSP34REF297, Robert Briscoe to Military Service Pensions, 9 October 1931.

[9] Clare Sheridan, *In many places* (London, 1923), 45.

[10] Gavin M. Foster, *The Irish civil war and society. Politics, class, and conflict* (London, 2015), 102.

29 MAY 1922

THE ARREST OF JOHN O DONNELL

INTERNMENT IN NORTHERN IRELAND

On 29 May 1922 John O Donnell was arrested following a crackdown on republican and nationalist activists in Northern Ireland. O Donnell, who had been a Volunteer in the Belfast IRA during the turbulent 1918–23 years, was imprisoned on the *HMS Argenta* until October 1923, when he was released in a 'dying state'.[1] By June 1925 he had succumbed to tuberculosis. His widow, Bridget O Donnell, penned a letter in 1932 to the minister for defence, Frank Aiken, applying for her dead husband's military service pension. Bridget related how John was 'unable to follow his usual occupation as dock labourer' following his release from the *Argenta*.[2] It was stated that he had been 'in perfect health previous to his internment', and his pension statement recorded that he died as a result of 'brutal and inhuman treatment' while on the ship. John O Donnell was not the only prisoner to suffer ill-health following internment on the *HMS Argenta*. Many of those interned on the ship would suffer the effects of their imprisonment for the rest of their lives.[3]

Internment was a feature of the Irish revolutionary years 1916–21 and continued during the Irish civil war of 1922–23. In Northern Ireland, David Fitzpatrick noted that political and sectarian violence peaked in early 1922, when some 300 murders were officially accounted for. As intercommunal violence increased, the Belfast administration introduced the Civil Authorities (Special Powers) Act in April. This provided the government with the powers to arrest and intern individuals whom it considered were acting in a manner prejudicial to the state.[4] What prompted the government to introduce wide-scale internment, however, was the assassination of the Unionist MP William Twaddell in May 1922. On the night of 22–23 May the authorities conducted sweeping arrests in Northern Ireland. Within a few weeks, some 300 persons, 'almost all Roman Catholic males', had been detained and served with internment orders. As the administration had only three prisons at its disposal (Derry jail, Belfast jail and Armagh prison), it purchased the *Argenta* and acquired Larne workhouse in order to meet the accommodation needs of the rising internee population.[5]

Pages from the autograph book of an internee imprisoned on the *HMS Argenta*, Belfast Lough, 1922–24.

Originally named the *SS Argenta*, this wooden steamer vessel was built in 1917 by the United States and launched in May 1919. Initially used as a cargo ship, the *Argenta* was purchased by the Belfast administration in May 1922, despite having been declared 'unseaworthy'.[6] The hard-line minister for home affairs, Sir Richard Dawson Bates, who specifically purchased the ship to ease the burden on the other state prisons, was hopeful that the prison ship would act as a deterrent for future political offenders. Observing that internees had become 'accustomed to enjoying the luxury of an internment camp', he remarked that prisoners would find the ship not quite so 'pleasant', and that many of the men had tried 'to avoid going on a ship'.[7] By 9 September 1922 there were around 340 internees on the now *HMS Argenta*. Bates acknowledged that many of these had not been tried and were, in fact, 'un-convicted' prisoners.[8]

Conditions on the *HMS Argenta* were significantly harsher than those experienced in internment camps, as prisoners were held in eight wire cages below deck. Former internee and Irish Volunteer, John Shields, described the ship as the 'most inhuman method of dealing with state prisoners' due to the overcrowding and unsanitary conditions. There were often up to 50 men interned in one cage, which measured 20 to 40 feet, resulting in conditions

When the Summers sun is setting
And your thoughs from cares are free
When of absent ones your thinking
Will you kindly think of me.
James Gallen. Friday Night. 11th Jan. 1924.
Larne Camp. Co Antrim. Late of
Garvagh Pullens. Castlederg. Co Tyrone
Lisnacloon. Platoon. and Derry Gaol.

BREAKFAST TIME PRISON SHIP "ARGENTA" 8.30

so 'congested' that there was little room for either tables or chairs. The latrines, positioned at either end of the deck, were regularly 'stopped up', which meant that the overflow often ran down by the cages.[9] The food was of an 'inferior quality' and was reportedly condemned by both the 'interned doctor' and the governor of the prison ship A.D. Drysdale. The men, who were served blackened potatoes for dinner, were provided with a sparse quantity of bread, margarine and butter for breakfast. Knives, forks and enamel mugs were supplied to the internees, but various reports emerged that prisoners had to eat their food 'while sitting on the floor'.

The internees had access to the upper deck for exercise during the hours from seven in the morning to eight in the evening. The exercise space, however, was overcrowded and covered with a wire enclosure to prevent internees jumping ship. Inside the cages, the sleeping arrangements were little better. Some internees were supplied with mattresses while others slept in swing hammocks. Appeals for additional clothing were not granted and, consequently, several men had to go 'through the winter with wet feet'. In these circumstances, many men succumbed to serious bouts of illness. Scabies broke out, and a lice infestation spread because of the lack of proper laundry facilities for clothes and bed linen. As a result of the spread of head and body lice, several prisoners had to be removed to isolation cells in Belfast prison. The atmosphere on the ship was most unhealthy; cases of tuberculosis and flu were reported among the prisoners.[10]

As early as October 1922 Dawson Bates conceded that 'the accommodation on the *Argenta* was not sufficient for purpose'. Nevertheless, these conditions persisted into 1923, and until the internees were finally removed from the ship. In 1933 Bridget O Donnell was granted a military service pension on account of her late husband's service during the conflict. Given Bridget's description of her husband's health, prior and subsequent to his incarceration, and in light of contemporary accounts of the *HMS Argenta*, it seems likely that his death resulted from the grossly substandard conditions on the ship. In later years, the former internee John Shields remarked that 'it was a marvel the men survived so long under such living conditions'. The last remaining *HMS Argenta* internees were transferred to Belfast prison, Derry jail and Larne camp in January 1924.[11]

by Anne-Marie McInerney

FURTHER READING

Denise Kleinrichert, *Republican internment and the prison ship Argenta 1922* (Dublin, 2001)

Seán McConville, *Irish political prisoners 1920–62: pilgrimage of desolation* (London, 2014)

William Murphy, *Political imprisonment and the Irish 1912–1921* (Oxford, 2014)

NOTES

[1] Military Archives, Military Service Pensions Collection (hereafter MA, MSPC), DP1178 John O Donnell, pension statement, 1932.

[2] MA, MSPC, DP1178 John O Donnell, Bridget O Donnell to Minister for Defence Frank Aiken, 10 August 1932.

[3] MA, MSPC, DP1178 John O Donnell; MSPC, DP4364 Hugh Hennon; MSPC, 24SP6738 John Morris; MSPC, DP612 Mathew Mongan.

[4] William Murphy, *Political imprisonment and the Irish 1912–1921* (Oxford, 2014), 106; David Fitzpatrick, *The two Irelands 1912–1939* (Oxford, 1998), 118–9; Kieran Glennon, *From pogrom to civil war: Tom Glennon and the Belfast IRA* (Cork, 2013), 260–61. Public Record Office of Northern Ireland (hereafter PRONI), Home Affairs, HA/5 files series, contains various internment orders for this period.

[5] Seán McConville, *Irish political prisoners 1920–62: pilgrimage of desolation* (London, 2014), 327; Denise Kleinrichert, *Republican internment and the prison ship Argenta 1922* (Dublin, 2001), 74; PRONI, HA/5/2028, Home Affairs minute sheet, 26 July 1922.

[6] Kleinrichert, *Republican internment*, 66-68.

[7] Northern Ireland parliamentary debates (hereafter NIPD), vol. 11, col. 1022 (12 October 1922).

[8] *Fermanagh Herald*, 16 September 1922; *Fermanagh Herald*, 28 April 1923.

[9] Kleinrichert, *Republican internment*, 68–84; MA, Bureau of Military History (BMH), witness statement (WS) 928, John Shields, 21–2.

[10] *Fermanagh Herald*, 26 September 1922; MA, BMH, WS 928, John Shields, 21–22; *Ulster Herald*, 11 November 1922; *Freeman's Journal*, 30 March 1923; *Freeman's Journal*, 5 August 1922; *Fermanagh Herald*, 16 September 1922; Kleinrichert, *Republican internment*, 82–111; *Freeman's Journal*, 5 August 1922; *Freeman's Journal*, 30 March 1923; *Irish Independent*, 13 July 1922.

[11] NIPD, vol. 2, col. 1010, 12 October 1922; MA, MSPC, DP1178 John O Donnell, report of the Army Pensions Board, September 1933; MA, BMH, WS 928, John Shields, 23; Kleinrichert, *Republican internment*, 239.

JUNE

3 JUNE 1922

'A VISIBLE SIGN OF OUR LOYALTY': THE ICONOGRAPHY OF PARTITION

On touring Belfast in the turbulent June of 1922, an English visitor to the city suggested to James Craig that there was 'just a little too much of the Union Jack in view in Belfast at the present moment to be healthy'. Unsurprisingly Craig was not impressed. Relaying this tale in an extended interview with the British tabloid *The People*, published on 3 June, the leader of northern unionism described the Union Jack as a symbol of loyalty that was being taken for granted by the English public, 'an outward and visible sign of our loyalty to the Throne and of our pride in Empire Citizenship'. This image of Belfast proudly demonstrating its attachment to the union was, for Craig, a crucial reminder of unionist loyalty in a period of grave anxiety. In particular, this display of fidelity was a reminder of what he saw as their 'duty as loyal representatives of a loyal people to say that we would have nothing more to do with the Boundary Commission'.[1] Writing in the wake of the Better Government of Ireland Act (1920) and the Anglo-Irish Treaty

(1921), Craig's plea to the British public was reflective of the deep insecurity about territory that then beleaguered the operations of his government.

Yet, in his search for symbolic currency, Craig was also reflecting a wider trend on the island. Jonathan Bardon writes that symbolism, primarily in the form of the oath of allegiance, had been 'the central issue' of the Treaty debates, despite Deputy Seán Mac Eoin's claim that these 'symbols, recognitions, shadows' held 'very little meaning' to the Irish public.[2] In the aftermath of the debates, however, icons and emblems took on a new significance, with the Irish Free State adopting already existing emblems and commissioning the production of new national symbols. From renaming streets to painting pillar-boxes, removing statues and developing a national coinage, outward and visible signs retained an enduring appeal to all sides of the 'Irish' question.

In the early years of partition, Robert Lynch has observed, both governments were haunted by 'a crippling lack of legitimacy', a problem exacerbated by the presence of significant religious and political minorities in each state.[3] As Craig's reference to the Boundary Commission suggested, territorial anxieties cast a long shadow over the operations of these new partition states, with each actively engaged in a dispute over the shape and status of the new border on the island. Perhaps foremost of the iconographies, emblems and flags adopted as weapons in this dispute were the various maps that had been published as state and anti-state propaganda since the question of partition had been raised. These maps, on display in state handbooks, in political pamphlets and at public exhibitions, were a more obvious intervention into the territorial dispute that had been engendered by the activities during previous decades. The Free State asserted its own territorial claims by commissioning a *Handbook of the Ulster question* (1923), with extensive maps and charts; the six-county government was, for its part, actively engaged in producing a periodical, the *Ulster Bulletin* (1922–25), and more generally courting the favour of British newspapers. All of these productions deployed maps detailing their claims and repudiating those of the opposition. In March 1922, for example, Craig had met with another English visitor, the *London Illustrated News* artist-correspondent L. Raven Hill. The artist, with the help of Craig, sketched a rough map of 'Ulster' and the iterations of its border as they had developed from 1914 to 1922, to which Craig added the signed comment: 'This is the boundary question'.[4]

For both states, however, imaging the boundary question went well beyond publishing maps and waving flags. As Peter Leary notes, Ireland's partitioning, a process established by acts of the Westminster Parliament with no Irish vote in favour, was

> neither the most desired nor most readily envisioned outcome to the conflicts that preceded its implementation. With the United Kingdom, Ireland, and even Ulster all divided, no previously 'imagined community' was left intact.[5]

The cultural traditions that had preceded the division of the island did not necessarily provide any pre-history for this division, but they were quickly recast by each new state as the precedent for their individual territorial claims. Binary constructions of urban against rural, Protestant against Catholic, idealism against realism, and many others, became a dominant motif across the political and cultural imaginations of these new states, and each sought historical and contemporary illustrations of their visions. The Irish Free State commissioned and displayed subject portraits by John Lavery and landscape paintings by Jack Yeats, while the northern state— beset, in part, by a perceived cultural impoverishment—deliberately sought to champion the art and artists of Belfast as a rival to Dublin. As an article in the *Ulster Bulletin*, praising the work of a new Belfast painter, had argued: 'until a few months ago the whole attitude in most political and cultural quarters was to belittle Belfast and all that to it pertained'.[6]

The artist to which this article had referred was William Conor, who had been commissioned by the 'Ulster' government to paint the first sitting of its parliament. Conor, also commissioned by the Free State in 1922, became known in this period primarily for his depictions of the industry of Belfast: the *Westminster Gazette* had called him 'the delineator of Ulster industrialism' in February 1922.[7] The evidence for this new title was plentiful: by then, Conor had turned away from his early entanglements with rural landscapes to paint the mills and shipyards that had so dominated the unionist imaginary in the early twentieth century, and that served for some as an artistic rendition of the social and economic benefits of the Union. His 'Men of Iron' (1922), which had appeared at the same time as his painting of the northern parliament, captured some of the dominant motifs within this imaginary. With the titular men placed in the foreground of the picture,

the perspective suggests their dominance as a subject of the painting. The faceless subjects on the right— the 'Queen's Islandmen', championed as symbols of the Belfast workforce—at once seem to be taller than the ship and gantries before them, but are also turned towards it. Perhaps most importantly, this ship carries a Union Flag on its jackstaff—very clearly locating the painting in the Belfast shipyards.[8] Taken together, the icons and emblems within 'Men of Iron'—the shipyard, the workers and the flag—bring to life many of the outward and visible signs that Craig and his government were trying to emphasise as proof of a distinct northern culture in an atmosphere of grave anxiety about the future of the northern state.

William Conor, 'Men of Iron' (1922).

by Stephen O'Neill

FURTHER READING

Róisín Kennedy, *Art and the nation state: the reception of modern art in Ireland* (Liverpool, 2020)

Peter Leary, *Unapproved routes: histories of the Irish border 1922–1972* (Oxford, 2016)

Robert Lynch, *The partition of Ireland 1918–25* (Cambridge, 2019)

NOTES

[1] Public Record Office of Northern Ireland, PM15/5, James Craig, 'Ulster and the Empire: the testing time has come' [text of an article that featured in *The People* newspaper].
[2] Jonathan Bardon, *A history of Ulster* (Belfast, 1992), 485.
[3] Robert Lynch, *The partition of Ireland 1918–25* (Cambridge, 2019), 138.
[4] Leonard Raven Hill, 'Our special artist in Ulster', *Illustrated London News*, 1 April 1922, 464.
[5] Peter Leary, *Unapproved routes: histories of the Irish border 1922–1972* (Oxford, 2016), 51.
[6] W.B.R., 'An Ulster artist', *Ulster Bulletin* 1 (3) (July 1923), 14.
[7] Trevor Allen, 'Belfast as an art centre: how it is growing', *Westminster Gazette*, 18 February 1922, 6.
[8] Significantly, this painting appeared after the Harland and Wolff and Workman Clark shipyard expulsions of 1920.

12 JUNE 1922

CONFLICTING IDENTITIES: MONARCHY, EMPIRE AND SOVEREIGNTY

'The ceremony was one of the most touching that I ever beheld', recalled John Fortescue, the librarian at Windsor Castle, describing the moment on 12 June 1922 when King George V received back the Colours of Irish regiments that were being disbanded following the establishment of the Irish Free State; 'The King read a message of farewell to each of the regiments and quitted the hall, leaving most of the officers and non-commissioned officers in tears'.[1] Men, who had been through the trenches of the First World War, wept. Colours were bestowed by the king to the regiments of his army to symbolise the British monarchy that their soldiers bled and died for on the battlefield. For Great War veterans, returning them crystallised that their

Opposite: King George V receiving the Colours of the disbanded Irish regiments, St George's Hall, Windsor Castle, 12 June 1922.

regiment was no more; even that its recent suffering in the theatres of the conflict had come to nought.

If Britain—and the men gathered at Windsor that day—had won the Great War, handing back the Colours embodied their Irish defeat. The ceremony was a powerful performance of monarchical retreat from the new Irish Free State: military service for the Crown was ending in these counties; the British army, engaged in a post-war cost-cutting exercise, saw these regiments as redundant. To soften the blow, the monarch had offered to care for their Colours in perpetuity. If George V remained the titular head of state, this ceremony highlighted that it was very much going to be a hollowed-out role. It marked the start of modern Irish military independence as clearly as those events that took place in Dublin as the British army handed over its former barracks and a new Irish army was founded. Men rarely wept in public in Britain and Ireland in this period. The emotion of those at the ceremony in Windsor suggests the profound upset that Irish monarchists felt at the Free State settlement. For Northern Irish unionists, the British monarchy was a central part of their identity and remained so. For their peers in the Free State a process of slow letting go of this deep-seated part of their culture now began.

Ireland had a long history of anti-monarchism. Its origins were closely linked to the traditional anti-Catholicism of the British monarchy, and it was a feature of folk music about peasant grievance and of the 1798 rebellion and its commemoration, particularly the centenary in 1898. Upon coming to the throne in 1910, however, King George V had reached out to Roman Catholics, dropping the anti-Catholic part of the Coronation oath and, during his 1911 visit to Ireland, visiting the National Seminary at Maynooth and meeting the Catholic Primate. Monarchist sentiment crossed the traditional sectarian divide; the rise of literacy, photography and access to newspapers resulted in human interest stories about the personal lives of royalty that attracted readers from all backgrounds. Although cultural loyalism was a visible feature of unionism, Irish Roman Catholics—in all parts of Ireland—were not all entirely indifferent to the monarchy by 1914.

The Home Rule party tread a fine line between opposing the monarchy and making an accommodation with it: it opposed the 1901 Civil List financial settlement for royals, but some of the party's support came from Catholic nationalists who favoured greater local Irish governance within the empire and monarchical system. The party's rapprochement with monarchism was clear by 1914. King George V's intervention in the Home Rule crisis, calling the Buckingham Palace conference in July

1914 to bring together John Redmond, leader of the Irish Parliamentary Party, and Edward Carson, leader of Irish unionism, was well-received as a peace-making gesture, and as a sign that the monarchy was newly inventing itself as a neutral arbiter on Ireland. The fact that the king signed the third Home Rule Bill that September, despite significant pressure from unionists who petitioned him to refuse it royal assent and trigger a constitutional crisis instead, was also appreciated. The outbreak of the First World War saw this rapprochement deepen.

This context helps to explain the remarkable radicalism of Irish republicanism's hostility to the British monarchy in the Irish revolution. The Irish Republican Brotherhood and Fenian movement had a long culture of opposing the British monarchy in Ireland. But through the Easter Rising and its aftermath, they successfully marketed this to the public mainstream. Radical anti-monarchism became a central part of their message, as a way of undermining the Home Rule position of wartime rapprochements with the monarchy and unionism, and as a way of breaking with Britishness. This set the IRB and the Fenians on a particular crash course with Ulster unionism, for whom monarchism was a revered core value, now sacralised with the blood of the First World War dead. It was also easy to utilise a grievance with an existing folk history—anti-monarchism—to increase support for advanced separatism. Doing so avoided more complex discussions about what precise type of future state an independent Ireland would be. Republicanism was a rarity in this period; America and France were the main models, and their versions of republican statehood were very different. The Proclamation read by Patrick Pearse outside the GPO in 1916, with its assertion that the people of Ireland were 'sovereign' in their own land, switched the locus of power from a living royal sovereign to the population—as befitted a republican understanding of statehood. This was a radical act in 1916 in a Europe still dominated by monarchical states. For Irish republicanism, anti-monarchism was also powerfully egalitarian, implying a state in which all citizens were in a horizontal bond with each other, without a vertical loyalty to a royal hierarchy.

Yet for all the mobilisation around anti-monarchism, George V's pre-war image as a well-disposed arbiter remained. It was most powerfully visible in his speech to open the Northern Irish devolved parliament in June 1921, when he appealed for a peaceful settlement in Ireland. Such a significant royal intervention pushed hawks on the British side to accept a truce and negotiations; it also undermined any potential protest from loyalists reluctant to oppose the king's will.

By 1922, however, the question of the relationship between monarchy and sovereignty would culminate in triggering Irish civil war. The Irish delegation to the Treaty talks was fully aware of the implications of including in the Anglo-Irish Treaty an 'oath of allegiance' to the British monarch for TDs in Dáil Éireann.[2] An oath acknowledged the nation as embodied in a living monarch. It was a tortuous focus of the negotiations. The Irish negotiators managed to get the wording of the oath watered down into an oath of 'fidelity' to the king, but the British monarch remained head of state of the new Irish Free State. The British for their part were adamant that the oath had to be part of the settlement. Every dominion parliament had an oath of allegiance to the king. Moreover, since 1917, the empire dominions were being reformulated as independent states, joined to Britain *solely* through its monarchy and its ties with their constitutions, and no longer also through Westminster and its civil service as had been the case before the outbreak of the First World War. For Prime Minister David Lloyd George, the oath of allegiance to the king was the principle 'upon which the whole fabric of the empire and every constitution within it are based'.[3] It was impossible for these reasons for Britain to conceptualise a republic as part of its empire in this period, although the Irish delegation suggested this as one possible compromise. This culture clash over monarchism profoundly undermined the Treaty.

Monarchism and anti-monarchism ultimately played a pivotal—and still understudied—role in mobilising and polarising Ireland during the Irish revolution. The emotional power of the cleavage over monarchism to trigger violence should not be underestimated. Its terminology— Crown forces, King's shilling, traitor, loyalist—intensified animosities and mobilised unionist against republican. In the debates around the 'oath of allegiance' it was powerful enough to help trigger an internecine civil war among nationalists. It was also one of the historic fault lines of the era. As monarchies fell across Europe in the wake of the Great War, Irish republicanism looked less opportunistic in its mobilisation of vitriolic anti-monarchism and more prescient. Embracing such very radical forms of hostile anti-monarchist discourse, however, doomed the Irish Free State settlement and helped ossify the division with unionism, creating a 'long' 1922 that lasted until Éamon de Valera's government dismantled the final elements of Treaty monarchic structures, and beyond.

by Heather Jones

FURTHER READING:

James Loughlin, *The British monarchy and Ireland, 1800 to the present* (Cambridge, 2007)

Brian Hughes and Conor Morrissey (eds), *Southern Irish loyalism, 1912–1949* (Liverpool, 2020)

Heather Jones, *For king and country. The British monarchy and the First World War* (Cambridge, 2021)

NOTES

[1] John Fortescue, *Author and curator: an autobiography* (Edinburgh, London, 1933), 236.
[2] Liam Weeks and Mícheál Ó Fathartaigh (eds), *The Treaty: debating and establishing the Irish state* (Newbridge, 2018).
[3] Parliamentary archives, London, Lloyd George papers, LG/F/29/4/77, copy sent to Stamford-ham of David Lloyd George reply to Éamon de Valera, n.d. [summer 1921].

Le Petit Journal

illustré

ABONNEMENTS

Trois mois Six mois Un an
FRANCE & COLONIES
4 fr. 7 fr. 50 14 fr.
UNION POSTALE
6 fr. 12 fr. 22 fr.

PARAISSANT LE DIMANCHE
33ᵉ Année - N° 1645

On s'abonne dans tous
les bureaux de poste

Les Manuscrits ne sont pas rendus

Un assassinat politique

L'histoire du conflit entre l'Irlande et la Grande-Bretagne a toutes ses pages tachées de sang. — Un nouveau chapitre dramatique vient d'y être ajouté. A Londres, le maréchal Wilson a été assassiné à coups de revolvers par deux fanatiques Irlandais. C'est un brave soldat et un ami de la France qui vient de disparaître.

22 JUNE 1922

THE ASSASSINATION OF SIR HENRY WILSON

'DYING BRAVELY AS SOLDIERS': AN IRISH TRAGEDY

At 2.20 p.m. on Thursday, 22 June 1922 Field Marshal Sir Henry Wilson, chief security advisor to the new Northern Irish government and former chief of the Imperial General Staff, was shot dead on the doorstep of his Belgravia home by IRA Commandant Reggie Dunne and Volunteer Joe O'Sullivan. Wilson's murder—the first assassination of a Westminster MP since Spencer Perceval was killed in 1812—shocked public opinion. It also hastened the onset of the Irish civil war: Winston Churchill warned Michael Collins that British troops would move against the anti-Treaty IRA leadership at the Four Courts, which he (wrongly) blamed for the outrage, if the Provisional Government failed to do so.

Opposite: *Le Petit Journal*'s dramatic depiction of Sir Henry Wilson's assassination by Irish Volunteers Reggie Dunne and Joe O'Sullivan.

The details of the assassination gripped public attention. Sensational press accounts described how Wilson—returning home after unveiling a war memorial at Liverpool Street Station—had drawn his ceremonial

sword in self-defence, making him Britain's only field marshal to die in action. 'You cowardly swine', he reportedly shouted, as he faced down his attackers, one of whom had a wooden leg.[1] Eyewitness, however, supported Dunne's more prosaic account:

> Wilson made for the door as best he could and actually reached the doorstep when I encountered him at a range of 7 or 8 feet. I fired three shots rapidly, the last one from the hip, as I took a step forward. Wilson was now uttering short cries and in a doubled up position staggered towards the edge of the pavement. At this point Joe fired once again and the last I saw of him he had collapsed.[2]

Vast crowds lined the streets to observe Wilson's cortège—which included among its pall-bearers Lord French, General Sir Nevil Macready, Field Marshal Sir Douglas Haig and Field Marshal Sir William Robertson—process to St Paul's Cathedral where the British establishment had gathered. Disavowed by both the Provisional Government and anti-Treaty IRA leadership, Wilson's youthful assassins came to a more ignominious end, in Wandsworth Prison on 10 August, at the end of a hangman's noose.

Discussion of Wilson's fate, one of the Irish revolution's great murder mysteries, has centred on the question of responsibility. Although Dunne and O'Sullivan claimed in court that their actions were a spontaneous response to the Ulster Special Constabulary's reign of 'Orange Terror' against Belfast Catholics, which they (wrongly) blamed on Wilson, republicans in London believed the killing had been ordered—whether as an IRA or IRB operation, before or after the truce—by Collins. Given the collapse of British and republican authority, and the resulting anarchy as reprisal and revenge prevailed across much of the country, Dunne's actions may best be understood as a desperate attempt to preserve both the unity of the IRA in London and his own authority, which had been diminished by his efforts to tread a neutral line.[3] This essay, however, explores a different facet of this notorious event, considering how the fate of Wilson and his killers illustrates the interconnected nature of the revolutionary decade's ostensibly disparate conflicts, the intimacy of the ties that bound

Ireland to Britain, and the dissonance between public narratives and family experiences of the violence that severed that union.

Wilson, who epitomised British imperial repression in Ireland, was born in Longford. His IRA killers were Londoners. All had served in the same army during the First World War, where O'Sullivan had lost his leg. Exemplifying the fluidity of wartime political allegiances, Dunne, who would lead the IRA in post-war London, enlisted in the British army after the Easter Rising. Addressing his jury, he attributed his actions in shooting Wilson in part to his role in the war fought for the right of small nations to self-determination: 'Those principles I found as an Irishman were not applied to my own country and I have endeavoured to strike a blow for it.'

Drawn to the music and dancing of Stamford Hill's Gaelic League branch, Dunne had embraced a powerful separatist Irish identity forged through cultural means, which politicised many among his generation of militant nationalists.[4] His victim belonged to a Protestant, landowning, unionist family, who believed 'themselves to be fully Irish, and as emotionally attached to the country as anyone',[5] and embodied an imperial Irish tradition that would not survive the revolutionary era.

As early as 1917 Wilson's brother, Jemmy, lamented how the 'oases of culture, of uprightness and of fair dealing' sustained by his landlord class, 'whose blood is so freely shed for the Empire, who for years have done their best to discharge their onerous & often thankless duties by their humble neighbours all over Ireland'—were giving way to 'a desert of dead uniformity where the poor will have no one to appeal to except the Priest or the local shopkeeper'. Reflecting on the 'Irish tragedy' that was Wilson's death, his biographer Keith Jeffery observed that although this romantic, solipsistic, anti-democratic vision of paternalistic conservatism was out of touch with the 'real' Ireland, in its 'combination of local, national, and imperial service' it 'exemplified the Wilsons' world view, and what they conceived their duty to be'.

Republicans regarded the family's fate less sympathetically. 'It was a good day for Ireland that day yourself and your hero of a companion went out and [s]layed the second Cromwell dead at your feet', Joe O'Sullivan was assured by his cousin. 'I have no regrets as it was done for the love of his faith and for Ireland', Joe's father confided to Seán T. O'Kelly, vice-president of the Executive Council of the Irish Free State, in 1933: 'we are very proud of his actions as he removed a dirty orange dog'.[6] All four

Wilson brothers had left Longford by the time of Henry's killing: the remaining physical traces of their presence there were obliterated by the burning of Currygrane House within days of the hanging of his killers. 'Our only crime', Major Cecil Wilson reflected plaintively in his claim for compensation to the Irish Grants Committee, 'was that we tried to help this country'.[7] But, like other multinational kingdoms across much of central and east Europe, that country had ceased to exist.

Whether considered poignant or deserved, Wilson's fate exemplifies one of the era's most enduring legacies, which continues to bedevil reconciliation in Ireland—the narrowing of identities effected by political violence. Drawing comparisons with Cathal Brugha, an equally zealous advocate of 'force and force alone', the liberal *New Statesmen* observed that Wilson, 'with his fanatical Orangeism', 'great military prestige' and 'inflammatory speeches', did more than any other man 'to promote that spirit of ruthless and stupid retaliation which had led to his own death'.[8]

Family experiences often diverged sharply from the political narratives that framed the public memory of the revolutionary dead. Although David Lloyd George reminded MPs at Westminster of his friendship with Wilson, his ministers were denounced as murderers by Lady Wilson, whose diehard husband never forgave their willingness to settle with the IRA. Despite Wilson's regret, shared by Edward Carson, at the sundering of the Union with Ireland, he was quickly claimed as a 'founding martyr for the Northern Ireland state'.[9]

Notwithstanding numerous appeals, the insistence of witnesses across the civil war divide that the assassins had acted on orders received, and the argument that the Irish government had 'a certain moral responsibility' given Collins's alleged promise 'that if anything happened to them their parents would be looked after', neither Dunne nor O'Sullivan's parents were judged to meet the criteria for the allowance paid to dependents of Volunteers who died in military service. Reggie's mother Mary, 'unhinged by her loss', continued to hope for 'some recognition from the Irish Government and the Irish People of her son's sacrifice for Ireland' until her death. Joe's elderly father campaigned in vain for their public recognition as 'soldiers of the Irish Republic who died bravely as soldiers'.[10]

On 8 July 1967, following a campaign for the return of their remains, Dunne and O'Sullivan finally received a public funeral befitting their status as heroic patriots. Despite the British government's concern, shared in Dublin, that the funeral might jeopardise 'the present delicate state of affairs in Northern Ireland',[11] the ceremony in Dublin's Pro-Cathedral was attended by representatives of the taoiseach and president. After the funeral, 'young men moving with military precision formed an escort party', while Londoner Sean Stephenson (who would become better known as Seán Mac Stíofáin, the Provisional IRA's founding chief of staff) provided the oration at Deansgrange Cemetery's Republican Plot. In Belfast, Ian Paisley roused a 'great Protestant demonstration' to protest Prime Minister Harold Wilson's decision to return the remains: 'While Dublin honours the murderers Belfast honours the martyr.'[12] The next morning, foreshadowing the bloodletting to come, three men fired a volley over the graves of Dunne and O'Sullivan.

by Fearghal McGarry

FURTHER READING

Keith Jeffery, *Field Marshal Sir Henry Wilson: a political soldier* (Oxford, 2006)

Peter Hart, 'Michael Collins and the assassination of Sir Henry Wilson', *Irish Historical Studies* 28 (110) (November 1992), 150–70

NOTES

[1] *Daily Mail*, quoted in *Belfast News-Letter*, 24 June 1922.
[2] *Sunday Press*, 14 August 1955.
[3] Peter Hart, 'Michael Collins and the assassination of Sir Henry Wilson', *Irish Historical Studies* 28 (110) (November 1992), 150–70: 167–8.
[4] Military Archives (MA), Bureau of Military History (BMH), witness statement (WS) 902, Mary McGeehin.
[5] Keith Jeffery, *Field Marshal Sir Henry Wilson: a political soldier* (Oxford, 2006), 297. Subsequent quotes are from this source unless specified.
[6] MA, WDP6925 Joseph O'Sullivan, John O'Sullivan to Seán T. O'Kelly, 23 February 1933.
[7] National Archives of the United Kingdom, CO762/64/6, Major Cecil Wilson to Alexander Reid Jameson, 9 August 1927. My thanks to Marie Coleman for bringing this source to my attention.
[8] *New Statesman*, 24 June 1922.
[9] Jeffery, *Wilson*, 287, 296.
[10] MA, WDP1462 Reginald Dunne; MA, BMH WS 902 (McGeehin); WDP6925 Joseph O'Sullivan.
[11] Brendan O Cathaoir, 'An Irishman's Diary', *The Irish Times*, 27 May 1997.
12 *Irish Independent*, 7 July 1967; *Evening Echo*, 8 July 1967.

28 JUNE 1922

DEFENDING THE REPUBLIC.
THE IRA FIELD ARMY AND THE CIVIL
WAR'S CONVENTIONAL PHASE

The Irish civil war began on 28 June 1922 when the National Army attacked the forces of the IRA Army Executive at the Four Courts in Dublin. The garrison surrendered on 30 June with comparatively few casualties, beyond the destruction of much of the Four Courts complex, including the invaluable Public Records Office. Subsequent IRA resistance took the form of a conventional phase of fighting, which lasted for roughly seven weeks, until early August 1922, followed by a longer phase of guerrilla war. This essay focuses on the first phase of combat, when the anti-Treaty IRA maintained an army in the field.

During the War of Independence, the Irish Republican Army (IRA) was a largely decentralised organisation. While IRA General Headquarters (GHQ) in Dublin issued broad policy guidelines and critiqued unit performances, it maintained little direct control over subordinate units beyond the capital. Individual brigades (subsequently superseded by divisions) practised collective decision-making at all levels. Units elected their own officers, armed and financed themselves, and planned their own operations. It should be emphasised that the provincial IRA leadership was not consulted before the Anglo-Irish Treaty was signed; many officers appear to have been shocked by the subsequent acceptance of dominion status, which disestablished the Irish Republic.

While precise figures are elusive, it can be estimated that roughly 70–75% of IRA members opposed the Anglo-Irish Treaty.[1] Their numbers included most of the IRA's guerrilla elite in Connaught and Munster. Following the ratification of the Treaty by Dáil Éireann, much of the country remained under the loose authority of the anti-Treaty IRA (hereafter called the IRA). In March/April 1922, the IRA's Army Convention renounced the organisation's allegiance to Dáil Éireann, elected a ruling Army Executive, and established a new general headquarters in the Four Courts. The Army Executive remained divided, however, over the best path forward. Militants such as Rory O'Connor and Ernie O'Malley wanted to overthrow the Provisional Government and establish an IRA military dictatorship to 'defend the Irish Republic'. If necessary, they would resume the war with Britain to reunify the movement. Moderates, especially Munster officers within Liam Lynch's powerful First Southern Division, recognised their lack of public support, opposed a dictatorship, and sought a peace settlement that retained national unity but protected the Republic.

Internally divided, the IRA surrendered the initiative to the Provisional Government, which was constructing a new National Army and expanding its civilian support via a highly efficient propaganda machine. The National Army relied on support from the pro-Treaty GHQ and active Dublin units, along with (largely ineffective) midland units, and more substantial brigades in Longford, East Clare, Donegal, and East Limerick. It also recruited from the wider public, including Irish First World War veterans.[2]

The Army Unification Agreement, a proposed peace settlement negotiated in May 1922, was opposed by hardliners on the IRA Army Executive, which openly split into moderate and militant factions. Briefly the IRA maintained two parallel headquarters and chiefs of staff (Liam Lynch and Joe McKelvey). Despite their belligerence, the militants made no practical preparations for hostilities with Provisional Government (hereafter called Free State) forces. At the outset of fighting in Dublin during late June 1922, the National Army essentially decapitated the IRA by capturing or killing

much of its leadership and headquarters staff inside the Four Courts and in the subsequent city fighting. As the IRA fought a losing battle in Dublin, it took a few days for the IRA to reorganise under the new Chief of Staff, Liam Lynch.[3] He reconstituted an army headquarters in Munster largely by repurposing his First Southern Division staff, and gathered what I call the IRA 'field army'.

The Four Courts façade: view from Merchants' Quay showing damage to the west wing.

The IRA enjoyed a numeric advantage in terms of overall personnel, but it was heavily outgunned by the National Army. At the start of hostilities, the National Army's strength was about 8,000 armed soldiers, a figure that grew to 14,000 by mid-August 1922.[4] Supplied by the British government, Free State forces possessed field artillery, numerous armoured cars and vehicles and an abundance of machine-guns, which amplified their firepower in subsequent engagements. Unlike the IRA, the National Army paid its soldiers, providing a financial incentive for enlistment. It also possessed the funds to purchase supplies, while the IRA was forced to commandeer them.

Though the IRA possessed a paper strength of almost 84,000 Volunteers on 1 July 1922, it could only arm a small portion of them. A reasonable estimate of IRA fighting strength during the conventional phase would be about 3,000–4,000 armed fighters, supported by tens of thousands of unarmed male and female combatants.

From the outset, IRA leaders debated whether to stand and fight the National Army in towns and cities, or to disperse and resume guerrilla tactics. While the IRA had been built as a guerrilla organisation, many leaders felt that a retreat without resistance would demoralise both the IRA rank-and-file and their civilian supporters. Liam Lynch sought to concentrate forces in Munster along a defensive line from Limerick city to Waterford city, which would absorb Free State pressure. IRA units elsewhere would use guerrilla tactics to weaken the National Army, while the Dublin IRA blockaded the capital to disrupt the flow of troops and supplies to different battlefronts. The plan faltered at the first hurdle, however, because the badly damaged Dublin IRA lacked the strength to seal off the city. Dublin became a secure base for the National Army to build up its strength, which was then deployed along interior lines of communication to hard-pressed locales.

IRA units initially defended their territory from Free State incursions, with varying degrees of success. The IRA in Sligo and Louth achieved noteworthy victories, while in Munster, columns of the IRA's First Southern Division fighters captured a number of National Army bases while clearing their area of Free State troops. The IRA quickly faltered, however, when units operated beyond their home areas, especially in places with weak IRA organisations. Determined IRA units in Mayo, Sligo, Louth and Wexford fought largely unsupported, and were soon pushed out of urban areas by Free State troops possessing superior numbers and firepower. Perhaps the most decisive moment occurred during the Battle of Limerick City, after hundreds of experienced Munster IRA fighters descended on the Free State forces there.[5] Instead of immediately attacking his outnumbered opponents, Liam Lynch agreed to a truce in an attempt to secure the neutrality of the Free State's forces in East Clare and East Limerick (via their commanders Michael Brennan and Donnacha O'Hannigan, an old friend of Lynch's). The truce allowed Free State reinforcements from Dublin to enter Limerick, attack the IRA, and drive them from the city after a week of tough fighting. Thereafter, the IRA fought on the defensive.

Only in the IRA-controlled 'Munster Republic' did the IRA manage to concentrate its forces adequately. There, the IRA formed a field army comprised of the fighting elite of its First and Second southern divisions from counties Cork, Kerry, Limerick, Tipperary and Waterford. For most of July it held a line from Limerick to Waterford. Battle fronts were defended by a number of flying columns from individual brigades and battalions, each of which usually numbered between twenty and one hundred armed fighters. They were relatively well-supplied with rifles, machine-guns and landmines, while lorries (seized from local businesses), and commandeered railways, allowed rapid movement. These forces were reinforced by poorly armed local units, which provided scouting, logistics and other support services. Cumann na mBan was also mobilised to carry messages, treat the wounded, collect information, scout, transport arms and feed and billet IRA troops.[6] Overall, the IRA field army performed poorly in Waterford city but fairly well during heavy fighting around Kilmallock in County Limerick and parts of Tipperary, when it managed to hold off superior Free State forces for a few weeks.[7] Yet, the overall republican effort was somewhat confused, haphazard and undermined by the IRA's decentralised structure, which made it difficult to command and control disparate, independently minded units and their leaders.

Throughout July, the IRA used Cork city as its unofficial capital, and took advantage of its amenities.[8] Critical funds (an estimated £100,000) were raised through the seizure of import and export duties at the Cork Customs House. This allowed the IRA to pay for its supplies instead of commandeering them from local businesses, which was unpopular. An IRA 'civil affairs' office issued steep income tax bills to local merchants who had been avoiding payment. IRA engineers began to produce numerous armoured cars in city workshops, while Erskine Childers and Mary MacSwiney used the *Cork Examiner* newspaper to, at least partially, offset the powerful Free State propaganda machine. Yet, the republicans made little effort to mobilise civilian support, and persistently underestimated how much the public was turning against them.[9]

The IRA in the Munster Republic was spread thin. The 'line fighting' sapped the IRA's fighting strength, while towns and cities had to be defended by weak units logistically supported by Cumann na mBan. Along its exposed southern coast, the IRA garrisoned ports and Coast Guard stations, and in late July started to destroy landing piers at potential landing spots in Cork and Kerry. These flimsy defences could not, however, prevent the Munster Republic from collapse in early August, following a series of Free State amphibious landings.

On 2 August the National Army landed 500 soldiers at Fenit, County Kerry, and seized Tralee after a brief but tough fight. A more spectacular operation occurred in county Cork in the early hours of 8 August. Led by Emmet Dalton, the National Army landed almost 500 soldiers at Passage West and advanced on Cork city. Simultaneously, 200 troops disembarked at Youghal, while another 180 landed at Union Hall. For three days in the Cork suburb of Douglas, the National Army battled up to 300 IRA Volunteers, most of whom had been rushed from different battle fronts. Like other set-piece contests, superior Free State firepower won the day, after its field artillery and armoured cars blasted republican defences. By then, the IRA had evacuated its Munster capital, and dispersed the IRA field army before it could be encircled by slow-moving Free State forces. Following IRA policy, retreating units systematically blocked roads, bridges and railways, and burned police and military barracks that could be used by the National Army; actions which only further antagonised the local population. Defeated and harried, the various IRA columns returned to their home areas and commenced a guerrilla campaign against the Free State.

IRA Chief of Staff Liam Lynch and his fellow commanders had never fully committed to a conventional warfare strategy. Even when the IRA stalled Free State advances in Limerick city, Kilmallock, and Douglas, Lynch avoided over-committing his fighting forces. Throughout this phase, he and his colleagues displayed a guerrilla warfare mind-set by disengaging and retreating whenever faced with superior forces. While this strategy had been successful against the British in the War of Independence, during the conventional phase of the civil war it thoroughly demoralised his IRA troops and their civilian supporters. IRA leaders underestimated their dependence on popular support. Its near collapse at the end of conventional fighting fatally compromised the ensuing guerrilla phase of the civil war. Within eight months, Liam Lynch was dead, the IRA organisation smashed, and the most committed republican fighters thoroughly defeated.

With many Volunteers unwilling to surrender, the IRA Chief of Staff Frank Aiken ordered his forces to 'dump arms' on 24 May 1923. The Irish Republic, which had briefly endured in Munster and the other provinces, was no more.

by John Borgonovo

FURTHER READING

Michael Hopkinson, *Green against green: the Irish civil war* (Dublin, 2004)

Charles Townshend, *The Republic: the fight for Irish independence, 1918–1923* (London, 2014)

John Borgonovo, *The battle for Cork: July–August 1922* (Cork, 2011)

NOTES

[1] Figures compiled from the Military Service Pension Collection's IRA membership series for the 26 counties that would become the Irish Free State show 83,910 IRA members to have been active at the start of the civil war, compared with 109,576 at the end of the War of Independence (or 76.4% of the 1921 total). The 1922 figures exclude members who joined the IRA during the truce (so-called 'Trucileers'), and likely includes some Volunteers who opposed the Treaty but later took a neutral stance in the civil war.

[2] Gerry White, 'Free State versus Republic: the opposing armed forces in the civil war', in John Crowley, Donal Ó Drisceoil and Mike Murphy (eds), *Atlas of the Irish revolution* (Cork, 2017), 691–7.

[3] Liz Gillis, *The fall of Dublin* (Cork, 2011).

[4] John Regan, *The Irish counter-revolution, 1921–1936: treatyite politics and settlement in independent Ireland* (Dublin, 1999), 102.

[5] Pádraig Óg Ó Ruairc, *The battle for Limerick city* (Cork, 2010).

[6] John Borgonovo, 'Cumann na mBan, martial women and the Irish civil war, 1922–1923', in Linda Connolly (ed.), *Women and the Irish revolution: feminism, activism, violence* (Dublin, 2020), 68–84.

[7] John O'Callaghan, *The battle for Kilmallock* (Cork, 2012).

[8] John Borgonovo, *The battle for Cork: July–August 1922* (Cork, 2013).

[9] Charles Townshend, *The Republic: the fight for Irish independence, 1918–1923* (London, 2014), 412–21.

JULY

7 JULY 1922

FREE STATE FORCES ATTACK SKEOG HOUSE

RESOLVE

On Wednesday, 6 May 1981, the *Detroit Free Press* sent staff reporter Robert H. Emmers to the Gaelic League bar on Michigan Avenue to get local reaction to events in Ireland. There, Emmers found an old man sitting at the end of the bar, drinking whiskey and pulling on Lucky Strikes, the smoke slowly curling above him. Opposite him on the wall was a greying poster of the 1916 Proclamation with portraits of its seven signatories. Surveying the dim lounge, Emmers saw another face, that of Bobby Sands, laughing up from fliers scattered around the bar; the fliers carried details of a memorial service—he had died the previous day at 27 years of age.[1]

The old man was George McCallion, who in 1925, also aged 27, had arrived in Detroit from Derry. The League had been established five years earlier, in 1920. Detroit's population had doubled over the previous decade, from 465,766 in 1910 to 933,678 in 1920, with the city becoming the US's fourth-largest urban centre after New York, Chicago and Philadelphia. Many of the newcomers were Irish, lured by the city's car factories. In the 1920s Detroit's population grew a further 58 per cent, hitting 1,568,662 in

1930, and went on rising until 1950, when it reached 1,849,568. Thereafter, it creaked into rust-belt decline.

George McCallion had seen the rise and fall of Motown, and, in Ireland's late twentieth-century Troubles, a tragedy long foretold.

McCallion was one of eleven children born to James McCallion (1848–1923), a stonemason, and Mary Ann Deeney (1863–1953). One of his siblings died in infancy and, in the 1920s, all but one of the remaining ten emigrated, eight settling between Dearborn and Detroit; their mother joined those in Michigan in 1928.

On that day in the Gaelic League, McCallion told Emmers that he had come to Detroit to find work, which was true. But it had been politics that made it hard for him to get work at home. McCallion (b. 1898) and a younger brother, Joseph Alphonsus (b. 1900)—Alfie in Ireland, but Joe in America—and an older one, Patrick (b. 1897), had been active republicans in the 1910s and early 1920s. They had fought against the Treaty and, after their defeat, the south was as cold a house as the north.

In truth, all the McCallions were republicans. Once, in October 1920, George and five brothers were arrested together, when the British army found weapons near their home on Berry Street. They passed their time in the cells singing songs.[2]

George did not mention that incident to Emmers. But on a day when 'it was all Irish republican talk' at the bar, the past was close to the present. So the old man did tell of how, in 1917, he had joined the Derry Battalion of the Irish Volunteers and participated in attacks on British convoys and barracks in 1919–21. He told too, as many IRA-men used to tell, a self-deprecating yarn about his lack of arms and training, when he went out to fight an empire. 'I remember one time', he said:

> We went over into Donegal to attack this police barrack. There was about six of us. Now, we didn't have many guns, but we did have the dynamite, and we tied it on a board and pushed it up against the barrack wall, thinking we'd blow up half of it. But it only went up in flames, and the police came out shootin' at us and we had to run like hell.

McCallion might have told Emmers a lot more. He might have told him how, in 1922, he had been the officer commanding IRA units that occupied Skeog House, a mansion near the Derry–Donegal county line, which had recently become 'the border'. And there, at Skeog, he proved himself a man of no mean resolve. At 4.00 p.m. on Friday, 7 July, Free State troops threw a cordon around the mansion and sent a courier, under a white flag, with a message demanding its surrender. The courier returned with a succinct reply:

> In receipt of your demand to surrender barracks to your men.
> I wish to inform you that, as soldiers of Ireland and the Irish
> Republic, we will defend the barracks and the cause for which
> we stand till the last. Signed: George McCallion.

A seven-hour gun-battle ensued, with the attackers using Lewis guns in efforts to dislodge the republicans. Finally, at 11.00 p.m., white flags were hoisted at the house and a gate lodge outpost. The Staters called ceasefire, and some fifty republicans, including one woman, marched out with their hands above their heads—they had exhausted their ammunition. Their only casualty was George McCallion, their officer commanding, who was 'severely wounded'.[3]

In 1981 Detroit's Irish community included supporters and critics of the Provisional IRA, with many of the latter ascribing to the notion, pushed by the Dublin government, that the 'men of violence' of the early 1900s were morally superior to those of the late 1900s.

On that day in the League, McCallion was critical of the Provisionals, yet not from any qualm about violence: 'But the fighting over there now, I don't like the way it's done', he told Emmers; 'The Provos don't seem to be of much value. In my day, there were no kids in the IRA'.

News reports showing children rioting may have prompted that remark. Certainly, it is the reflection of an old man. His brother Alfie wrote a memoir detailing his own ideological formation: he became politically conscious in childhood, joining the IRB at fifteen, and then at sixteen the Volunteers.[4]

A faded photograph of Terence MacSwiney was passed along the bar. 'There was a famous man', McCallion told Emmers, 'He knew what it was about'. He was alluding, the reporter averred, to the hunger-striker's dictum: 'It is not those who can inflict the most, but those who can suffer the most who will conquer'.

And so on that day in 1981, when the world's gaze turned to Ireland as it had turned when MacSwiney died in 1920, an old man in Detroit sat transfixed by similarities, discomfited by differences, real and imagined, between past and present. In youth, he had apprehended that his generation's failure to resolve matters meant war would come again to Ireland; and then, when that war did come, when he was old and far away, he understood that it would be a long war.

'The Treaty of 1921 was a bad treaty', McCallion told the man from the *Free Press*, 'and I am still bitter about it. It's going to go on and on'.

The fight in his youth and the fight in his old age were the same fight, he was saying. And clear to him was the pity of it all—young people dying when he, who had seen it all, could see where it would end: a conference table and a treaty or, treaty being a dirty word, an agreement, to repair the injustice that had issued from the 'bad treaty' that sent him to Skeog House in 1922.

That at least is what he says to me.

by Breandán Mac Suibhne

FURTHER READING

Adrian Grant, *Derry: the Irish revolution, 1912–23* (Dublin, 2018)

Okan Ozseker, *Forging the border: Donegal and Derry in times of revolution, 1911–1925* (Newbridge, 2019)

NOTES

[1] *Detroit Free Press*, 8 May 1981. All details of the conversation in the bar are from Emmers's article ('The Irish lament far from home'). For sharing recollections of George McCallion, I am grateful to Harry McAuley, Detroit, and I am grateful too to several members and connections of the extended McCallion family, most especially Ted Zimbo, for clarifying some details.
[2] On the McCallions' republicanism, see, Ted Zimbo, *McCallions in the IRA* (privately published for a family reunion, 28 July 2019).
[3] *Derry Journal*, 10 July 1922. Military Archives, Military Service Pensions Collection/A39/42, Brigade activity series, Derry City Battalion, 'Statement of activities and operations', 15 September 1939.
[4] The memoir, written in 1942, was either never completed or else all but the first chapter is lost. Ted Zimbo kindly supplied me with a copy of it.

13 JULY 1922

'HEARTSTRINGS BOUND TO IRELAND': DIASPORIC NATIONALISM IN NORTH AMERICA

On 13 July 1922 the newly established Irish Republican League of Canada (IRL) organised a lecture by Irish republican labour activist Jim Larkin at Montreal's Auditorium Hall. Over the course of a raucous evening, a woman in the audience tore down a Union Jack and threw it on the floor—an action that spurred an angry editorial in Toronto's ultra-loyal *Mail and Empire*, which was later reprinted as far away as Abbotsford, British Columbia.[1] This turbulent and controversial event demonstrated the intergenerational diaspora's continuing, and frequently contested, esteem for their ancestral homeland in the closing stages of Ireland's 'global revolution'.

The transnational movement for Irish freedom had reached its zenith in mid-1921 but, beginning with the signing of the truce between British forces and the Irish Republican Army in July, and accelerated by the signing of the Anglo-Irish Treaty in December and the subsequent outbreak of civil war, the organisational networks of Irish diaspora nationalism began to break down. Although an attitude of disillusionment prevailed, individuals of Irish descent followed news from Ireland closely, and their continued, though diminished, participation in the nationalist movement reflected a wide range of opinions. In some cases, the tremendous upsurge in public expressions of Irish nationalism and identity that took place from 1919 to 1921 helped breathe new energy into intergenerational Irish cultural and associational life in 1922 and after, setting the stage for how those of Irish descent would remain connected to one another and to the 'old land' over the following decades.

In the United States, where republican Irish nationalism ran deep, the schism between pro- and anti-Treaty factions split the country's foremost nationalist associations, and these divisions frequently reflected pre-existing tensions within Irish American nationalism. The final, turbulent months of Éamon de Valera's American tour of 1919 and 1920 resulted in his bitter falling out with some of the foremost leaders of the Friends of Irish Freedom, particularly John Devoy and Justice Daniel Cohalan. Despite their strong ideological republicanism, they refused to support de Valera's stance against the Treaty, and eventually became overt supporters of the Irish Free State.[2] The American Association for the Recognition of the Irish Republic (AARIR), which had been established by de Valera to regain control of the mass movement for Irish independence, supported the Treaty in the early months of 1922, but by May had been taken over by anti-Treaty nationalists and continued to raise funds and lobby for the IRA 'irregulars'. Most members did not follow the organisation down this path, and from its peak of over 700,000 in mid-1921, the AARIR's membership had dropped to less than 14,000 by 1924.[3] Smaller, more radical groups, like the MacSwiney clubs that were active in New England, tended to be more open in their opposition to the Treaty, but these remained marginal after 1922.[4]

In the dominion of Canada, circumstances were somewhat different, as notions of Catholic respectability were closely connected to expressions of imperial loyalty. Nevertheless, the pattern of a gradual breakdown of formal Irish nationalist networks was repeated. Most branches of the Self-Determination for Ireland League (SDIL), which had been established in May 1920 as an independent Canadian alternative to the Friends of Irish Freedom, shut down over the course of 1922. The overwhelming majority of Irish-Catholic Canadians supported the Treaty, and saw the Irish Free State as achieving the SDIL's publicly stated objectives: granting the Irish people the ability to dictate their own affairs and comparable freedoms—within the structures of the British empire—to those that they enjoyed in Canada. The editor of London, Ontario's *Catholic Record* noted that he disagreed with Irish American anti-Treaty contributions to the paper—specifically a weekly column on Ireland by the Donegal-born, New York-based author

Seumas MacManus—stating that they failed 'to see through Canadian eyes because they lacked Canadian experience'.[5] The same paper also referenced the intergenerational nature of Irish Canadian engagement with Irish affairs, noting on 22 March 1922 how:

> Irishmen abroad and the children of Irishmen to the third and fourth generation, whose heartstrings are bound to Ireland as no other motherland binds to herself the loving allegiance of her children, are keenly, poignantly, interested in the prospects of acceptance or rejection by the Irish people of the measure of independence guaranteed by the Anglo-Irish Treaty.[6]

As in the United States, there was considerable disillusionment among Irish Canadian nationalists as Ireland descended into civil war, but most mainstream opinion—reinforced by Catholic newspapers across the country—regarded the military actions of the Free State forces as necessary.[7] There were, of course, exceptions. In Montreal, which had been the hotbed of republican Irish nationalism in Canada, prominent Irish Montrealer John Loye led a branch of the IRL—a resolutely anti-Treaty organisation that held public meetings throughout 1922. Overall, however, despite drawing the ire of segments of Canada's imperially oriented newspaper press in the aftermath of Jim Larkin's lecture, the IRL was a relatively minor organisation and attracted only a fraction of the support—and opposition—of the old SDIL.[8]

In the small, then-independent Dominion of Newfoundland, continued expressions of Irish identity in 1922 and 1923 provide an intriguing example of the ongoing construction and evolution of intergenerational ethnicity, as well as of the reconfiguration of global Irish networks that took place in the aftermath of the revolution. By the early twentieth century, the Irish community of Newfoundland's capital and chief port, St John's, was several generations removed from Ireland—a product of late-eighteenth and early-nineteenth century migration from the Irish south-east. Despite this significant, and growing, generational distance, nationalist associations thrived in the city in 1920 and 1921 as thousands of people attended the meetings, lectures and rallies sponsored by the local branch of the SDIL.

Following the signing of the Anglo-Irish Treaty, organised SDIL activity declined considerably, but the branch remained active until mid-1923, continuing to serve as the primary point of contact between those of Irish descent in St John's and the broader currents of diaspora nationalism. In early 1922, for example, the branch raised funds locally to send a marathon

runner, Jack Bell, to participate in the inaugural 'Irish Race Olympics'—Aonach Tailteann—scheduled for August in Dublin. Bell arrived in Ireland only to find the meet cancelled owing to the escalating circumstances of the civil war, and returned

to St John's without competing.[9] Similarly, it was through the structures of the SDIL that a young St John's law student at Oxford, William J. Browne, was selected to represent Newfoundland at the 1922 Irish Race Congress. His contributions in Paris were enthusiastically reported in the local press.[10]

By far the most intriguing shift in the Irish-Catholic associational sphere in St John's was the establishment of the Newfoundland Gaelic League in late 1922. This group, which had no formal affiliation with Gaelic Leagues in Ireland or elsewhere in North America, took over many of the social functions of the declining SDIL. It organised Irish language classes, put on Irish plays, sponsored lectures about Irish history, politics and literature and even had an association football team by the beginning of 1923. The League maintained a robust presence in the town until at least 1925, when references to its activities in the local press finally began to fade.[11]

The example of the Newfoundland Gaelic League, a body comprised almost exclusively of men and women three or more generations removed from Ireland, demonstrates how the upsurge in Irish identity that accompanied the mass movement for Irish independence evolved over the subsequent years. As reports of the brutal violence of the civil war reached North America, the networks of Irish nationalism ceased to function as a unifying basis for the construction of a broader diasporic identity, as only a small proportion of the continent's Irish ethnic communities remained involved with the movement after 1922. Ultimately, with the decline of the Friends of Irish Freedom, AARIR, SDIL and other nationalist associations, it was left to other groups, such as the Gaelic League or the transnational Ancient Order of Hibernians, to forge and promote diasporic connections into the mid-twentieth century.

by Patrick Mannion

FURTHER READING

David Brundage, *Irish Nationalists in America: the politics of exile, 1798– 1998* (Oxford, 2016)

Patrick Mannion, *A land of dreams: ethnicity, nationalism, and the Irish in Newfoundland, Nova Scotia, and Maine, 1880–1923* (Montreal, 2018)

Robert McLaughlin, *Irish Canadian conflict and the struggle for Irish independence, 1912–1925* (Toronto, 2013)

NOTES

[1] *Montreal Gazette*, 14 July 1922. See, also *Abbotsford Post* [British Columbia], 8 September 1922.
[2] David Brundage, *Irish nationalists in America: the politics of exile* (Oxford, 2016), 168–9.
[3] Brundage, *Irish nationalists in America*, 169. See, also Gavin Wilk, *Transatlantic defiance: the militant Irish republican movement in America, 1923–45* (Manchester, 2014), 13–4.
[4] Damien Murray, *Irish nationalists in Boston: Catholicism and conflict, 1900–1928* (Washington, 2016), 207–12.
[5] *Catholic Record* [London, Ontario], 4 February 1922.
[6] *Catholic Record* [London, Ontario], 25 March 1922.
[7] Robert McLaughlin, *Irish Canadian conflict and the struggle for Irish independence, 1912–1925* (Toronto, 2013), 176–83.
[8] Simon Jolivet, 'Entre nationalismes Irlandais et Canadien-français: les intrigues Québécoises de la Self Determination for Ireland League of Canada and Newfoundland', *Canadian Historical Review* 92 (1) (2011), 43–68: 64; Pádraig Ó Siadhail, 'The Self-Determination for Ireland League, 1920–1922: some notes on the league in Nova Scotia', *An Nasc* 15 (2003), 15–30: 29.
[9] *Daily News* [St John's], 17 February 1922; *Daily News*, 8 July 1922; *Daily News*, 12 August 1922.
[10] An account of Browne's contribution to the Irish Race Congress is included in his memoirs: William J. Browne, *Eighty-four years a Newfoundlander: memoirs of William J. Browne* (St John's, 1981), 71–86. See, also [St John's] *Evening Telegram*, 26 January 1922.
[11] Patrick Mannion, *A land of dreams: ethnicity, nationalism, and the Irish in Newfoundland, Nova Scotia, and Maine, 1880–1923* (Montreal, 2018), 211–4.

AUGUST

3 AUGUST 1922

THE ABANDONED TAILTEANN GAMES

PLAYING UNDER THE NATIONAL FLAG: SPORT, NATIONALITY AND PARTITION

The plan was a clear one: on 3 August 1922 the new Irish Free State would stage the opening ceremony of a major two-week sporting and cultural festival. That festival—the Tailteann Games—was to be modelled on the modern Olympic Games and planning for it began in earnest at Cabinet meetings in February 1922.

While the modern Olympic Games were the model, the inspiration for the Tailteann Games was rooted deep in the traditions of Irish nationalist history and mythology. The Tailteann Games were presented as a revival of a festival supposedly held at Tara, from 632 BC until the last record of the event in AD 1168—just before the 'English invasion' of 1169. The Games were said to have involved athletic and equestrian events and cultural contests in poetry, music and dancing, held on a peaceful, unified island. The historical record does not sustain these claims, but the message was clear:

despite centuries of invasion and oppression (political, economic and cultural) the Irish had survived and so had their unique culture.

J.J. Walsh, an Easter 1916 veteran appointed to the Cabinet position of Postmaster General, was the driving force behind the Tailteann Games. In Walsh's vision, they would be open to Irish-born people and to people of Irish descent around the world.[1] Even as disagreement over the Anglo-Irish Treaty deepened from split to civil war, plans to stage the Games progressed. Eventually, though, as violence worsened, the American team sent a cable that its members would not travel, and postponement became unavoidable.[2]

The programme for the games had emphasised the fault-lines of Irish sport. The competitions comprised Gaelic games, athletics and a range of Olympic sports—but no soccer or rugby. This was an exclusion based on a mentality that understood as an 'imperative the expression of nationality through sport'. This mentality had led the Gaelic Athletic Association (GAA) to operate a series of rules that banned from its membership those who played or watched rugby, soccer, hockey or cricket. J.J. Walsh was entirely in sympathy with this approach; it was a mentality, however, that was unable to accommodate the many who, in their sporting choices, 'were swayed by personal conviction and social context', and not by matters of politics or identity.[3]

Under the initiative of Walsh, a sum of £10,000 had been made available to redevelop Croke Park, the home of the GAA, to host the opening and closing ceremonies of the Tailteann Games. It was the first in a series of government decisions in the 1920s that privileged the position of the GAA in the Irish Free State.

For their part, those who controlled rugby reacted to partition by pretending it was not happening; the provincial structure of rugby permitted an independence of local action that suited those who organised rugby in Ulster. But the overarching ambition to preserve the unity of Irish rugby was challenged by practicalities relating to the international team. The emergence of international sporting competitions in the nineteenth century as a key marker of national identity, replete with the symbols of statehood, created obvious problems. What nation did the Irish team now represent? On which side of the border would it play its international matches? What flag would fly? What anthem would be played?

That a significant constituency of its membership was unionist in its politics created obvious difficulties; that rugby's leadership appeared similarly unionist in its sympathies created further tensions. In October 1922 a delegate from Bective Rangers club told the AGM of the Leinster Branch of the Irish Rugby Football Union (IRFU) that the men who controlled rugby were unrepresentative and impeding the game's progress:

> Rugby football could be made the national pastime of Ireland, but not until its control had been democratised. It had been deliberately excluded by the organisers of the Tailteann Games. He, personally, regarded that as a humiliation, but he, and no doubt many others, guessed the reason. It was because the present control was undemocratic, unsympathetic and almost un-Irish.[4]

But the old administration was not about to give way. There was no change to the jersey. In terms of grounds, the IRFU developed Ravenhill in Belfast; Ireland's home matches would now be split between Dublin and Belfast.[5]

More problematic was the flag. Although the IRFU designed its own flag in 1925, critics argued that 'when Ireland played at Lansdowne Road, she should do so under the national flag'.[6] This was objected to by committee members who noted that popular interest in rugby was drawn from opposing political traditions and that only the flag of the IRFU should fly at home matches. There the matter lay until 1932 when a popular campaign from certain southern rugby clubs, politicians and members of the public saw the IRFU agree that the tricolour would fly beside the IRFU flag at international matches in Dublin.[7]

Rugby's fine balancing act drew occasional criticism: in 1936 the decision to postpone a match between Cork Constitution and Sunday's Well because it fell on the day of the funeral of King George V was condemned by a Cork Constitution delegate as pandering 'to satisfy a certain section'.[8]

Soccer, alone of the major sports, assumed a new partitioned structure of governance, with the Irish Football Association (IFA) in Northern Ireland and the Football Association of Ireland (FAI) in Irish Free State. In 1922 the most immediate manifestation of change came in the Irish Cup. Until 1922 that was an all-Ireland competition, played annually since 1881 between the island's leading soccer clubs. Then, in spring 1922, two Irish Cup finals were played within a fortnight of each other, one in Dublin and the other in Belfast.

There was extreme bitterness between the IFA and the FAI. Something of a working compromise emerged, in time, for domestic competitions—the

IFA controlled competitions north of the border and the FAI controlled the south. The international aspect, however, proved much more difficult. In 1922 the government of the Free State recognised the legitimacy of the FAI and supported sending a team to represent Ireland at the 1924 Paris Olympics. But the IFA rejected this legitimacy, its attitude later encapsulated in a memorandum: 'The Irish FA functioned harmoniously until a political movement inspired by a religious element caused a re-adjustment of relations between Ireland and the British Government.'[9]

Ultimately, both associations fielded teams called 'Ireland' and claimed the right to draw international players from wherever they wished on the island. Indeed, it was only in the 1950s that this practice ceased; by then, more than forty players had lined up for 'Ireland' teams selected by both competing soccer bodies; matters of identity could be suborned to the desire to win matches.

Time and again, it was this idea of the love of play, of watching play, of organising sport, of trying to win, that undermined the attempts of ideologues to infuse sport with a specific meaning.

This was manifest when the Free State government finally staged the Tailteann Games in 1924. What emerged was the biggest sporting event in the world that year, bigger even than the Paris Olympics. There was no soccer or rugby, but this did not ensure a triumph for Gaelic games. Instead, it was modern mechanised sports—motorcycle, speedboat and aeroplane races—that were the most popular, wooing people fascinated by speed and danger. Big favourites with the crowd were the northern competitors, J.W. Shaw and Joe Craig.[10] It was a reminder that partition mattered when it came to sport—except when it didn't matter at all.

by Paul Rouse

FURTHER READING

T.H. Nally, *The Aonach Tailteann and the Tailteann Games: their origin, history and development* (Dublin, 1922)

Mike Cronin, 'The Irish Free State and Aonach Tailteann', in Alan Bairner (ed.), *Sport and the Irish: histories, identities, issues* (Dublin, 2004), 53–84

Paul Rouse, *Sport and Ireland: a history* (Oxford, 2015)

NOTES

[1] National Archives of Ireland (NAI), Department of the Taoiseach, S1592, memorandum on Tailteann Games, n.d., and Department of Finance, letter to J.J. Walsh, 25 September 1922.

[2] NAI, S8970, memorandum on Tailteann Games for Department of Finance, 10 August 1928.

[3] Liam O'Callaghan, *Rugby in Munster: a social and cultural history* (Cork, 2011), 164.

[4] University College Dublin Archives, Leinster branch of the Irish Rugby Football Union (hereafter UCDA, LB IRFU), annual general meeting minutes (uncatalogued), 24 October 1922.

[5] Edmund Van Esbeck, *One hundred years of Irish rugby* (Dublin, 1974), 98.

[6] Van Esbeck, *Irish rugby*, 107.

[7] UCDA, LB IRFU, minute book, 15 and 30 January 1932 and 5 February 1932; and NAI S2950, *passim*.

[8] O'Callaghan, *Munster*, 173.

[9] H.F. Moorhouse, 'One state, several countries: soccer and nationality in a "United" Kingdom', in J.A. Mangan (ed.), *Tribal identities: nationalism, Europe, sport* (London, 1996), 55–74: 62.

[10] *The Irish Times*, 11 August 1924 and Alistair McCook, *Days of thunder: the history of the Ulster Grand Prix* (Belfast, 2004).

9 AUGUST 1922

THE BATTLE FOR CORK

LANDSCAPES OF COUNTER-MEMORY

On Wednesday, 9 August 1922, an Irish Free State soldier named Flood was shot by anti-Treaty forces who had taken up positions in the hills overlooking Rochestown and Douglas, hoping to obstruct the advance of the National Army on Cork city.[1] Flood was one of a detachment of troops advancing across a field in a bid to outflank a group of IRA Volunteers positioned at a sharp bend in the road. Emerging through a gate onto the road, he was hit by a burst of IRA machine-gun fire. As Flood lay dying, Frank O'Donoghue, a republican who had fought alongside him in the War of Independence, broke cover, running out to take his hand and to say an Act of Contrition in his ear. This moment epitomises the bitter ironies of the civil war that have made it such a difficult episode in Ireland's recent history.

In this essay, we wish to highlight the forgotten landscapes of the civil war. Like other elements of Ireland's post-1700 heritage, the landscapes of the civil war are afforded no statutory protection. This is compounded by the particular challenges around remembering and coming to terms with this contentious period in Ireland's recent revolutionary past. Yet, the material residues of the civil war have significant potential to illuminate the details of the conflict. More than this, though, they speak powerfully of the texture of human emotion

Overleaf: National Army soldiers in Passage West prior to their advance on Cork city.

and experience, not only of those who fought and died, but also of the civilians caught up in the conflict. The sharp bend in the road at which Frank O'Donoghue and his comrades were positioned has now been bypassed, but it survives as a quiet lane with modern housing on either side. The iron gate through which Flood passed is still present. Known locally as the 'battlefield gate', its frame is pierced with bullet holes that stand as testament to the ferocity of the fighting that took place here.

The 'battlefield gate' signposts the archaeological potential of civil war landscapes, specifically in this case the area between Passage West and Cork city, which witnessed some of the most intensive clashes of the conflict.[2] Although the docks at Passage West have been significantly reworked since the Free State landings there in the early hours of the morning on Tuesday, 8 August 1922, much of the historic streetscape remains intact. It is little surprise, then, that features such as bullet-impact scars survive in the fabric of some of these buildings. On the wall of the Criterion Bar and its surrounds, the damage caused by bullets fired by National Army troops remains visible. They were created as Free State forces emerged from the docks and returned the fire of republicans positioned on high ground above them. Other buildings tell the opposite side of the story: the houses of Somerville Terrace display the evidence for incoming republican bullets, a reminder of the harassing fire they discharged from across the channel in Carrigaloe, on Great Island.

The heaviest fighting took place in the vicinity of Rochestown on Tuesday and Wednesday, and most casualties in the battle for Cork were recorded in this area.[3] Two eye-witness accounts—one by Dr James Lynch, a local doctor who tended the wounded, and another by Fr Michael OFM, a priest in the Capuchin monastery at Rochestown—provide richly textured detail on the events of those days.[4] Combining these with contemporary newspaper accounts, the second edition Ordnance Survey maps and the 1911 census data, it is possible to identify many of the key sites of the engagement, to assess how the opposing forces moved through the landscape, and crucially to examine the extent to which buildings and other landscape features that appear in accounts of the conflict have survived into the present.

The authors have conducted an initial phase of fieldwork to assess the archaeological survival of the buildings, boundaries and features associated with this 1922 conflict landscape.[5] Many of these survive today. For example, the road bridge at Rochestown, which was blown up by anti-Treaty troops on Tuesday morning, lies to one side of the modern road; the rebuilt central section remains clearly visible. Many of the buildings occupied and routes followed by both sides through the landscape are still extant. Among them are Dr Lynch's house, which served as a key National Army position and field hospital during the heaviest fighting, and which is today part of the Garryduff sports centre. The cottage of William and Mary Cronin, where three republican soldiers, famously including Scottish Volunteer Ian 'Scottie' McKenzie Kennedy, made a 'last stand', also appears extant, though likely much altered.[6]

The Cronin cottage and nearby 'battlefield gate' were at the vortex of the heaviest fighting of all in Rochestown. Among the most important surviving features in this area are the field boundaries that the republicans used as defensive positions, and from where they laid down intensive machine-gun fire. Some of the National Army men advancing over the exposed ground from the Lynch house towards these positions were First World War veterans, and that day's experience must have been traumatically reminiscent of the Western Front. Some of the injuries certainly were, as attested to by applications in the Military Service Pensions Collection. Ex-British soldier James Gavigan was struck in the head during the attack, and only 'lived a short time' afterwards. When the firing ceased, his Mullingar comrades knelt around his body and 'prayed for the happy repose of his soul'. Fellow Free Stater James Madden's section suffered particularly heavy casualties at the hands of the machine guns. Madden was killed instantly when he was 'hit in the forehead'. On the anti-Treaty side, nineteen-year-old republican Christopher Olden lingered for two days after being struck in the intestines during the Rochestown fighting, before succumbing to shock and hemorrhaging in the South Infirmary.[7] The engagement had a lasting impact on the civilian population as well, not least the elderly Cronins who 'screamed and called while the Staters surrounded the cottage', a building Scottie McKenzie and fellow anti-Treaty Volunteer James Maloney died defending.[8] A photograph published in the *Cork Examiner* on 23 August shows the Cronins standing forlornly outside their shattered home holding possessions riddled with bullet holes.

The railway and maritime heritage of the area between Passage West and Cork city is widely known and appreciated among the public today: the old

route of the Cork, Blackrock and Passage Railway, for instance, is a popular local walk, while the recently established Passage West Maritime Museum showcases the area's history. Yet, the momentous events of the civil war that took place here remain underexplored, their memory all but invisible in the contemporary landscape. At Passage West, the only memorial to an incident during the revolutionary years commemorates the death of a member of Cork No. 1 Brigade during the War of Independence. Garryduff woods, a public recreation area owned by Coillte, lies at the heart of the battlefield, but there is no signage to indicate the historical significance of the area—indeed no such signage exists anywhere in Passage West or Rochestown. In what is an almost ubiquitous issue with respect to revolutionary-era conflict sites, the landscape features that survive—with the possible exception of the 'battlefield gate'—have done so by accident rather than design.

The 'battlefield gate', Rochestown, Co. Cork: close-ups display where the frame was pierced by bullets.

Combining archaeological methods with archival evidence, it is possible to address these deficits, and employ the material remains of the past to provide insights into the events and experiences of conflict. The Irish civil war has been marked by forgetfulness—the eliding of a past that has been too painful to remember—but such acts of forgetting have political consequences, for they paper over dissonances in memory and experience in an effort to create a past that is uncontentious. As we approach the centenary of the civil war, it is all the more important to record its fragile and undocumented sites and landscapes and to recognise the damage that can be done to them by modern development.

Engaging with these landscapes can help to make visible the traces of repressed pasts and to ensure that discourse around difficult histories remains in the public sphere. Beyond this, however, the material residues of the past have restorative and redemptive potential. Sites of conflict have an enduring affective presence, foregrounding the humanity and suffering of those caught up in these events. The material remains of the past open spaces for reflection that make possible new dialogues and new ways of seeing the 'other'. As we approach the centenary and beyond, there is potential for such places to act as pivots around which to recount and come to terms with difficult histories, through practices of meaning-making, recognition and accountability that facilitate social repair in the present.

by Joanna Brück and Damian Shiels

FURTHER READING

John Borgonovo, *The battle for Cork: July–August 1922* (Cork, 2012)

NOTES

[1] Archives of the Capuchin Franciscans Province of Ireland (hereafter Capuchin Franciscans Archives), folder 33, letter from Fr Michael OFM, Capuchin Franciscan College, Rochestown, to Winifred Etheridge, 27 January 1923 (particular thanks to John Borgonovo for sharing his knowledge of Fr Michael's account).

[2] John Borgonovo, *The battle for Cork: July–August 1922* (Cork, 2012).

[3] Borgonovo, *The battle for Cork.*

[4] Cork City Library, Local Studies department, Dr James Lynch, typescript, 'The battle of Douglas' (n.d.). Reference courtesy of John Borgonovo. Capuchin Franciscans Archives, Letter from Fr Michael.

[5] We are very grateful to John Borgonovo, Andy Bielenberg, Niall Murray, Joe Healy and Robert Allison for assistance in identifying the battle sites on the ground.

[6] Capuchin Franciscans Archives, letter from Fr Michael.

[7] Military Archives, Military Service Pensions Collection, files 2D383, 2D82 and DP2702.

[8] Capuchin Franciscans Archives, letter from Fr Michael.

9 AUGUST 1922

THE REOPENING OF CLERY'S DEPARTMENT STORE

THE MUNDANE AND THE TRAUMATIC: ORDINARY LIFE IN EXTRAORDINARY TIMES

On Wednesday, 9 August 1922, an advertisement for Clery's department store adorned the full front page of the *Irish Independent*, announcing the store's reopening in Dublin. 'New Clery's' was in the same location on lower O'Connell street as the earlier store, which had been built in 1853 but suffered extensive damage in the Easter Rising. A British shell hit a barricade on Lower Abbey Street causing a fire, which spread to Clery & Co. and destroyed the entire building. After six years' occupation of a temporary warehouse during the 'many trials and difficulties that have beset us since 1916', the largest department store in Ireland was ready to open its doors again. Clery's sold all the luxury items one might want—hosiery, silk, ribbon and flowers, millinery, carpets, tailoring and much more. The original shop had been the first of Dublin's larger stores to fit electric lights, installing them in 1892 to support evening shopping. 'New Clery's'

EVENING HERALD
Largest Net Paid Sale of any Dublin Evening Paper.

DUBLIN: WEDNESDAY, AUGUST 9, 1922.

Irish Independent

VOL. 31. No. 167.
Price—
TWO PENCE

OUR OBITUARY AND SPECIAL NOTICES COLUMN WILL BE FOUND ON PAGE TWO.

We have pleasure in announcing the opening of our new building in Lower O'Connell Street to-day after six years' occupation of a temporary Warehouse in Lower Abbey Street.

New Clery's is a notable addition to the fine street it adorns, and this great enterprise is a monument to Irish craftsmanship and native skill.

It is the largest establishment of its kind in the country, and has been designed in every detail with especial care for the service and convenience of our customers.

Throughout the many trials and difficulties which have beset us since 1916, we have maintained, unimpaired, the efficiency of our great buying organisation, which handles the products of the world as well as the manufactures of our own country.

In our new home the resources and prestige of the firm will always be utilised to make Clery shopping the last word in comfort and honest value, combined with Clery's well-known standard of quality.

August 9, 1922.   CLERY & CO., Ltd.

INDUSTRY

COMMERCE

CLERY & Co.
DUBLIN   LTD.

The drawing from which this advertisement appears is by the well-known Irish artist, Oswald Cuningham.   The engraving is by Irish Photo-Engraving Co., Dublin.   Designed and produced by Corrigan Adservice, Dublin

continued this trend, advertising its modern facilities—electric passenger lifts and 'beautifully appointed
toilet rooms for both lady and gentlemen customers'.
Clery's had also led the way with the introduction of
its internal phone system and switchboard some years
previously, and an earlier advert on 5 August noted
they now had a new telephone number with five sep-
arate lines.[1] The principal owner of Clery & Co. in 1922 was Dr Lombard
Murphy, the son of William Martin Murphy, and the family retained ownership of the *Irish Independent* newspaper, hence its prominent placing of
adverts for the store.[2]

Opposite: Front-
page advert for
the reopening
of Clery's
department store,
Irish Independent,
9 August 1922.

The *Evening Herald*, another Murphy family publication, described on
9 August how Rev. Father Flanagan from Marlborough street visited and
blessed the premises before the doors opened to let in the waiting crowds,
who enjoyed their shopping as a 'first-class orchestra' played in the background. The reopening of this modern, glamorous building seemed to
herald new beginnings after destruction. The only slight allusion to the
events that destroyed the original Clery's premises and the ongoing conflict was the emphasis placed on providing the new building with immu-
nity from fire. The building's walls were fire-proof, the windows had fire-
resisting glass and the sprinkler system covered every room from the roof
to the basement. Its owners did not want to risk the damage experienced in
the Rising, during which one eye-witness, Oscar Traynor, described seeing
the 'huge plate-glass windows of Clery's stores run molten into the channel
from the terrific heat'.[3]

The new building cost £400,000, half of which came from British government compensation for damage inflicted during the Rising. Clery's
availed of modern technologies in rebuilding the store, providing a bridge
between the traditions of its origins and the future it looked towards. It
was described by *The Irish Times* on 10 August as 'one of the most important works of reconstruction in Dublin'. *Irish Life* magazine reported in
September 1922 that Dubliners were 'very proud of the new Clery's which
had risen up to adorn poor, knocked about Sackville street'. The confident view of Dublin it represented, however, was still notably precarious in
August 1922. Heavy fighting had taken place in Dublin just over a month
previously, with areas of Upper O'Connell street again destroyed in the
'Battle of Dublin'. The reconstruction of Clery's was fortunate to escape a
further fire: another building on the street, the Hamman Hotel, was utterly

destroyed by shells and fire and many others suffered very significant damage.[4]

The ruins of Clery's
department store,
O'Connell Street, 1916.

Dublin city began to assess the damage and
once again began the process of reconstruction
in the aftermath, but the civil war fighting continued in other counties of
Ireland with no clear resolution in sight. Notices about Clery's reopening
jostled for space with reports of a raid by 'Irregulars' of the train from
Enniskillen to Sligo, photographs of Free State troops departing Dublin,
and a map of 'the war area in the south'.[5] In addition, Clery's had re-opened
at a time when 'nearly everyone is suffering financially by the disorder in
the economic life of Ireland', making it difficult for the store to prosper.[6]
Many firms were on the verge of bankruptcy by August 1922, having suffered from the 'blockading of roads, the cutting of railway communication
and the wrecking of bridges'.[7] Merchants were having difficulty securing
payments from their customers and supplying goods due to the civil disorder. The increased cost of living was also having a negative impact, inevitably resulting in less disposable income available for the sort of commodi-
ties sold by Clery's.[8] The greatest threat, however, came from the ongoing
conflict in Ireland. The opening of the new premises was also reported in
the *Nenagh News* on 12 August in a short article immediately following a

The restored Clery's department store, c. 1924

report of a meeting of the Ballybrophy branch of the National Union of Railwaymen, at which the actions of the 'irregulars' were roundly condemned. The chairman of the meeting asserted that

> the foundation on which civilisation rested was ordered government—that the security of life, the security of person, individual rights, development and progress rested on a well-ordered government established by the people and failing that they could only view the future with despair.

This mingling of the mundane and the traumatic is evident in *Irish Life* magazine in 1922. In August the magazine reported that the general topic of conversation was the Dublin Horse Show and the good news that, despite rumours of postponement or cancellation, it was to proceed in the middle of the month. The reporter argued that for 'Ireland to have been deprived of its greatest carnival would have been an unthinkable calamity'. He viewed the horse show as an opportunity to 'forget the dark clouds that are slowly dispersing' and to 'imagine we are back once more in those grand and wonderful days when men and women breathed freely'. The following month

Irish Life carried an image of Michael Collins on its front cover with the caption 'The dead leader'. The 'Town and Country column' lamented the loss of Collins, worrying that the bullet 'is out to kill the Treaty and blast Ireland'. The columnist, however, quickly moved to other matters, notably the success of the Dublin Horse Show. Despite the deaths of Arthur Griffith and Michael Collins, the Horse Show did go ahead, along with the annual Liffey Swim, which had been postponed in July due to the fighting.

A few short weeks after the reopening of Clery's, O'Connell street thronged with thousands of people as they watched the coffin of Michael Collins being brought from City Hall to Glasnevin Cemetery. It is believed that 500,000 people came out to pay their respects for his funeral on 28 August. Postcards reproduced in the months afterwards reveal the huge crowds in the city. For nine hours people filed past his body as it lay in state at City Hall. Once again the mundane and the political intertwined: Dublin builders gained a temporary postponement on promised wage cuts out of respect for the loss of Collins.[9] Businesses were closed across the city as 'no one had the heart to engage in business of any kind' and 'no one felt any inclination for feasting or amusement'.[10] The excitement and optimism generated by the opening of the new Clery's store stood in stark contrast to the communal mourning evident in Dublin a few short weeks later, with Collins's death serving as a grim reminder of the difficulties of achieving peace.

by Fionnuala Walsh

FURTHER READING

John Dorney, *The civil war in Dublin: the fight for the Irish capital, 1922–1924* (Dublin, 2017)

Padraig Yeates, *A city in civil war, Dublin 1921–4* (Dublin, 2015)

Diarmaid Ferriter, *A nation and not a rabble: the Irish revolution 1913–1923* (London, 2015)

NOTES

[1] Stephanie Rains, *Commodity culture and social class in Dublin, 1850–1916* (Dublin, 2010), 135, 170, 206.

[2] Peter Costello and Tony Farmar, *The very heart of the city: the story of Denis Guiney and Clerys* (Dublin, 1992), 55.

[3] Rains, *Commodity culture*, 206.

[4] 'Ireland's tragic week: a record of the Four Courts battles in Dublin', in *Irish Life*, 7 and 15 July 1922, 11–15.

[5] *Evening Herald*, 9 August 1922, 1–2.

[6] 'Hopes and fears for Ireland', *Irish Homestead*, 12 August 1922, 490.

[7] 'Problems for an Irish government', *Irish Homestead*, 19 August 1922, 506.

[8] 'National indebtedness', *Irish Homestead*, 7 October 1922, 593.

[9] Anne Dolan and William Murphy, *Michael Collins, the man and the revolution* (Cork, 2018), 282–5.

[10] 'At home and abroad', *Irish Life*, September 1922, 78.

12 AUGUST 1922

TRANSIENT EMINENCE:
THE FADING OF ARTHUR GRIFFITH

Arthur Griffith's sudden death at the age of just 51 on 12 August 1922 was an enormous shock to his Provisional Government colleagues and to Treaty supporters in Ireland and beyond. A printer and jobbing political journalist, he lived and died a poor man: his widow had to fight for adequate state support for his young family.[1] Michael Collins died less than a fortnight later; ever since, Griffith's death has been addressed largely as a prelude to the 'Big Fellow's' dramatic end. Collins's death still overshadows Griffith's memory, clouds the reality that Griffith's death was world news when it happened, and hampers evaluation of how Griffith might have influenced national economic development in succeeding years.

Founder of Sinn Féin and populariser of separatist arguments based on economic as well as political grounds, Griffith in 1919–20 was left holding the reins of the revolutionary underground Dáil government in Dublin.[2] Meanwhile President Éamon de Valera squandered nineteen months on a diplomatically futile American tour. 'The Chief's' acolytes later dismissed

Griffith as an inadequate figure who yielded to temptation during the Treaty negotiations, intoxicated by the chance of seizing the top job. Griffith's longstanding advocacy of 'dual monarchy' was taken as evidence that he was never a thoroughgoing separatist. Yet de Valera's failed compromise 'Document No. 2' was a refinement rather than an abrogation of that approach, because it reserved a limited place for the British Crown in a new Ireland's constitutional framework.

Griffith was a vigorous and sometimes abrasive defender of the Treaty settlement he had done so much to forge. Others around the Provisional Government table may have regarded the Treaty as the least bad option: not Griffith. When he succeeded Collins as chairman of the Provisional Government after civil war erupted, he bluntly informed an American journalist that 'the Irish people want peace. They want peace even to the extent of accepting an alliance with Britain'.[3]

The dominions mourned Griffith as a constructive statesman who turned the necessity of compromise with Britain into a positive element not only in Anglo-Irish but in dominions relations. Some newspapers recalled a man who died disappointed, yet others pointed to his remarkable achievements as a political thinker, from the founding of Sinn Féin to the securing of effective independence for most of Ireland. Most of his political dreams had become reality, the tragic issue of Ulster apart. Australian and New Zealand newspapers lamented the loss of a man of integrity and intelligence. The 'friends of Ireland in Australia will place a wreath' on his grave 'no matter what their politics may be...his good faith has been as conspicuous as his courage'.[4] The South African leader General Smuts, who had helped clear the way for the truce of July 1921, termed Griffith 'quite the strongest man of the Sinn Féin party'.[5]

In New York, Griffith was described as 'the brain of the Irish movement for freedom', and de Valera's antagonist, Judge Daniel Cohalan, mourned

> one of the greatest men of his generation, the father of Sinn Féin and a scholar...I believe the work in Ireland will go on. His work and life will be an inspiration...I know he felt that the Free State was only a step towards ultimate freedom.[6]

The *New York Tribune* said of him that 'beloved of no one class, the rock of the revolution had come to be respected by all, from the somewhat frightened old Unionists of the Kildare Street club to the impatient youths in the Free State green'. Another newspaper accorded Griffith's death a banner headline and a collage of three photographs, one of him walking with his two children. His passing was discussed not only in major urban newspapers, but in obscure small towns such as Paragould, Arkansas, and Hartford, Kentucky, while his image appeared on the front page of the *Capital Journal* of Salem, Oregon.[7] Reporters wrote of the enormous crowds that assembled in Dublin to pay their respects as his funeral procession passed. Newsreels, one inaccurately terming him 'first President of the Irish Free State', recorded the occasion.

Expressions of regret from King George V and the British Cabinet reflected genuine feeling. In British eyes Griffith had become the embodiment of reasonableness in discourse and negotiation. He traded on this to secure acceptance, with very limited and symbolic elements of fealty to the Crown as required under the 1921 Anglo-Irish Treaty, of the draft constitution of the Irish Free State. That constitution was secular and democratic in the institutions it prescribed. It also, albeit unintentionally, turned out to prove a significant stepping stone towards complete independence: it was under its provisions that from 1932 de Valera was able successively to remove the elements of subjugation most obnoxious to republicans.

Lord Birkenhead, who sparred with Griffith during the Treaty negotiations, praised a remarkable man, 'dour and placid' but 'courageous and honest', who 'perished of sheer exhaustion and overwork'. It is difficult to say if hard work was a decisive factor, on a par with his heavy smoking and lack of exercise.[8] Fourteen men served as ministers of the Dáil and Provisional governments between January and December 1922. Excluding Michael Collins (shot in 1922, aged 31), Kevin O'Higgins (shot in 1927, aged 35) and Patrick Hogan (killed in an accident in 1936, aged 45), five died in their eighties, two in their seventies, two in their sixties, and only two, including Griffith, as early as their fifties. This was despite the imprisonment, hardship and the threat of violent death all experienced from 1916 onwards.

In February 1922 Lord Midleton commended Griffith's understanding of the concerns of southern unionist landowners, and in May the Provost of Trinity College contrasted Griffith with Michael Collins, who had not 'kept faith'. Griffith came to be seen as a moderate on Northern Ireland: upon news of his death, a unionist grandee on Derry Corporation proposed a vote of sympathy.[9] Yet his sensitivity towards minority concerns in the emerging Irish Free State was not matched by insistence upon legislative measures to protect the long-term interests of the nationalist minority in newly created Northern Ireland.

Had death not intervened, Free State economic policy under President Griffith might have been far more ambitious and adventurous, and less in thrall to conventional thinking than under his more conservative and fiscally orthodox successor W.T. Cosgrave. The paradox is that his key ideas were embraced most enthusiastically not by his pro-Treaty allies, but by his civil war opponents under de Valera in the 1930s. Popular memory, dazzled by the glamour of Michael Collins and fascinated by the enigmatic figure of Éamon de Valera, overlooks how important a political leader Griffith was when he died, and how influential his ideas remained in both constitutional and economic affairs. Of the key thinkers and actors who re-invented Irish nationalism at the turn of the twentieth century and who achieved separation from Britain, only Bulmer Hobson (1883–1969) has fared worse in public memory than the stocky bowler-hatted printer, polemicist, ideologue and statesman Arthur Griffith.

by Eunan O'Halpin

FURTHER READING

Colum Kenny, *The enigma of Arthur Griffith: 'Father of us all'* (Dublin, 2020)

Michael Laffan, 'Griffith, Arthur Joseph', in James McGuire and James Quinn (eds), *Dictionary of Irish biography* (Cambridge, 2009), 277–86

Owen McGee, *Arthur Griffith* (Sallins, 2015)

NOTES

[1] *New York Herald*, 13 August 1922; *Evening World*, 14 August 1922; Anne Dolan, *Commemorating the Irish civil war: history and memory, 1923–2000* (Cambridge, 2005), 114–16. Griffith's wife and two children were featured in a Reuters newsreel captioned 'photocall in garden' issued on 10 February 1922. See, British Pathé, 'Republic of Ireland/politics: family of Arthur Griffith (1922); available at: www.britishpathe.com (accessed 19 April 2021).

[2] Risteárd Mulcahy, *Richard Mulcahy (1886–1971): a family memoir* (Dublin, 1999), 148–50.

[3] *Washington Times*, 31 August 1922.

[4] *Daily Express* (Waga Waga, New South Wales), 14 August 1922; *Gisborne Times*, 15 August 1922; *Poverty Bay Herald* (New Zealand), 14 August 1922; *Freeman's Journal* (Sydney, New South Wales), 17 August 1922.

[5] *New Zealand Herald*, 17 August 1922.

[6] *New York Herald*, 13 August 1922.

[7] *New York Tribune*, 13 August 1922; *Evening World* (New York), 12 August 1922; *Paragould Soliphone* (Paragould, Arkansas), 14 August 1922; *Capital Journal* (Salem, Oregon), 12 August 1922; *Hartford Herald* (Hartford, Kentucky), 16 August 1922.

[8] *Belfast News-Letter*, 24 August 1922; Mulcahy, *Richard Mulcahy*, 129–31.

[9] British Library, Bernard papers, Add MSS 52781, Midleton to Bernard, 27 February, and Bernard to Midleton, 23 May 1922; *Belfast News-Letter*, 22 August 1922.

13 AUGUST 1922

THE DESTRUCTION OF MITCHELSTOWN CASTLE

THE IRISH REVOLUTION AND COUNTRY HOUSE BURNINGS

On 13 August 1922 Mitchelstown Castle in Cork became the largest Irish country house to be destroyed during the civil war. Early histories of the War of Independence and civil war in Ireland make no reference to this event, and little mention of the burning of around 300 Irish country houses, here defined as the (former) residences of Irish landlords. Nor, indeed, was serious consideration given to a related issue, the growth in agrarian disorder.[1] While it can legitimately be argued that the foremost desire of revolutionaries was to secure Ireland's sovereignty, sight should not be lost of the fact that the chaos of the 1920–23 period created local conditions in which republicans and agrarian activists, often one and the same, staged their own micro-revolutions that had ulterior social ambitions, most notably the redistribution of lands. Case studies of country house burnings can be useful in elucidating this.[2]

Less than two months before, on the evening of 29 June 1922, Mitchelstown Castle was commandeered by anti-treatyite forces led by

Commandant Patrick Luddy, a farmer's son from Coolyregan, who, during the War of Independence, had been an officer in the Mitchelstown Battalion of the IRA.[3] The castle was an ideal billet to accommodate his men, while its strategic location provided a sweeping view of the town and surrounding countryside. To Luddy, the castle was also a symbol of alien culture; as a youth he had been reared on fireside stories of how 'the men and women of the Mitchelstown district took strong and active steps to ensure that the landlord's men were effectively dealt with', and years after its destruction, he is said to have boasted about his role in the burning, 'that he was avenging centuries of landlordism and English occupation, as well as erasing what little was left of the Kingston presence in Mitchelstown'.[4] Thus, his memory ascribed the motivation not to the wanton destruction that characterises civil wars, or any grand military scheme, but to historical grievances located in the expropriation of lands by colonial usurpers; it was an important myth to justify the return of these lands to native ownership.

Mitchelstown Castle was no different from most of the other houses burned during 1920–23, when motivations were web-like in their complexities,

Mitchelstown Castle after the fire of August 1922.

rooted in the historical past as well as the revolutionary present. In this case, Mitchelstown Castle represented a very significant site of ancestral grievance: on 9 September 1887 three civilians were shot by the RIC during a nationalist demonstration—'the Mitchelstown massacre'—organised in opposition to William Downes Webber's estate-management policy. Col. Alex King-Harman, who inherited the estate in 1924, reflected on the memory of this event and the role of his ancestor: 'The disasters here [in 1922] were inevitable. I think, at the time, there was great bitterness.... . He put it in the position where people wanted to burn down the castle.'[5]

The bulk of the Webber (formerly Kingston) estate had long been sold by 1922, but the neo-Gothic extravaganza was still surrounded by hundreds of acres of demesne and untenanted lands, much of it prime agricultural land. The burning of the castle dissuaded King-Harman from ever returning; his solicitor claimed: 'The social standing of the district had been entirely changed in the rebellion and he said he would not come to live there.'[6] King-Harman had, therefore, no option but to sell his lands to the Irish Land Commission, which he eventually did in 1936, and Patrick Luddy was one of the allottees who received a farm, rewarded by the Fianna Fáil government for his role in the War of Independence.[7] This was certainly not unusual. Since the passing of the 1923 Land Act, the rhetoric and reality of land redistribution had been a major catalyst in the change from disorder to order. The act legislated for the compulsory acquisition of lands, targeting the former landed elite, but that was diplomatically tempered by offering payment in land bonds, it was not expropriation. Simultaneously, the process threatened to punish those who stood against the state by denying them access to land in redistribution schemes, while also holding out the prospect of reward to loyal supporters.[8] This is a dimension of the Irish revolution that can only be understood if we look well beyond 1923, but to do so, and to fully comprehend the Irish revolution in all its complexities, access must be provided to the Irish Land Commission files to allow scholars to examine post-independence redistribution schemes systematically.

The story of Mitchelstown Castle also reveals the extent of country house looting. Before and after the burning, eyewitnesses described men and women dragging furniture from the house, 'putting stuff behind trees and bushes', while the newly established Civic Guard used warrants to search several premises in the town where valuable silver pieces were recovered.[9] The paintings were not recovered, but, in 1957, Sir Cecil King-Harman received a letter from a native of Limerick informing him that 41 paintings had been sold at Sotheby's in London for almost £101,000; the author believed, 'in the light of information given to him by one of the castle's Republican garrison in 1922', that they had come from Mitchelstown Castle.[10] In 2000 Bill Power controversially claimed that before the burning some of the paintings had been 'taken away by a Republican lawyer for his personal pleasure and advantage'.[11] While looting is part and parcel of warfare, and may be regarded as another step in the despoilment of the coloniser's residence, it is also driven by ambitions of personal enrichment.

In the wider national context, looting and a multitude of other crimes had become so widespread by August 1923 that the Irish Free State government introduced a Public Safety (Emergency Powers) Act. This worked in tandem with the 1923 Land Act and the Damage to Property (Compensation) Act of May 1923 to coerce and conciliate; a strategy very familiar in rural Ireland. The latter provided for compensation, appeasing the British government, but frustrating the country-house owners who generally regarded awards as inadequate and punitive. For example, in the case of contents stolen, an owner had to prove that thieves had been acting 'on behalf of any combination or conspiracy for the overthrow of the Provisional Government'. During the Mitchelstown Castle compensation hearing, Judge Kenny concluded that the looting had been carried out by 'ordinary thieves', not members of the anti-Treaty forces.[12] Neither was the government in a position, even if it had the desire, to compensate country house owners on the levels claimed.[13] Judge Kenny awarded £27,500, a fraction of the £149,000 claimed for Mitchelstown. The minister for finance 'made it plain' to King-Harman 'that he would not grant full restoration compensation, that it was absurd to rebuild such a vast house in those days'.[14] King-Harman invested the award in building seventeen houses in the Dublin suburbs, altering the urban landscape. The Cistercian monks of Mount Melleray in County Waterford used the salvage of the castle to build a new abbey, while in the 1940s Mitchelstown Co-operative Agricultural Society built a milk-processing factory on the site of the castle ruins. Both abbey and co-op were symbols of the newly imagined independent Ireland, while their construction meant that the symbol of the old colonial order was completely erased from the physical and cultural landscape.

by Terence Dooley

FURTHER READING

Gemma Clark, *Everyday violence in the Irish civil war* (Cambridge, 2014)

Terence Dooley, *The decline of the big house in Ireland* (Dublin, 2001)

Terence Dooley and Christopher Ridgway (eds), *The Irish country house: its past, present and future* (Dublin, 2011)

NOTES

[1] For recent scholarship, see, Terence Dooley, *The decline of the big house in Ireland* (Dublin, 2001), 171–207; Terence Dooley, *'The land for the people': the land question in independent Ireland* (Dublin, 2004), 26–56; Gemma Clark, *Everyday violence in the Irish civil war* (Cambridge, 2014), 54–97; Gavin Foster, *The Irish civil war and society: politics, class, and conflict* (London, 2015).

[2] Anne O'Riordan, *East Galway agrarian agitation and the burning of Ballydugan House* (Dublin, 2015); James S. Donnelly Jr, 'Big house burnings in county Cork during the Irish revolution, 1920–21', *Éire-Ireland* 47 (3 and 4) (Fall/Winter 2012), 141–97; Ciaran J. Reilly, 'The burning of country houses in Co. Offaly, 1920–3', in Terence Dooley and Christopher Ridgway (eds), *The Irish country house: its past, present and future* (Dublin, 2011), 110–33.

[3] Military Archives (MA), Bureau of Military History (BMH), witness statement (WS) 1,151, Patrick Luddy, 1–2.

[4] MA, BMH, WS 1,151, Patrick Luddy, 1–2. The second quote is from Bill Power, *White knights, dark earls: the rise and fall of an Anglo-Irish dynasty* (Cork, 2000), 225.

[5] Quoted in Power, *White knights*, 247.

[6] The National Archives of the United Kingdom (hereafter TNA), Records of the Colonial Office, CO 762/29/1, Anthony Carroll, sol. to Major A. Reid Jameson, 14 December 1927.

[7] Power, *White knights*, 245; see, Dooley, 'The land for the people', 99–131.

[8] Dooley, 'The land for the people', 57–98.

[9] National Archives of Ireland (NAI), Board of Works files, 2D/62/73, claim of Arthur Webber, Mitchelstown Castle, Co. Cork, December 1925.

[10] Quoted in Power, *White knights*, 240.

[11] Quoted in Power, *White knights*, 240.

[12] *The Irish Times*, 29 April 1926.

[13] Dooley, *Decline of the big house*, 197–207.

[14] TNA, CO 762/29/1, Alex King-Harman to Irish Grants Committee, 31 March 1928.

17 AUGUST 1922

THE DISBANDMENT OF THE ROYAL IRISH CONSTABULARY

REVOLUTIONARY LOSERS: SOUTHERN IRISH LOYALIST EXPERIENCES OF MIGRATION

On 17 August 1922 Joseph Cashman photographed a small crowd of men and women outside Dublin Castle. Three were in Royal Irish Constabulary (RIC) uniform, with two standing among the discarded jackets and trousers of their colleagues. Less dramatic, perhaps, than men marching in formation, formal salutes, or flags being lowered and raised, the photograph nonetheless captures a symbolic moment in the shift to the new order in the Irish Free State. At 12 o'clock that day, the new Civic Guard (later An Garda Síochána) took charge of Dublin Castle and the RIC was, as *The Irish Times* put it, 'fairly disbanded and put into civil life'.[1] The process had begun in April, with men gathered in central barracks and camps before being gradually dispersed. For these former policemen and their families, the consequences lasted well beyond the five months or so it had taken to dismantle the RIC.

A majority of the Irish-born members who remained in the force by 1922—whose numbers included some of the Black and Tans recruited from 1920—stayed in Ireland (on both sides of the new border) and attempted to settle into 'civil life'. Further policing opportunities were available in the Royal Ulster Constabulary, but among a couple of hundred ex-RIC listed in a Civic Guard register in 1922 and 1923 (by which time recruitment of ex-RIC seems to have effectively ceased), only nine were disbanded men. The remainder had retired, resigned or been dismissed from the RIC by 1921, with some subsequently joining the Irish Republican Army.[2] As Seán William Gannon has found, a large minority—over one-third—chose to leave Ireland, either temporarily or permanently.[3]

Individual motivations are difficult to disentangle, but this migration took place in the context of what British civil servant Andy Cope described as a 'concerted movement for a wholesale expulsion' of ex-policemen and their families. While this was ultimately something of an exaggeration, and violence and intimidation was sporadic and localised, threats, raids and shooting were regularly reported.[4] On the night of 25 April 1922, for instance, five armed and masked men entered the home of ex-Sergeant Michael Flynn and ordered him to leave within 48 hours. His family had already packed for a move to Castletownbere, County Cork, but shortly after arrival there they received another letter ordering them to leave. Flynn immediately travelled to Dover, followed five days later by his wife Annie and six young children. Annie Flynn, he later claimed, had received 'such a fright that she is not the same since'. Finding 'no prospect of employment', and with a pension that was 'not sufficient to meet my demands', Flynn had returned to Cork by 1924. In 1930 he was living in Bandon, unemployed, and claimed to have 'no other means of getting the money as Ex R.I.C. men wont [sic] get any employment on account of remaining in the force until disbandment'. The last recorded details in Flynn's post-disbandment file— the only one of its kind to survive—were unsuccessful applications to have a portion of his pension commuted to pay off some debts, replace a cow that had died and purchase a pony and trap to bring his children to school.[5]

Such challenges were also shared by many of the southern loyalists who left Ireland around 1922, whether because of violence, intimidation, economic concerns, or personal preference. Neither leaving nor returning offered any guarantees. The exact scale of the 'exodus' is difficult to discern. In May 1922 the British government established an Irish Distress Committee for 'persons ordinarily resident in Ireland who, for reasons of personal safety, have come to Great Britain and are represented to be in urgent need of assistance'. By March 1923 it had dealt with 7,500 applications for loans or grants, including 5,600 for 'immediate assistance' of which 4,330 were approved. Not all of those who arrived in Britain sought aid, but a large proportion of applicants were married men with wives and children. Nor were these 'refugees' all Protestant: it was recorded that 598 grants were awarded to Protestants and 1,063 to Catholics between May and October 1922; most, but not all, from the Irish Free State. These included, as the committee's chairman Sir Samuel Hoare put it, 'ex-service men, members of the Royal Irish Constabulary, ex-civil servants in our service in Ireland ...who cannot return to Ireland'.[6]

While it is problematic to label all Irish members of the RIC as loyalists, Michael Flynn was just one who labelled himself as a southern loyalist when applying for compensation to the Irish Grants Committee in the late 1920s. As a particularly well-documented group, their post-migration challenges are thus illustrative. Periods of separation were common—often much longer than the Flynns' five days apart—as men travelled alone in search of work and suitable accommodation, which was often difficult to afford in the absence of new employment. Wives were left to settle up affairs and sell off property as best they could, remaining vulnerable to boycotting, threat and harm. British and dominion police forces were extremely reluctant to take on men with service in Ireland and the stigma could extend to other employers, making work difficult to find in Britain (as Michael Flynn discovered). Other ex-RIC who applied to the Irish Grants Committee were similarly living off pensions and creditors well into the 1920s.

That said, the disbanded RIC had access to supports unavailable to other southern Irish loyalist refugees—including retired rather than disbanded RIC—arriving on British shores around the same time. The latter could apply to the Irish Distress Committee or seek aid from the privately funded Southern Irish Loyalists Relief Association (SILRA). Under the terms of disbandment, meanwhile, some 7,000 'disturbance allowances' and 886 'separation allowances' were disbursed to disbanded RIC. Any who felt in danger at home were entitled to a free travelling warrant to move anywhere in Ireland or Britain, and the RIC tribunal granted thousands of small awards in cases of 'exceptional hardship'. It further facilitated the loading of pensions to allow a man to 'live and maintain his family without other employment', and it adjudicated on applications to commute a portion of a pension to emigrate, establish a business, purchase a farm or in some cases a house. The Irish Office also set up an accommodation bureau; local police commissioners were asked to provide any assistance they could, and the government secured a boarding house in London 'as an emergency measure' for families with children.[7] SILRA, founded in July 1922 for 'the relief of distress amongst the Southern Irish Loyalists' in Britain, operated

RIC members and onlookers gather around dumped uniforms, Dublin, 17 August 1922.

its own RIC Relief Committee and claimed to have 4,000 ex-RIC on its books by September (presumably both Irish and British-born).[8] Ex-RIC interest groups in Britain provided camaraderie through reunion dinners and dances throughout the 1920s.[9]

Ultimately, there was no uniform experience of life after disbandment. Ex-Sergeant Benjamin Stafford told locals that warned him to leave his home in Cavan that he hoped to be 'as good a Free State citizen as any they had', but a cold reception from many of his neighbours, a further threatening notice, and damaged property convinced him to leave permanently for County Down. In November 1926 ex-Constable Patrick Meara applied to the Irish Grants Committee for compensation but insisted that 'If this claim is to go to anything belonging to the Free State, I will forego it at once, as I do not want any wrangling or business of any sort with the Free State'. A colleague grumbled about his own treatment compared to other 'civil officers of the State', who remained in the Free State and 'lived in peace and quietness'.[10]

It is, however, the losses and grievances that are most often recorded. Those who did not suffer or put themselves forward as victims, living quiet and ordinary lives, remain harder to account for. Patrick Shea, son of a policeman in Clones, insisted that 'disbanded members of the Royal Irish Constabulary were not made to feel unwanted in the Irish Free State. I think we could have gone to live anywhere in the country without fear of molestation'.[11] But as one of many sets of 'losers' of the Irish revolution, the afterlives of the ex-RIC, their relatives and other loyalists—good, bad and indifferent—warrant further exploration.

by Brian Hughes

FURTHER READING

Kent Fedorowich, 'The problems of disbandment: the Royal Irish Constabulary and imperial migration, 1919–29', *Irish Historical Studies* 30 (117) (1996), 88–110

Seán William Gannon, *The Irish imperial service: policing Palestine and administering the empire* (Cham, 2019)

Mo Moulton, *Ireland and the Irish in interwar England* (Cambridge, 2014)

NOTES

[1] 'R.I.C. disbandment, Civic Guard to take over Dublin Castle', *The Irish Times*, 17 August 1922. The last remaining members were disbanded from Gormanston a few days later.
[2] Garda Museum and Archives, Dublin Metropolitan Police and Civic Guard (Garda Síochána) Personnel Registers, Civic Guard (Garda Síochána) temporary register, 1922–1924 (available at: https://doi.org/10.7925/drs1.ucdlib_53466, accessed 19 April 2021). In one other case a man had been discharged from the RIC as 'unsuitable' in January 1922, having joined in 1910.
[3] According to the available data, 2,348 of a sample of 6,354 Irish-born men disbanded from the force left Ireland, not including men who moved from the Irish Free State to Northern Ireland. I am grateful to Dr Gannon for sharing these figures, part of an ongoing research project.
[4] Brian Hughes, *Defying the IRA? Intimidation, coercion, and communities during the Irish revolution* (Liverpool, 2016), 192–200.
[5] The National Archives of the United Kingdom [hereafter TNA], Home Office, HO 144/22575, 'Ex-member of Royal Irish Constabulary ordered to leave area by Irish Republican Army'.
[6] *First interim report of the Irish Distress Committee* (London, 1922); *Irish Grants Committee second interim report* [Cmd. 2032], HC, 1924; *Hansard 5 (Commons)*, vol. 154, col. 2160 (31 May 1922).
[7] Brian Hughes, 'The disbanded Royal Irish Constabulary and forced migration, 1922–31', *Irish Studies Review* (2021), 212–28.
[8] Public Record Office of Northern Ireland, Irish Unionist Alliance papers, D989/B/1/3, minutes of meeting to found Southern Irish Loyalists Relief Association, 30 May 1922; 'The work of relief', *Belfast News-Letter*, 19 September 1922.
[9] See, for example, events in London, reported in *The Irish Times*, 26 April 1924, 3 June 1925 and in Sheffield, reported in the *Weekly Irish Times*, 26 November 1938; Mo Moulton, *Ireland and the Irish in interwar England* (Cambridge, 2014), 209.
[10] National Archives of Ireland, post-truce compensation claims, FIN/COMP/381/153(2), Benjamin Stafford; TNA, Colonial Office, Irish Grants Committee, CO 762/42/9, Patrick Meara.
[11] Patrick Shea, *Voices and the sound of drums: an Irish autobiography* (Galway, 1981), 91.

26 AUGUST 1922

THE KILLING OF SEÁN COLE AND ALF COLLEY

STATE TERROR

Dublin on Saturday, 26 August 1922 was a city in mourning. In City Hall thousands filed past the body of Michael Collins, killed just three days before. In Marino, to the north of the city centre, however, a group of young men had gathered to reorganise the anti-Treaty Fianna in the city. Twenty-one-year-old Alfred (Alf) Colley had brought along two revolvers for instruction purposes. After the meeting, Colley, a tinsmith, and his nineteen-year-old comrade Seán Cole, who had just completed his electrical apprenticeship, walked home to the inner city together. At Newcomen Bridge near North Strand they were stopped at a checkpoint operated by men wearing a mix of National Army uniforms and plainclothes.[1] After a search the revolvers were found and witnesses saw the two men bundled into a Ford car and driven off. Their bodies were left dumped at the Yellow Lane, near Whitehall. Witnesses, including a British soldier, had seen them struggling with the men before being shot.[2]

On the same day, another republican, Bernard Daly, a grocer's assistant, was also abducted, shot, and his dead body left in Malahide. The state forces denied any knowledge of these killings. Indeed, pro-Treaty sources suggested that the IRA had killed the men themselves. But suspicion began to fall upon a group of National Army Intelligence officers and members of the Criminal Investigation Department. Based at Wellington Barracks on the South Circular Road and Oriel House on Westland Row, these men were soon dubbed the 'Murder Gang' by republicans.

These were not the first cases of unarmed prisoners being killed by state forces. Harry Boland had been shot during his arrest in early August, while eighteen-year-old Joe Hudson was killed in a raid on his home on 10 August. In the month following the killings of Colley, Cole and Daly, four more IRA Volunteers died in dubious circumstances in Dublin. Two, Leo Murray and Rodney Murphy, were killed during a raid, but, it was alleged, after their surrender. In the cases of James Stephens and Michael Neville two weeks later, there was no suggestion of a gun battle. Stephens was taken from his lodgings in Gardiner Street and driven to the Naas Road, where he was shot and fatally wounded. Neville, a native of Clare, was picked up at the pub where he worked on Eden Quay and his body later found at a cemetery at Killester.

The killings established a pattern, discernible from over twenty deaths in the city during the war. Victims were abducted from their homes or workplaces and their bodies dumped in locations on the outskirts of the north or south side of the city. They sometimes bore the marks of ill-treatment. State forces denied any knowledge of the shootings and often sought to muddy the waters about the circumstances.

Controversial killings were not confined to Dublin. On 28 August Michael Danford, a Limerick IRA officer, was taken from his home by army officers and his body was found later on the Tipperary road. On the same day another Limerick IRA man, Harry Brazier, was shot dead by troops trying to arrest him at his workplace. In Cork on 8 September the body of Timothy Kenefick, an IRA member whose corpse bore signs of torture, was found. Witnesses described seeing troops arresting Kenefick earlier that day and the inquest returned a verdict of 'wilful murder'. A week later, another IRA prisoner, James Buckley, was shot after seven soldiers had been killed

"Father, Forgive them, for they know not
what they do."

Sean Cole, Alf. Colley
Boy Scouts of the FIANNA
Murdered Aug 26. 1922.

in a mine attack.[3] On 19 September Bertie Murphy, a labourer, was killed in custody in Killarney. Like Buckley, seventeen-year-old Murphy was shot in retaliation after two soldiers had died in an ambush. Some killings then, were unplanned and spur-of-the-moment reactions to the death of comrades. Those of Kenefick and Buckley, however, shared something in common with the deaths of Cole and Colley. The National Army commander in Cork, General Emmet Dalton, confirmed to Headquarters that members of Michael Collins's elite 'Squad' were responsible for them. Dalton made clear that he approved of their actions, but many of his men did not, and troops in Cork threatened to mutiny unless the Dubliners were withdrawn.[4]

The 'Murder Gang' was largely (though not entirely) composed of men who had been central to the IRA's campaign in Dublin prior to the truce. John Dorney has offered the best analysis of this group.[5] They were intensely loyal to Michael Collins and this, over any other factor, had guaranteed their support for the Treaty. After Collins's death they were overwhelmed with a desire for revenge, but also robbed of the one leader who could control them. They usually killed in retaliation for the loss of close comrades, and they had long memories. In June 1922 two army officers were killed in an ambush in Dublin. Over a year later anti-treatyite Noel Lemass was kidnapped, tortured and killed in revenge.

The group often displayed contempt for the fighting record of their enemies; their targeting of young republicans may have been influenced by this. While the majority of IRA Volunteers in Dublin, after the Easter Rising at least, never engaged in armed action again, the 'Squad' had been fulltime activists, constantly on the run and living on the edge. There is no doubt some of them were brutalised by the experience. Prior to the civil war many of the group had already gained a reputation for heavy drinking and erratic behaviour. But they were a vital factor in holding Dublin during the fighting in June 1922. Though republicans often pointed to the presence of former British servicemen in the state forces, the worst outrages against them were carried out by men with impeccable IRA records. The Squad's former commander, Paddy O'Daly, who had led from the front in the IRA's campaign in Dublin, was responsible for several brutal atrocities in Kerry. Though much of this violence was not formally authorised, it served a purpose for the state, augmenting the policy of official executions.

Those in government were certainly aware of the 'Murder Gang's' activities. Members of W.T. Cosgrave's personal escort arrested Bobby Bonfield at Stephen's Green in March 1923. Cosgrave was present when Bonfield, a UCD student, was taken away after a struggle. The IRA man's body was found at Clondalkin a few hours later.[6] (Bonfield was strongly suspected of involvement in the killing of pro-Treaty politician Seamus O'Dwyer in December 1922.) The Free State leader had himself suggested in February 1923 that, if in order to survive, the state has 'to exterminate 10,000 republicans then the 3 millions of our people are bigger than the ten thousand'.[7] So, while the civil war took place, those engaged in these activities faced little prospect of sanction. Indeed, the involvement of the Army's Director of Intelligence, Michael J. Costello, in the last such killing, of military policeman and IRA informant Joe Bergin in December 1923, was covered up.[8] There came a time when these activities were no longer tolerable, and many of the 'Murder Gang' would ultimately attempt to challenge the state themselves during the abortive 'Army Mutiny' of March 1924. Terror, official and unofficial, played an important role in the victory of the Irish Free State over its republican enemies.

by Brian Hanley

FURTHER READING

John Dorney, *The civil war in Dublin: the fight for the Irish capital 1922–1924* (Newbridge, 2017)

NOTES

[1] Military Archives (MA), Military Service Pensions Collection (MSPC), DP3749 Sean Cole.
[2] John Dorney, *The civil war in Dublin: the fight for the Irish capital 1922–1924* (Newbridge, 2017), 177–8.
[3] MA, MSPC, W19, Timothy Kenefick.
[4] Peter Hart, *The IRA and its enemies: violence and community in Cork, 1916–1923* (Oxford, 1998), 122.
[5] Dorney, *Civil war in Dublin*, 177–90.
[6] MA, MSPC, DP23999 Robert Bonfield.
[7] Diarmaid Ferriter, *A nation and not a rabble: the Irish revolution, 1913–1923* (London, 2015), 281.
[8] Dorney, *Civil war in Dublin*, 260.

SEPTEMBER

LOVE
OF
IRELAND

5 SEPTEMBER 1922

JOHN LAVERY PRESENTS HIS PAINTING, 'MICHAEL COLLINS, LOVE OF IRELAND' TO THE LONDON PRESS

PAINTING THE NATION-STATE

On 5 September 1922 John Lavery presented his painting, 'Michael Collins, Love of Ireland' (1922, Hugh Lane Gallery), to the press in his London home. His actions spoke volumes for his diplomatic aspirations and his hopes for the persuasive function of art. His friendship with Collins had been formed in the house where the painting was shown, and this personal connection to the subject added a poignant note to the work and to Lavery's ambition to provide a befitting imagery of the foundation of the new Irish state, sublimating its brutality and carnage into more refined representations of valour and stability.

Opposite: John Lavery, 'Michael Collins, Love of Ireland' (1922).

John Ruskin asserted that 'Great nations write their autobiographies in three manuscripts, the book of their deeds, the book of their words, and the book of their art'.[1] The book of the new Irish state's art opened on a promising page in January 1922 when a major exhibition of Irish visual and decorative art was shown in Paris as part of the World Congress of the Irish Race.[2] Just a few weeks prior to its launch, however, the minister for Fine

Arts, Count Plunkett, had resigned in protest at the Treaty, and the ministry was abolished. The second Dáil went on to eliminate drawing as a subject in national schools, a decision that had a detrimental impact on the future understanding of art and design in Ireland.

The painter, Jack B. Yeats spoke at the Race Congress on the relationship between the artist and the nation, declaring in uncharacteristically forthright terms that

> the roots of every art must be in the country of the artist, and no men can have two countries; and this applies with greater force to the artist than to anyone else, for the true painter must be part of the land and of the life he paints.[3]

While landscape and genre scenes dominated the painting section, some of the exhibits at Paris, such as John Lavery's 'Funeral of Terence MacSwiney, Mayor of Cork', referred to the impact of violence and militarism on Irish life. But they did so in a noble and elevating fashion. Yeats's 'Bachelor's Walk, In Memory' (1915, National Gallery of Ireland), exhibited for the first time since it was painted in 1915, depicts a graceful flower girl on the Dublin quays. Isolated from the other figures in the painting, she alone mourns those killed in the aftermath of the Howth gun running. The work empathises with the complex situation of the ordinary citizen in the face of civic disintegration. Yeats's ability to elevate commonplace scenes into epic moments of human history endeared his work to many.

Lavery's work, by contrast, takes a more elevated view, focusing on the great figures of Irish political and religious life and on moments of pomp and splendour. A consummate painter of British imperial pageantry, he put his skills to great effect in the grand baroque painting of the funeral of MacSwiney (and later of Collins). His 'Blessing of the Colours' (1921, Hugh Lane Gallery), a version of which was shown in Paris, depicts an archbishop standing on the altar of a cavernous church, identified as the Pro-Cathedral.[4] He is consecrating a tricolour, held by a kneeling soldier. The immense flowing form of the flag symbolises the new state, and the obsequious young man expresses the allegiance of its citizens to the state and to the Roman Catholic Church. The prominent inclusion of a deacon holding the prayer book adds to the hierarchical arrangement of symbols and figures and conveys order and stability.

A Belfast-born Catholic of modest origins, John Lavery had become an extremely successful portraitist in London. Knighted in 1918, he and his society hostess wife, Hazel, played an important role in facilitating informal interactions amongst the Treaty delegates over the course of the negotiations. As a result, Lavery was the artist most closely associated with the political establishment of the new state in the immediate aftermath of the Treaty. His portrait of Hazel as Kathleen ní Houlihan graced Irish Free State banknotes from 1927. In 1928, he had hoped to replace his friend, Timothy Healy, as Governor General.

Lavery painted 'Michael Collins, Love of Ireland' while Collins's body lay in the mortuary chapel in St Vincent's Hospital. He later recalled that

> Any grossness in his features, even the peculiar little dent near the point of his nose, had disappeared. He might have been Napoleon in marble as he lay in his uniform, covered by the Free State flag, with a crucifix on his breast. Four soldiers stood round the bier. The stillness was broken at long intervals by someone entering the chapel on tiptoe, kissing the brow, and then slipping to the door where I could hear a burst of suppressed grief. One woman kissed the dead lips, making it hard for me to continue my work.[5]

Collins is depicted as Commander-in-Chief of the Irish Free State army, in full uniform with the tricolour across his body and a crucifix placed prominently. The badly wounded head, shown bandaged in contemporary photographs of the body, appears untouched in Lavery's painting. The words 'Love of Ireland' are inscribed in the vacant space to the right of the figure. They confirm in plain terms Collins's patriotism, and, like the prominent symbols of state and religion, refute any notion of the man as a renegade. The solitary nature of the body recalls Christian iconography of the Passion. It is also akin to established representations of heroic deathbed scenes, such as the French academic painter, Horace Vernet's 'Napoleon on his Deathbed' (1825), in which the laurel-crowned Napoleon expires alone with a crucifix resting on his chest. One journalist proclaimed of Collins that 'the pallor of death adds nothing terrible. It seems only to bring out the spiritual aspects of the features'.[6]

The fact that 'Michael Collins, Love of Ireland' was formally exhibited for the first time at the Paris Salon in October 1922 heightened the international importance of its subject matter, reflecting Lavery's ambition to be perceived as a significant maker of contemporary history painting. He had arranged for the painting to be reproduced as a colour print by George

Pulman and Sons, part of his pretext for showing it to the press on 5 September.[7] This has been interpreted as a ploy to profit from Collins's now legendary status, but the reproduction of paintings in print form accords with a long-standing convention and was more likely motivated by a genuine desire to make the image accessible to a wider public.[8] (Many of Lavery's paintings of Irish affairs were reproduced in this way.) The picture could now be hung in private homes, perhaps becoming part of the pantheon of Irish martyrs. More significantly, the circulation of the image would facilitate a new official iconography of Irish nationalism, one that marked an allegiance to the new Irish state and the principles of personal sacrifice, military discipline and Roman Catholic faith on which it was founded. This differentiated it from earlier imagery of rebels and insurgents, as well as countermanding the negative representations of the Irish that dominated British visual culture.

Opposite: John Lavery's 'Blessing of the Colours' (1922) depicts the archbishop of Dublin blessing the tricolour.

Lavery intended that both 'Michael Collins, Love of Ireland' and 'Blessing of the Colours' would, along with his portraits of Irish leaders and events, become part of the collection of the National Gallery of Ireland. There, like the artworks in the recently established Imperial War Museum in London, the traumas and triumphs of contemporary history would be commemorated for future generations. The gallery did not accept work by living artists, so Lavery lent the paintings to the Dublin Municipal Gallery of Modern Art; in 1935 he bequeathed the paintings to that institution, in memory of Hazel Lavery. He also donated a separate collection of portraits and works of art to the Belfast Art Gallery, where they were housed in a special Lavery Room in 1929.

by Róisín Kennedy

FURTHER READING

Róisín Kennedy, 'Art and uncertainty: painting in Ireland 1912–1932', in Brendan Rooney (ed.), *Creating history: stories of Ireland in art* (Dublin, 2016), 154–71

Sinéad McCoole, *Passion and politics. Sir John Lavery: the salon revisited* (Dublin, 2010)

NOTES

[1] John Ruskin, *St Mark's rest. The history of Venice* (New York, 1877), v.

[2] Exposition d'art Irlandais, Galeries Barbazanges, Paris, 28 January to 25 February 1922.

[3] Jack B. Yeats, *Modern aspects of Irish art* (Dublin, 1922), 3, reprinted in Fintan Cullen and Róisín Kennedy (eds), *Sources in Irish art 2. A reader* (Cork, 2021).

[4] The version shown at Paris is now in the Crawford Art Gallery, Cork. William Shortall, Art and the Irish Free State—visualizing nationhood (1922–34). Unpublished Ph.D. thesis, Trinity College Dublin (2020), 2, 20.

[5] John Lavery, *The life of a painter* (London, 1940), 217.

[6] *Evening Echo*, 5 September 1922, 4.

[7] *Evening Echo*, 5 September 1922, 4.

[8] Anne Dolan, *Commemorating the Irish civil war: history and memory, 1923–2000* (Cambridge, 2003), 76.

12 SEPTEMBER 1922

THE DÁIL DEBATES UNEMPLOYMENT

A GAELIC ECONOMY?
FINANCING THE IRISH STATE

At a sitting of the third Dáil on 12 September 1922, as the government's handling of the civil war came under attack, long-time Sinn Féiner Darrell Figgis criticised President W.T. Cosgrave's refusal to provide an economic plan upon his election as president of the Executive Council and demanded he set an early date to discuss taxation policy. As the deputies continued to debate the economic direction of the new state, Minister for Agriculture Patrick Hogan, not particularly known as a Gaelic enthusiast or Sinn Féiner, said, 'I hope we are not going to slavishly copy England. I hope we have some Gaelic social and economic ideals'.[1] Hogan was echoing earlier musings of Michael Collins, who wrote, 'We want a modern edition of our old Gaelic Social polity—a thing that...grows naturally out of our own Irish character and requirements'.[2] When the government produced its first official budget in 1923, George Gavan Duffy told the Dáil, 'let it not be forgotten that we are laying the foundations of a new Irish fiscal system'.[3]

The belief that the Irish Free State would create a fiscal system that would be both post-colonial and Irish was widely held. These anticipated

economic changes were part of what revolutionaries called the 'Gaelic state'. Although efforts
to revive the Irish language and Irish literature
received the most pre-revolutionary attention,
the Gaelic state was also assumed to encompass
an Irish fiscal system and an Irish political system.

Opposite: 'At the crossroads', a front-page cartoon from the *Voice of Labour* (17 February 1923) advocating a workers' republic.

This Irish fiscal system was usually left undefined, but revolutionaries assumed that such a system would express an Irish way of doing things and right the perceived wrongs of the colonial era.

Taxation, colonialism and identity have always been intertwined in Ireland, and Sinn Féin certainly emphasised these connections in its revolutionary propaganda.[4] The party argued that Irish economic development had been deliberately sabotaged by the metropole through over-taxation, expensive Dublin Castle government, and dumping of British-manufactured goods.[5] Its supporters promised to reverse this underdevelopment by means of tariffs. Sinn Féiners were also eager to demonstrate that a post-colonial Irish state would be sufficiently successful to reverse perceptions of the Catholic Irish as incapable of self-government. While generally most Irish politicians of the era agreed that Ireland was over-taxed and underdeveloped, there was no consensus on the necessary remedies.

Once the Treaty was ratified, politicians began articulating the shape of their desired fiscal system. These views were built on different interpretations of what constituted Irishness and what colonial remnants needed most to be dismantled in order to promote an 'Irish' system. The resulting debates were therefore tied to larger questions of the nature and identity of the new state and its inhabitants. Cumann na nGaedheal, the governing party, saw Ireland as a small European nation like Denmark or Belgium: an agricultural exporter seeking wider markets. The government was also obsessed with attracting investment and balancing the budget, believing such fiscal prudence would refute colonial stereotypes of the Irish as irresponsible and ungovernable.[6] Introducing the Irish Free State's first annual budget, Cosgrave said:

> I think it is a matter of some satisfaction that we have passed
> through the troubled year just ended without serious embar-
> rassment. The anticipated deficit for the coming year is, no
> doubt, serious, but it is not such as to cause any misgiving as
> to the financial future of the Free State and the credit of the
> country.[7]

AT THE CROSS ROADS.

He proudly boasted during a 1927 election speech that the Free State had a better credit rating than Belgium, indicating that his government had reversed the Irish reputation for unruliness and joined the ranks of fiscally responsible small European nations.[8]

Opposition parties, unsurprisingly, held completely different views. The Labour party believed that an 'Irish' fiscal system would develop Irish industries and ease the plight of labourers while moving toward a workers' republic. To this end, Labour advocated policies that rewarded investment in Irish industries and purchases of Irish goods. Their proposals included tax penalties on investments outside of Ireland and stipulations that those receiving government salaries must purchase Irish-made goods. Labour leaders also recognised that the colonial period had restricted the Irish economy and prioritised the financial markets of the metropole, but wanted to use tax law and fiscal penalties, rather than patriotic volunteerism, to remedy this. Labour also wanted to reduce taxes on staples and everyday consumables, the remnants of a tax system that they felt disproportionately affected the working classes.

The Farmers' party took very different lessons away from the colonial period. The Farmers saw Ireland as an agrarian country whose gains through land purchase were threatened by high taxes, especially local rates, and uncompetitive labour costs. They wanted a post-colonial Ireland with low taxes and rates, a minimal central state and spending priorities that reflected Ireland's fundamentally agrarian nature, such as agricultural education and marketing. Their vision of an 'Irish' fiscal system was one of reversing the British legacies of over-taxation and centralised government.

Anti-Treaty Sinn Féin also articulated a different fiscal vision, although it took socialist-leaning politicians such as Seán Lemass and Constance Markievicz some time to convince republicans to focus on issues other than the Free State's imperial ties.[9] Anti-treatyites embraced Arthur Griffith's notion of developing Irish industry behind tariff walls. Like the Farmers, republicans envisioned a state substantially less centralised and less dependent on career officials. The anti-treatyites' interpretation of an 'Irish' tax code emphasised breaking remaining economic ties with Britain through tariffs and the withholding of land annuities. They also wanted to reward investment in, and purchases from, Irish industries. In fact, what became the Fianna Fáil vision for an Irish fiscal system was a combination of the Farmers' attack on expensive career officials, Labour's promotion of Irish industry and Griffith's arguments for tariffs.

These broad disagreements were revealed through specific clashes on issues that transcended mere budgetary questions. Sinn Féin dissenters like Figgis and Gavan Duffy attacked the government for its wholesale adoption of the British taxation and tariff system that protected industries not extant in Ireland. Instead, they promoted an 'Irish' taxation system that fostered particular Irish industries. The taxation of Irish citizens who had invested in London markets also stirred debate. The government proposed relief from double taxation on such investments, while Labour bitterly opposed what it considered unpatriotic and unproductive capital flight. Labour instead argued that wealth that was not used to promote Irish economic development should be taxed heavily, thus reversing what they saw as colonial dependence on metropolitan financial markets. Cumann na nGaedheal and the Farmers both sought a system that remedied over-taxation, but the Farmers saw local agrarian ratepayers as the hardest hit by the phenomenon, while Cumann na nGaedheal often designed its tax cuts to attract British wealth and investment. As Ernest Blythe said, 'if we could only induce one millionaire to come here to die, the [fiscal] advantages would be very great'.[10]

By the later 1920s the performance of the post-independence economy was at least as important as constitutional issues in electoral campaigns. The need to focus on economic matters was recognised as early as 1922, even given the initial attention directed toward dealing with various remnants of the imperial system. Each party drew fiscal lessons from aspects of revolutionary ideology and the perceived legacies of the colonial period. While the economic shortcomings of Cumann na nGaedheal are well-known, the initial debates over taxation demonstrate a shared desire to make the new state's fiscal system Irish, and an inability to agree on a definition of such a system.

by Jason Knirck

FURTHER READING

Mary E. Daly, *Industrial development and Irish national identity, 1922–1939* (Syracuse, 1992)

Ronan Fanning, *The Irish Department of Finance 1922–58* (Dublin, 1978)

Niamh Puirséil, *The Irish Labour Party, 1922–73* (Dublin, 2007)

NOTES

[1] *Dáil debates*, vol. 1, no. 3, 'Ceisteanna-Questions: Finance and taxation' (12 September 1922), 'An amendment' (12 September 1922); available at: https://www.oireachtas.ie/en/debates/ (accessed 20 April 2021).

[2] University College Dublin Archives, Richard Mulcahy papers, P7/B/28, notes by Collins, 'Change of situation and outlook', *c.* summer 1922.

[3] *Dáil debates*, vol. 3, no. 9, 'Finance Bill 1923, Second stage' (3 May 1923); available at: www.oireachtas.ie/en/debates/ (accessed 20 April 2021).

[4] See, generally, Douglas Kanter and Patrick Walsh (eds), *Taxation, politics, and protest in Ireland, 1662–2016* (London, 2019) and specifically the chapter by Charles Ivar McGrath, 'Politics, parliament, patriot opinion, and the Irish national debt in the age of Jonathan Swift', 43–87.

[5] A Sinn Féin leaflet claimed that Ireland's government took in three times more in taxes than it spent in Ireland, with the remainder filling Britain's coffers; see, Boston College Archives, Burns Library, Thomas Clarke collection, MS 2001–7 (Folder 2/13), Bond certificate campaign, 1919.

[6] The best account of these stereotypes is Michael de Nie, *The eternal Paddy: Irish identity and the British press, 1798–1882* (Madison, WI, 2004).

[7] *Dáil debates*, vol. 3, no. 2, 'Committee on Finance - Financial resolutions' (13 April 1923); available at: www.oireachtas.ie/en/debates/ (accessed 20 April 2021).

[8] *Irish Independent*, 8 June 1927.

[9] Republican Sinn Féin's embrace of a clearly defined economic policy as a way to power is analysed in a brilliant series of essays by Tim O'Neil. See, for example, Timothy M. O'Neil, 'Reframing the Republic: republican socioeconomic thought and the road to Fianna Fáil, 1923–26', in Mel Farrell, Jason Knirck and Ciara Meehan (eds), *A formative decade: Ireland in the 1920s* (Dublin, 2015), 157–76.

[10] *Dáil debates*, vol. 7, no. 1, 'Financial statement' (25 April 1924); available at: www.oireachtas.ie/en/debates/ (accessed 20 April 2021).

22 SEPTEMBER 1922

CLASS, SOCIAL REVOLUTION, AND REPUBLICANISM IN THE CIVIL WAR

On 22 September 1922, roughly three months into the Irish civil war, both the *Irish Independent* and the *Freeman's Journal* reprinted IRA correspondence recently smuggled out of Mountjoy jail.[1] They did so at the behest of the Provisional Government, which instructed its publicity department to circulate the intercepted material to the pro-Treaty press, accompanied by an official statement.[2] Only one of many targets in the nascent regime's propaganda campaign against the anti-Treaty cause, the so-called 'Notes from Mountjoy' or 'Jail Notes', acquired a historical and historiographical influence far beyond their limited impact during the 1922–3 conflict.

Their author was Liam Mellows (1892–1922), in Provisional Government custody since 30 June when the republican garrison in Dublin's Four Courts fell following two days of heavy fighting that started the civil war. Mellows had been an exceptionally energetic republican activist during the preceding decade, with a reputation as one of the more forward-thinking and (relatively) socially conscious IRA leaders. Pre-1916 he had been a key organiser for Na Fianna Éireann, the IRB and the Irish Volunteers, while during Easter Week he helped lead the mini-rising in Galway. After several years promoting Sinn Féin in the US, he returned home in 1920, taking a place on the IRA's HQ staff and representing County Galway in the Dáil. Mellows achieved national prominence for his principled arguments against the Treaty during Dáil debates and in public speeches that preceded the civil war.[3] Amidst the anti-Treaty camp's failing military and political fortunes throughout July and August, Ernie O'Malley—who was among a number of high-profile republicans growing dissatisfied with IRA Chief of Staff Liam Lynch's rigidly martial outlook—solicited Mellows's advice on policy ideas that might rescue the republican cause from irrelevance and defeat. Contacted in Mountjoy on 18 August, Mellows wrote up his suggestions in a series of notes, producing part one on 26 August and part two on 29 August, with a short postscript on 11 September. With two slightly different versions and several copies smuggled out, a set of the notes fell into the hands of Provisional Government authorities, leading to their subsequent release to the press.[4]

Mellows's 'Jail Notes' were shaped by discussions he held with fellow anti-Treaty prisoners, including northerner Joseph McKelvey, Corkman Richard Barrett, Donegal republican-socialist Peadar O'Donnell and several other republicans in the trade-union movement. The radical tenor of their musings was influenced by the *Workers' Republic*, the then Communist Party of Ireland newspaper run by Roderick Connolly, carrying on his late father's legacy.[5] The miniscule communist party had been virtually alone in southern Ireland in cheering on the country's slide towards civil war, based on the ideological logic that the conflict could break 'bourgeois' control over the independence movement and lead to a socially revolutionary situation in Ireland. It relentlessly advocated a radical policy turn for republicans, entailing a worker-run state with full control over banks, natural resources, public utilities and all private property, especially large land holdings.[6] In his messages back to O'Malley (and Austin Stack), Mellows approvingly quoted a summary of the Communist Party of Ireland programme from the 22 July issue of *Workers' Republic* (the same issue to which he contributed a piece chastising pro-Treaty labour for compromising with imperialism and capitalism and betraying James Connolly.)[7]

Much of Mellows's schematic 'Jail Notes' concerned propaganda. Its suggested themes included imperialism (the 'Irish Free State as a Colony'); the reality of the 'Republic' as manifested in Dáil Éireann's administrative activities and President de Valera's political 'miracles' abroad; the pro-Treaty Roman Catholic Church hierarchy's 'abandonment of principle';

and South Africa's object lessons for Ireland. He also devoted passing attention to India, communications, courts, by-elections and the Fianna. His most substantive ideas, however, dealt with republican political organisation and social policy; unusual priorities for a 'die-hard' on the military side of the movement. He stressed the urgent need for a 'Provisional Republican Government' ('even if it is unable to function') to provide a 'rallying centre' for supporters and to challenge the legitimacy of treatyite institutions. On social policy, he argued that since official labour had 'deserted the people for the flesh-pots of Empire', republicans must assume the vanguard with a radical industrial-economic programme tied to land redistribution. Although he endorsed 'something like' the *Workers' Republic* formulation mentioned above, he insisted that such a policy was not a departure for republicans, only a belated effort to translate the Dáil's 1919 Democratic Programme 'into something definite'. In his most memorable lines, Mellows dramatically articulated the historical stakes and class implications of the civil war for the anti-Treaty cause: 'We are back to [Theobald Wolfe] Tone—and it is just as well—relying on that great body, "the men of no property". The "stake in the country" people were never with the Republic'.[8]

In its statement introducing the 'Jail Notes' in the press, the Provisional Government predictably pounced on the 'avowedly' communistic inspiration behind Mellows's ideas. Its main critique, however, was that his was an opportunistic and disingenuous 'fall back…plan' for beleaguered republicans, a desperate gambit to 'bribe' (and fool) the landless and unemployed with 'plunder' 'from another section of the people'. Accused by Mellows of becoming 'Imperialist and respectable', the official labour movement was, unsurprisingly, ill-disposed to his notion that unemployment, starvation, and recent strikes might be advantageously 'utilized for the Republic'. It persevered in its balancing act of pushing for labour reforms inside the treatyite parliament, while freely criticising both sides in the split. Only the Communist Party of Ireland (CPI) and a few left-leaning republican commentators publicly hailed Mellows's policy ideas at the time.[9] Crucially, his appeal failed to gain traction inside the anti-Treaty movement, apart from the setting up of a notional Republican Government that had little impact or influence before the IRA abandoned its moribund campaign in May 1923.

When Lynch escalated the IRA's campaign by ordering assassinations to counter government executions, Mellows, along with McKelvey, Barrett and imprisoned Four Courts commander Rory O'Connor, became collateral victims. Immediately following an IRA attack that killed pro-Treaty TD Seán Hales (while wounding Pádraic Ó Máille), 'Rory, Liam, Dick and Joe' were selected for reprisal execution by the executive council of the newly christened Irish Free State and shot by firing squad on the morning of 8 December. Despite the mutual hostility between the Labour party and anti-treatyites, labour deputies Thomas Johnson and Cathal O'Shannon delivered blistering condemnations of the government's legally questionable action.[10]

In his religiously infused final letters, Mellows welcomed the 'greatest human honour' of joining Tone, Emmett, Pearse and Connolly in republican martyrdom.[11] He subsequently achieved legendary status within the anti-Treaty republican tradition, especially among iterations of left republicanism, from Republican Congress and Saor Éire in the 1930s, to the CPI and Official IRA in the 1960s and '70s, to republican-socialist factions that hold commemorations at his grave in Wexford to this day. Peadar O'Donnell extolled his friend as 'the richest mind our race had achieved for many a long day', while Mellows's biographer, British socialist activist and historian C.D. Greaves, concluded that with his republican fighting credentials, staunch anti-imperialism and dawning class-consciousness, Mellows was the worthiest successor to Connolly in the revolution.[12]

Later Marxist and revisionist historians have challenged Mellows hagiography by sharply questioning his alleged conversion from Pearsean idealism to Marxist materialism, the coherence of his class analysis, and the prospects for republican-led social revolution in 1922.[13] This debate tends to ignore some of the more perceptive insights in his 'Jail Notes', such as his suggestive references to respectability and status—as opposed to rigid class identities—as underlying factors in the Treaty split. Moreover, his assumptions about the salience of agrarian, labour and other social discontents in the civil war also proved prescient, as evidenced by the explosion of social unrest throughout 1922–3. Ultimately, the turmoil on the land proved too chaotic and diffuse to be harnessed for anti-Treaty political ends (while the wave of industrial strikes was connected to organised labour, from whom republicans had been violently estranged at least since the former's April 1922 'general strike' against 'militarism'.) At moments, however, such unrest blurred and overlapped with the IRA's insurgency, while it also exercised a powerful influence over treatyite perceptions of 'irregularism'.[14] One hundred years on, the famous 'Notes from Mountjoy' continue to inspire questions, debate and counter-factual speculations about Liam Mellows and the relationship between class, social revolution and republicanism in the Irish civil war.

by Gavin Foster

FURTHER READING

C.D. Greaves, *Liam Mellows and the Irish revolution* (London, 2004 edn)

Conor McNamara, *Liam Mellows, soldier of the Republic: selected writings, 1914–1922* (Newbridge, 2019)

Gavin Foster, *The Irish civil war and society: politics, class and conflict* (Basingstoke, 2015)

NOTES

[1] The date is often inaccurately given as 21 September, perhaps because that date appears in C.D. Greaves's influential 1971 study, *Liam Mellows and the Irish revolution* (London, 2004 edn), 375.

[2] National Archives of Ireland, Provisional Government Cabinet minutes, PG 10(a), 20 September 1922.

[3] 'Major General Liam Mellows', *Republican War Bulletin*, 23 December 1922. See, Marie Coleman and William Murphy, 'Mellows, William Joseph (Liam)', in James McGuire and James Quinn (eds), *Dictionary of Irish Biography* (Cambridge, 2009), 477–9. Greaves, *Liam Mellows, passim*.

[4] Greaves, *Liam Mellows*, 354–69. Michael Hopkinson, *Green against green: the Irish civil war* (Dublin, 2004), 186–8.

[5] Greaves, *Liam Mellows*, 362. Donal Ó Drisceoil, *Peadar O'Donnell* (Cork, 2001), 26–9.

[6] *Workers' Republic (WR)*, 'Lesson of the split', 29 January 1922; 'A forward move', 11 March 1922; 'No peace possible', 5 August 1922; 'Our policy in detail' series: 29 January and 4, 11, 18 and 25 February 1922.

[7] Greaves quotes the 22 July *WR* editorial in full: see, *Liam Mellows*, 358. Mellows's article, 'The Irish Republic is the people's republic', is reprinted in Conor McNamara, *Liam Mellows, soldier of the republic: selected writings, 1914–1922* (Newbridge, 2019), 133–6.

[8] 'A republican policy', *Irish Independent*, 22 September 1922, 7. 'Mr. Mellows' policy', *Freeman's Journal*, 22 September 1922, 1. A copy can also be consulted in Military Archives, lot 210(1/b), captured documents. The 'Notes' are partially republished in Greaves, *Liam Mellows*, 362–9, and fully in McNamara, *Liam Mellows, soldier of the Republic*, 136–49.

[9] 'Republican leaders adopt our programme', *Workers' Republic*, 30 September 1922; 'Liam Mellows' programme', *Fenian*, 2 October 1922.

[10] 'Keen debate' and 'Executed as reprisal', *Freeman's Journal*, 9 December 1922.

[11] Greaves, *Liam Mellows*, 386–8.

[12] For example, George Gilmore *et al.*, *The Irish Republican Congress* (1934; reprinted 1974 by Cork Workers' Club); and *Notes from Mountjoy Jail*, pamphlet published by the Irish Communist Group, n.d. [1960s?], National Library of Ireland, IR 3359 P38. Peadar O'Donnell, *The gates flew open* (London, 1932), 88. Greaves, *Liam Mellows*, 392–3.

[13] For example, Henry Patterson, *The politics of illusion: a political history of the IRA* (London, 1997), 25–8; Pat Walshe, *Irish republicanism and socialism: the politics of the republican movement 1905–1994* (Belfast, 1994), 22–3; Richard English, *Radicals and the republic: socialist republicanism in the Irish Free State, 1925–1937* (Oxford, 1994), 'Introduction'.

[14] Gavin Foster, *The Irish civil war and society: politics, class and conflict* (Basingstoke, 2015).

OCTOBER

7 OCTOBER 1922

THE KILLING OF TEENAGERS EAMONN HUGHES, BRENDAN HOLOHAN AND JOSEPH ROGERS

TRAUMA AND THE LEGACY OF VIOLENCE

In the early morning of 7 October 1922 a dairyman found the bodies of two 'respectably-dressed men' lying on the side of Monastery Road, Clondalkin; a third was nearby on quarry land. Eamonn Hughes and Brendan Holohan had been shot multiple times, then shot again after falling to the ground. On Joseph Rogers's body, a doctor counted sixteen wounds. These 'respectably-dressed men' were teenagers, sixteen and seventeen years old, identified by their families as studious, religious, hardworking; they were apprentices making their way in the world; they were coming men, the eldest with a cigarette holder in his pocket, a gold ring on his finger and a monogrammed watch on his wrist. After going out together to paste up anti-Treaty handbills, they were seen getting into a car with three National Army officers on Clonliffe Road. What happened between then and when the dairyman found them remains unclear.[1]

These deaths, days before the Special Powers Resolution came into force, and over a month before official executions began with the deaths of three more teenagers and a man of twenty-one, have a very particular civil-war context, but they are also part of a longer continuum of violence. Irishmen had been killing Irishmen in this way for well over two years, nearly three, by this point, and perhaps that may explain the assumptions that have been made about these deaths in October 1922. When the killings of Hughes, Holohan and Rogers are mentioned, Charles Dalton's responsibility is presumed more than proved. These deaths are taken as a type of unfortunate proof of the toll all he had seen and done since becoming a Volunteer at the age of fourteen had taken on him by 1922. Although two other army officers, Nicholas Tobin and Sean O'Connell, were with Dalton on Clonliffe Road, Dalton, the one-time GHQ intelligence officer and by then commandant in the new state's army, had the reputation to fit a very particular understanding of violence, one that rather neatly supposes that Hughes, Holohan and Rogers were victims of how one young man had been brutalised by his war.

This view of Dalton has been confirmed since the release of his military service pension application. While he was a patient in St Patrick's and Grangegorman hospitals between 1939 and 1943, doctors wrote that 'his impressions and hallucinations' all 'referred back to those earlier years'; that he was 'hearing voices which accuse him of murder'; that 'his own active part…preyed on his mind and conscience so that in the following years he has gradually lost his reason'. One old comrade, Frank Saurin, reminded the pension assessors that Dalton 'was a mere school-boy when he commenced his career as a "gun-man"', and that he had once found Dalton cowering from 'imaginary potential executioners' in his own home. The same file notes the time Dalton spent in different hospitals and the worry of his wife, with four young children, who sought assistance in 1940 for the medical treatment that she could not afford.

Dalton's file has become noteworthy because an old civil-war opponent, Seán Lemass, took the time when minister for supplies in wartime 1941 to pen a five-page, hand-written letter in support of Dalton's case, but even more so because his file provides medical evidence of 'postcombat stress and despair' amongst those who fought.[2] Because Dalton's application is not the only one, because there are others who describe what they endured as 'shell-shock' or 'neurasthenia', because more stumble it out as 'nerves went astray after' or 'cracked up as a consequence', assumptions have been made—extrapolating from the experience of some to the many—that 'one of the major themes of the aftermath of the revolution is...trauma'.[3] Such a conclusion is not, however, without its challenges and its consequences.

Having reviewed the psychiatric files of 450 German veterans of the Second World War, Svenja Goltermann argues that 'the concept of "trauma" is a problematic tool for historians', and she even refuses to use it 'on the grounds of anachronism'. Goltermann's reservations reflect the contested nature of trauma and post-traumatic stress disorder within the fields of psychology and psychiatry certainly, but also her unwillingness to pronounce beyond her capacity as a historian.[4] Psychiatrists would hesitate to diagnose trauma without direct clinical examination of their patients, so should historians be so quick to pathologise? Joanna Bourke has argued that 'the cultural history of warfare' has become 'obsessed with trauma', despite 'the fact that most men coped remarkably well with the demands being made upon them in wartime'. Nigel Hunt has gone further, suggesting that 'we have now almost reached the stage where we expect people to break down after a traumatic event, and there is something wrong if they do not'; that silence is read too straightforwardly as anguish. For Yuval Harari, the 'soldier-as-victim' of 'the psychological damage' of war is now so ubiquitous as to be 'clichéd'.[5] Dalton is one very specific case, with very clear clinical evidence, but his pension application speaks eloquently of no one else's distress but his own.

Crucially, distress was not his only response. He left hospital; he went home; he wrote newspaper articles about his war; he finished his Bureau of Military History statement in 1950 cherishing the 'very strong spirit of comradeship' that survived long beyond 1922.[6] His relationship with his own past was neither static nor clear. Given that what was intended to be private has been made public in the release of his and other pension applications, it begs questions about what historians can assume to write about another's torment in the past. But the ethical challenges are broader than that. C.F. Alford argues that trauma 'helps us see the world through the victim's eyes', and Dalton comes from the pages of his application as a victim of what happened to him, of what he was made do; barely even an actor in his own wars.[7] It is a concern that troubles some historians of violence who, in response to the expansion of victimhood to include war's perpetrators, urge 'differentiation between the experiences of perpetrators, victims, and bystanders, as both an ethical and historical imperative'.[8] Unfortunately, perpetrators and victims are not always as easy to disentangle as that.

Application for (Gratuity) Relief.

Under Army Pensions Act 1932. (See A. P. 52.)
Made on behalf of the Parents of Sergeant Eamonn P.
Hughes (deceased) late of 'K' Coy. Batt. II Dublin Brigade
I.R.A.   Statement by G. W. Hughes (brother of deceased)

On the night of 6th October 1922 Sergeant Eamonn Hughes
(along with Volunteers Brendan Holohan and Joseph Rogers) left
his home at 107 Clonliffe Road Drumcondra Dublin. The next
morning he was found shot to death near the 'Red Cow' Clondalkin

Subsequently after a five days inquest inquiry the Jury returned
a verdict of wilful murder against persons unknown.

Extensive details of case were published in Press.

No previous claim has been made by any member of family under the
Army Pensions Acts 1923-7. The grounds on which this application
is made is based on the manner of deceased death and its effects
on the lives of his parents. The parents always facilitated their
sons aspirations and activities in spite of danger and home
disturbance. They are now both broken down completely physically and mentally and unable to support themselves.

Mrs A. J. Hughes (Mother of deceased) who is a qualified music
teacher had over thirty pupils which was reduced to a few two years after
the tragedy and finally her frequent mental collapse caused her to
abandon her profession altogether, later Rheumatic Arthritis set in and
now only special medical attention and other advantages which are not
available might effect recovery. Her local medical attendant has been
Dr. McKee of Dalymount Phibsborough. She has not been able to go
outside house for past three years. Her mental condition is variable.

Mr. Mark J. Hughes (Father of deceased) aged 61 years also had a
complete breakdown physically about two years after the tragedy and
had to give up his position as clerk in Ministry of Industry and Commerce
since August 1924 and has been attended by Dr. MacCarthy of Earl Street
for Valvular disease of the heart.

Indeed, Dalton captures the challenge of this. While he strikes a sympathetic figure in his own application, so too do the parents of Eamonn Hughes when an application was made on their behalf for a dependents' allowance. Described as 'both broken down completely physically and mentally', Mark Hughes was the clerk who could no longer work, Annie Hughes the music teacher who could no longer teach, because their teenage son had been killed, possibly by Charles Dalton, on 7 October 1922. In 1933 the Pension Board was requested not to even send letters about the application to their home, because 'mention of his name to them would serve no good purpose'; over a decade after they still could not bear reference to the circumstance of their son's death.[9]

Opposite: Extract from a statement by Gerald Hughes applying for a dependents' allowance for his parents in respect of his dead brother Eamonn Hughes, 6 April 1933.

If trauma is to be a means to consider the long-term consequences of violence, is it an agile enough concept to accommodate Eamonn Hughes's parents alongside Dalton? Given what can now be known from the sources, historians incur responsibilities 'when resurrecting the pain and suffering of people in the past'.[10] In light of what remains unknown, Dalton and the Hughes should be left to speak for no one but themselves.

by Anne Dolan

FURTHER READING

Melania Terrazas Gallego (ed.), *Trauma and identity in contemporary Irish culture* (Berlin, 2020)

C.F. Alford, *Trauma, culture and PTSD* (New York, 2016)

Efrat Ben-Ze'ev, Ruth Ginio and Jay Winter (eds), *Shadows of war: a social history of silence in the twentieth century* (Cambridge, 2010)

NOTES

[1] *Irish Independent*, 9 October 1922, 5; *Irish Independent*, 14 October 1922, 5, 8; *Sligo Champion*, 14 October 1922, 8; *Evening Herald*, 18 October 1922, 1; *Freeman's Journal*, 19 October 1922, 5, 8. Eamonn Hughes is also recorded as Edwin Hughes.

[2] Military Archives (MA), Military Service Pensions Collection (MSPC), 24SP1153 Charles Dalton; Eunan O'Halpin, *Irish Times*, 15 February 2016, 11.

[3] MA, MSPC, 34A6 Ernest O'Malley; MA, MSPC, MSP34REF2396 John O'Donnell; Diarmaid Ferriter, quoted in *Irish Independent*, 16 December 2018.

[4] Svenja Goltermann, 'On silence, madness, and lassitude: negotiating the past in post-war West Germany', in Efrat Ben-Ze'ev, Ruth Ginio and Jay Winter (eds), *Shadows of war: a social history of silence in the twentieth century* (Cambridge, 2010), 91–112: 93–4.

[5] Joanne Bourke, 'Effeminacy, ethnicity and the end of trauma: the sufferings of "shell-shocked" men in Great Britain and Ireland, 1914–39', *Journal of Contemporary History*, 35 (1) (January 2000), 57–69: 57; Nigel C. Hunt, *Memory, war and trauma* (Cambridge, 2010), 123; Yuval Harari, 'Martial illusions', *Journal of Military History*, 69 (1) (January 2005), 43–72: 47.

[6] MA, MSPC, 24SP1153 Charles Dalton; *Sunday Independent*, 25 August 1946, 3; MA, Bureau of Military History, witness statement 434, Charles Dalton.

[7] C.F. Alford, *Trauma, culture and PTSD* (New York, 2016), 23.

[8] Howard G. Brown, *Mass violence and the self: from the French wars of religion to the Paris Commune* (Ithaca, 2018), 16.

[9] MA, MSPC, DP4559 Eamonn Patrick Hughes.

[10] Stuart Carroll, 'Introduction', in Stuart Carroll (ed.), *Cultures of violence: interpersonal violence in historical perspective* (Basingstoke, 2007), 1–43: 38.

10 OCTOBER 1922

THE BISHOPS CONDEMN THE REPUBLICAN CAMPAIGN

WEAPONISING THE SACRAMENTS: THE ROMAN CATHOLIC CHURCH AND CIVIL WAR

On 10 October 1922 the Irish Roman Catholic hierarchy issued a pastoral letter that strongly condemned the anti-Treaty republican side in the Irish civil war and upheld the Anglo-Irish Treaty of 1921. Abjuration of violence, obeisance to the legally constituted government, condemnation of partition, advocacy of majority rule, and support for order and social stability characterised the political stance of the hierarchy between 1918 and 1923. The bishops' influence on public opinion during the turbulent Irish revolution should not be overstated, however. Powerful denunciations of violence, whether perpetrated by republicans or the British government, went unheeded during the War of Independence and did not halt killing, destruction of property or dislocation of law and order. While this also pertained during the civil war, the situation differed in one vital respect: for the first time, the Catholic hierarchy was 'sustaining' and reinforcing the authority of an *Irish* state.[1]

Predictably, the bishops welcomed the Treaty and favoured its ratification. On 13 December 1921 the hierarchy issued a careful statement that praised the 'patriotism' and 'honesty of purpose' of the Irish negotiating team and expressed the hope that when Dáil Éireann began its deliberations (the following day) its members would 'have before their minds the best interests of the country'.[2] As opposition to the settlement intensified during increasingly bitter parliamentary debates, Cardinal Michael Logue, archbishop of Armagh and primate of All Ireland, and his brother prelates exerted political and moral pressure on TDs to uphold majority opinion and support the Treaty. For example, Archbishop Edward Byrne of Dublin tried, unsuccessfully, to persuade Éamon de Valera to accept the agreement. On New Year's Day 1922 Logue declared that the settlement gave everything necessary for the progress of the country and prayed that God would preserve Irish people from 'the disaster that rejection of the Treaty would bring'.[3]

Although the Treaty was ratified by the Dáil on 7 January 1922, the deteriorating political and military situation alarmed the hierarchy. Acutely conscious of the political opportunities at stake, many bishops used their February Lenten pastorals to bolster support for the Treaty. For Archbishop John Harty of Cashel, the benefits of the Treaty far overweighed its limitations, none more so than 'England's renunciation of its claim to govern Ireland'. Likewise, Archbishop Byrne emphasised that the 'unintelligent rule of men alien to us in blood and traditions' would be replaced by one with 'knowledge of our people's needs' and 'a real interest in solving the many problems that concern our people's well-being.' Archbishop Gilmartin of Tuam prayed for deliverance from the curse of disunion, a theme put more forcefully by Bishop Michael Fogarty of Killaloe: 'Ireland is now the sovereign mistress of her own life. The rusty chains of bondage are scrapped for ever—unless, indeed, by our own folly we put them on again.'[4]

With only a few exceptions, the most experienced elements of the pre-truce IRA opposed the Treaty as a subversion of the Republic. This position crystallised in late March 1922 at the General Army Convention, which effectively revoked the authority of Dáil Éireann by electing a sixteen-member army executive. On 14 April anti-Treaty forces seized the Four Courts and other buildings. Anguished at the increasing lawlessness and looming threat of a military coup or civil war, the hierarchy's standing committee issued an uncompromising statement on 26 April. While supporting the Treaty, the bishops recognised that it was a political question to be settled by the national will at the forthcoming general election. That any part of the army had the moral right to declare itself independent of all civil authority was, the bishops maintained, 'a claim to military despotism and subversive of all civil liberty. It is an immoral usurpation and confiscation of the people's rights.'[5] Supreme national authority resided only in the Dáil and the Provisional Government. Although his name was appended to the statement, Archbishop Byrne was absent from the meeting. Together with the lord mayor of Dublin he had attempted, in vain, to bring pro- and anti-Treaty sides together in conference at the Mansion House in April.

Fearing anarchy, the hierarchy unequivocally upheld the authority of the Provisional Government on the outbreak of civil war and was committed to the survival of the Treaty settlement. Throughout the summer individual bishops repeatedly decried violations of moral law. In September a draconian emergency powers resolution was introduced, under which military courts were empowered to impose the death penalty for a range of offences. Before this came into operation in mid-October, the government offered republicans an amnesty and deployed the moral authority of the hierarchy. A trenchant, partisan and hastily written pastoral, dated 10 October, was published in the press the following day to coincide with the amnesty offer.

The pastoral had four objectives and strongly echoed the hierarchy's April statement. The first was to strip the republican campaign, which attacked its own country 'as if she were a foreign Power', of any legitimacy. This argument was reinforced by the electorate's overwhelming endorsement of the Treaty in June. What republicans called a war was 'only a system of murder and assassination of the National forces', destruction of property, criminality and the 'demoralization of the young whose minds are being poisoned by false principles'.[6] The pastoral's use of terminology like 'irregular' mirrored government anti-Treaty propaganda. The second goal, repeated throughout the letter, was an appeal for civic obedience to government authority, because 'no one is justified in rebelling against the legitimate Government... set up by the nation and acting within its rights'.[7] The third aim was to deny those engaged in unlawful rebellion, who nevertheless claimed to be good Catholics, absolution in confession or admission to Holy Communion. To republicans this was tantamount to weaponising the sacraments. Furthermore, priests sympathetic to the anti-Treaty position were warned against being 'false to their sacred office' on pain of suspension. Republicans were outraged and de Valera protested to the Vatican at the end of October. He denounced the hierarchy's attempt to use religious sanctions to enforce a political standpoint on a constitutional matter. Lastly, the bishops enjoined

republicans to pursue grievances through constitutional
action and to avail of the amnesty. Those conflicted by
an oath to the Republic were counselled that 'no oath
can bind any man to carry on a warfare against his own
country in circumstances forbidden by the law of God'.[8]

It is difficult to assess the effectiveness of the bishops'
intervention. For many it simply went unheeded. As Patrick Murray suggests, it may have emboldened the government and clergy to take a sterner
stance against republicans.[9] Privately, some bishops were alarmed at the
executions in November and December 1922. Patrick O'Donnell, coadjutor
archbishop of Armagh, appealed unsuccessfully for clemency for Erskine

W.T. Cosgrave
with archbishops
John Harty and
Edward Byrne,
Blackrock
College, 1929.

Childers. In a letter to W.T. Cosgrave, Archbishop Byrne deemed the policy of reprisal executions on 7 December 'not only unwise but entirely unjustifiable from the moral point of view. That one man should be punished for another's crime seems to me to be absolutely unjust'.[10] However dismayed the bishops were in private at the excesses of the Irish government or the National Army during the civil war, no public condemnation was issued. In this there was an element of pragmatic self-interest. The creation of Northern Ireland under a unionist government inimical to Catholic interests filled the bishops with foreboding. That increased their determination to secure the Irish Free State and the opportunities that it promised, not least for the Church.

by Daithí Ó Corráin

FURTHER READING

Patrick Murray, *Oracles of God: the Roman Catholic Church and Irish politics, 1922–37* (Dublin, 2000)

John Privilege, *Michael Logue and the Catholic Church in Ireland, 1879–1925* (Manchester, 2009)

NOTES

[1] See, Patrick Murray's authoritative, *Oracles of God: the Roman Catholic Church and Irish politics, 1922–37* (Dublin, 2000), 34.
[2] *Irish Catholic Directory* 1923, 538.
[3] *Irish Catholic Directory* 1923, 543.
[4] *Irish Catholic Directory* 1923, 551–3.
[5] *Irish Catholic Directory* 1923, 598–600.
[6] *Freeman's Journal*, 11 October 1922.
[7] *Freeman's Journal*, 11 October 1922.
[8] *Freeman's Journal*, 11 October 1922.
[9] Murray, *Oracles*, 77.
[10] Dublin Diocesan Archives, Byrne MSS 466, office of the president of the Executive Council, 1922, draft Byrne to Cosgrave, 10 December 1922, cited in Michael Laffan, *Judging W.T. Cosgrave* (Dublin, 2014), 122.

23 OCTOBER 1922

THE BURNING OF TULLAMAINE CASTLE

EVERYDAY VIOLENCE IN THE IRISH CIVIL WAR

'Another Tipperary castle destroyed', reported the *Nenagh Guardian* on 23 October 1922, detailing the burning, during the previous week, of Tullamaine Castle, near Fethard, County Tipperary. In what was becoming a familiar military strategy—razing former or potential barracks as National Army troops advanced—the castle had been occupied by a 'large force of Irregulars' (anti-Treaty republicans engaged in guerrilla warfare with the nascent Irish Free State). The subsequent damage, estimated at £60,000, to one of the county's 'finest private mansions' (*Nenagh Guardian*) did not, however, garner much further attention from the local press.[1] The historic and political significance of the anti-Treaty IRA's campaign against these former seats of British loyalist and Protestant power was not lost on contemporaries, and has been much interpreted since, in culture and academia. Yet, from the burning of small hayricks to fiery spectacles on huge demesnes, arson—alongside other acts of 'everyday' violence and intimidation (assault, boycotting, animal maiming, circulation of threatening notices)—had become commonplace in Ireland during 1922, serving two key functions in the war over the independence settlement with Britain: community regulation and land redistribution.

With its 'long hall' and 'battlemented screen wall with turrets',[2] Tullamaine Castle, constructed in its current style in 1835–8, on the site of a Norman structure, had in common with other 'big houses' in rural Ireland its size and striking appearance. Typically these residences—built in the Georgian era and evoking Palladian elegance—had asserted an 'imperial domestication of a wild Irish countryside'.[3] Their destruction, by fire, thus represented the undoing of the English Plantation: smouldering mansions and blackened shells of former settler-privilege are strong motifs of Irish and postcolonial fiction.[4] (Unlike other 'big houses' in the county, Rapla House and Graguenoe Park, which were abandoned following their burning,[5] Tullamaine was repaired and resold many times in the decades that followed. A 1982 *Irish Times* advertisement offered the estate at the 'bargain price' of £300,000, noting that substantial spending on modernisation had rendered Tullamaine 'one of the most liveable castle[s] in Ireland'.)

The intensification of 'big-house' burning during the civil war, as compared to the earlier War of Independence, poses interesting questions about the motivations of the warring sides. In Tipperary, a hotbed of 'everyday' violence, four 'big houses' were burned during January 1920–July 1921, compared to twenty-nine during January 1922–April 1923.[6] In common with many mansion dwellers—and the already dwindling landlord class—who had fled Ireland earlier in the revolution, Major Edward Clement Morel, Master of the Foxhounds, had departed Tullamaine in summer 1921. Perhaps the October 1922 burning of the lavish hunting lodge can be seen, then, as a final routing of English culture; foxhunting had been identified since the late nineteenth-century land wars as the 'embodiment of landlordism'— and hunts historically were disrupted by protesters (although, Tipperary's apparently ran 'most successfully' on Morel's estate 'for two years').[7] Morel's British military credentials, and an earlier War of Independence encounter at Tullamaine, also may have marked out Edward for a future act of revenge; scholars of civil war around the globe observe that the opportunity to act on old vendettas is often realised by, and against, civilians during intra-state conflict. In January 1921 a flying column of the Third Tipperary Brigade made a hasty escape from the castle when the armed men realised that Mrs Morel, while apparently preparing the meal demanded by them of 'the lady of the house', had 'sent a messenger to Fethard for the [British] military'.[8]

It is likely that various personal and political grudges, as well as local military considerations, intersected in the burning of Tullamaine; we see the complexities of civil-war violence not only in large-scale attacks on seemingly obvious symbols of former British rule, but also in the burning of more modest properties. On 15 October 1922, a week before the fire at Tullamaine, and around eight miles north of the castle, Hugh O'Brien's hay barn, in Ballincurry, Thurles, was destroyed by fire. O'Brien's loss, the basis of a compensation claim to a British government committee, fit a wider pattern; accounting for 28% of arson attacks in Tipperary, crops and outhouses were the most common category of property burned in the county during the civil war. Yet, perhaps to bolster his chances of financial remuneration, O'Brien explains the episode not in terms of the land hunger driving violence across the county but rather his political allegiances, stating himself to have been 'very friendly with the RIC [the Royal Irish Constabulary] and the army'. Information O'Brien supplied to the authorities had allegedly 'saved a party of soldiers' from an IRA ambush and 'before the hay was burned we got a letter threatening to drive us out after the British'.[9]

Violence profoundly shaped individual lives, causing physical injury, financial hardship and forced relocation. By analysing collectively the thousands of acts of intimidation, arson and other forms of harm that took place in Ireland in 1922–23, we understand also the ideological and strategic functions of violence against civilians during the civil war. Republicans protested the Treaty's maintenance of a link with Britain by punishing the Protestant minority and driving out former 'loyalists' of all denominations. While the building most commonly burned during the civil war was the small- to medium-sized house (accounting for 16% of all arson attacks in Tipperary), 'big houses' like Tullamaine Castle were disproportionately targeted during the conflict (accounting for 15% of all burnings). Looking at Tipperary in a wider context (with Munster neighbours Limerick and Waterford), 25% of buildings burned were 'big houses' and 19% of arson attacks were attributable to the claimant's 'allegiance to the United Kingdom'.[10] Yet, as the burning of O'Brien's barn also shows, politicised violence over land had clearly not ended with the land war and subsequent empowerment of tenants via British and Irish Free State land-purchase legislation. Revolutionary social agendas that did not necessarily align with anti-Treaty or anti-British feelings also persisted in independent Ireland, as republican and rural agitators intimidated farmers and graziers to enact land redistribution. These myriad local conflicts over political loyalties, religious and cultural identities, land and economic resources typified the disorder of 1922 in many areas—with violence continuing up to and beyond the end of the civil war in May 1923.

by Gemma Clark

FURTHER READING

Gemma Clark, 'Violence in the Irish civil war', in John Crowley, Donal Ó Drisceoil and Mike Murphy (eds), *Atlas of the Irish revolution* (Cork, 2017), 732–5

James S. Donnelly Jr., 'Big house burnings in County Cork during the Irish revolution, 1920–21', *Éire-Ireland* 47 (3 and 4) (Fall/Winter 2012), 141–97

Stathis N. Kalyvas, *The logic of violence in civil war* (Cambridge, 2006)

NOTES

[1] *Waterford News and Star*, 27 October 1922.
[2] Mark Bence-Jones, *Burke's guide to country houses* (3 vols; Burke's Peerage, 1978), vol. i: *Ireland*, 277.
[3] Vera Kreilkamp, 'Fiction and empire: the Irish novel', in Kevin Kenny (ed.), *Ireland and the British empire* (Oxford, 2004), 154–81: 175.
[4] Gemma Clark, *Everyday violence in the Irish civil war* (Cambridge, 2014), 54, 73–4.
[5] Clark, *Everyday violence*, 76–7, 81.
[6] Terence Dooley, *The decline of the big house in Ireland: a study of Irish landed families, 1860–1960* (Dublin, 2001), 286–7.
[7] *Irish Independent*, 7 January 1921; Neal Garnham, 'Fox hunting', in Sean J. Connolly (ed.), *The Oxford companion to Irish history* (Oxford, 2002), 214–5.
[8] Bureau of Military History, witness statement 1647, John J. O'Brien, 25.
[9] The National Archives of the United Kingdom, Records of the Colonial Office (CO), Records of the Irish Office, Irish Grants Committee, files and minutes, CO 762/19/10, O'Brien, Tipperary.
[10] Clark, *Everyday violence*, 89.

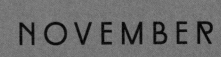

NOVEMBER

4 NOVEMBER 1922

MARY MacSWINEY'S HUNGER STRIKE

THE SANCTITY OF OATHS

The imprisonment and three-week hunger strike of Mary MacSwiney, which began in Dublin on 4 November 1922, generated national and international controversy. The episode illuminated key themes relating to the civil war, including the political divide prompted by the Anglo-Irish Treaty, the strategies and rhetoric adopted by both sides, gender, religion, emotion, and the internationalising of the Irish question. Revisiting the MacSwiney hunger strike of 1922 offers an opportunity to examine the extent of distortion, caricature and the fashioning of contentious and partisan narratives arising from that most controversial of years.

Opposite: Mary MacSwiney, Sinn Féin TD for Cork Borough, was a vehement opponent of the Anglo-Irish Treaty.

MacSwiney, who first came to prominence as a suffragette, was elected to the Dáil for Cork city as well as being a member of Cumann na mBan's national executive. She was one of six female Sinn Féin TDs in the Dáil in 1921, all of whom voted against the Treaty. A teacher, experienced public orator and eminently quotable debater, she spoke for two hours and forty minutes during the Treaty debate; the longest contribution of anyone.

Alongside her harsh words for supporters of the Treaty on account of their 'gross betrayal' of the Republic, another weapon in her armoury was the ghost of her brother Terence, who had died in Brixton prison in 1920 after a 74-day hunger strike. She was the keeper of his flame and her name carried weight because of that as she embarked on an extensive seven-month tour of the US in 1921, incorporating 58 cities and over 300 meetings.

Her resort to her own hunger strike in Mountjoy Prison in November 1922 brought her further prominence and notoriety. For supporters, her protest underlined her purist republican credentials, marking the continuation of her brother's sacrifice; for her detractors—her hysteria and incorrigibility.

It was often through these lenses that the women on the anti-Treaty side of the civil war were viewed, but MacSwiney was much more than the prolongation of her brother's spirit, and her career to that point had revealed much about women's extensive political range during the revolutionary period. What is striking about 1922, however, is the extent to which its convulsions facilitated a strident simplification of complex figures.

Part of this had to do with MacSwiney's reliance on sacred rhetoric. There is little doubt she equated her republicanism with a spiritual quest, and she framed her beliefs in that context. This has been negatively described by Tom Garvin as amounting to 'aggression, hysterical energy and rage', or by Michael Laffan as 'lengthy diatribes' fixated on dead martyrs.[1] These late twentieth-century views continued a long tradition of stripping women of reason, notably by contemporaries such as P.S. O'Hegarty who, in his 1924 book *The victory of Sinn Féin*, referred to such women as 'the Furies' and suggested they 'were largely responsible for the bitterness and the ferocity of the civil war'.[2]

Politics or ideology as faith in 1922, it seems, came to be something to be despised and even mocked, but that is a poor historical reading of the mindset of that generation and their declarations, vulnerabilities, pieties, arrogance and aspirations as explored, for example, in Roy Foster's *Vivid faces: the revolutionary generation in Ireland 1890–1923* (2014). Their zealousness needs to be seen in its broader European context; a product of that 'generation of 1914' who could be almost messianic in their rejection of the established order and very moved by images of martyrdom.

MacSwiney was adamant in April 1922 in writing to Joseph McGarrity that 'one thing is certain: the Army of the Republic will not tolerate the subversion of the Republic'.[3] This has been directly translated as an assertion that 'the soldiers would not allow civilians to decide Ireland's future' and that therefore the civil war was 'between those who believed that the morally

superior should rule regardless of majority preferences, and others who believed in majority rule'.[4] But the divisions of 1922 were not necessarily as clear-cut as that. Ascribing a monopoly of democratic virtue to one side

(From second-left) Maud Gonne MacBride, Mary MacSwiney and Charlotte Despard protest outside Mountjoy jail, *c.* 1922.

is unconvincing, given the failure of both sides to find a workable compromise, and what MacSwiney referred to as the 'sanctity of oaths' should not be dismissed as unreasonable given the sacrifices and atmosphere of that era, and the extent of the reservoir of support for MacSwiney's stance.

While anti-treatyites indulged in their share of recklessness, to suggest as Ernest Blythe did in June 1922 that there was only 'one logical and defensible line' in Irish politics at that point, and that was 'full acceptance of the Treaty', was disingenuous.[5] True, de Valera became increasingly exasperated with MacSwiney in September 1922, telling her

> I have done my utmost to be angry with you, but it is impossible—you are incorrigible! As long as you keep on the plane of Faith and Unreason…no one can ever possibly weaken you. …Unfortunately for me, Reason rather than Faith has been my master.

He was also firm in subsequently telling her there was a 'difference between desiring a thing and having a feasible programme for securing It'.[6] Yet he clearly admired her consistency, something he was struggling to emulate, and if there was one thing MacSwiney was, it was consistent.

That stubbornness became a stick with which to beat her, but this was also because of her capacity to exercise considerable influence and generate embarrassment by directly challenging the new state and the Roman Catholic Church as well as by raising the international profile of the Treaty divide in 1922. MacSwiney chastised the Catholic archbishop of Dublin, Dr Edward Byrne, for 'supporting one political side against another', which was clearly true. Byrne preferred to focus on her perceived breaking of divine law by embarking on a hunger strike: 'all who participate in such crimes are guilty of the gravest sins and may not be absolved nor admitted to Holy Communion'.[7] But that contradicted the support Catholic bishops had shown for her brother Terence in 1920, when they had publicly condemned his treatment. Privately, Archbishop Byrne pleaded with Cosgrave to ensure Mary did not die, pointing out that she had not been tried or convicted of any offence.

MacSwiney also had the capacity to complicate the government's efforts when it came to pro-Treaty diplomacy in the US, as her hunger strike seemed to reinvigorate the anti-Treaty side there. Joseph Connolly, the Consul General of Ireland in the US, believed that prior to her hunger strike the political activities of the Irish Americans were 'dying quickly', but with the MacSwiney affair there was 'an old time revival of interest in the AARIR [American Association for Recognition of the Irish Republic]', and that to allow her 'to indulge her idea of heroic self-sacrifice was going to destroy our work' in the US.[8] A Brooklyn representative of the AARIR maintained that 'millions of Americans will hold President Cosgrave responsible for murder if she dies'.[9] She was released from prison, ostensibly on grounds of ill-health.

MacSwiney was undoubtedly influenced by Terence's *Principles of freedom* (1921), in which he had suggested that man often 'wavers on the verge of the right path', but that woman could be nobler and that it was 'frequently the case she can lift him to her level'. She directly raised this question of gender with her opponents; when Tomás Mac Aodha, of the Director of Intelligence Office of the National Army, refused permission for her sister Annie to visit her, she responded:

I am reluctantly forced to the conclusion that the action of your authorities in this matter is one of vindictiveness against women whose spirit you cannot break any more than you can kill the Republic for which they stand.[10]

While debate will continue about the legitimacy and appropriateness of her actions, understanding rather than dismissing her mindset and what it represented is essential to gain a full appreciation of the dilemmas and divisions of 1922.

by Diarmaid Ferriter

FURTHER READING

Charlotte H. Fallon, *Soul of fire: a biography of Mary MacSwiney* (Cork, 1986)

Tom Garvin, *1922: the birth of Irish democracy* (Dublin, 1996)

Joanne Mooney Eichaker, *Irish republican women in America: lecture tours, 1916–1925* (Dublin, 2003)

NOTES

[1] Tom Garvin, *1922: the birth of Irish democracy* (Dublin, 1996), 96; Michael Laffan, *The resurrection of Ireland: the Sinn Féin party, 1916–1923* (Cambridge, 1999), 375.

[2] P.S. O'Hegarty, *The victory of Sinn Féin: how it won it and how it used it* (Dublin, 1924), 104.

[3] Laffan, *Resurrection of Ireland*, 375.

[4] Laffan, *Resurrection of Ireland*, 376.

[5] Ronan Fanning, *Independent Ireland* (Dublin, 1983), 35.

[6] University College Dublin Archives (UCDA), Eamon de Valera papers, P 150/657, de Valera to Mary MacSwiney, 11 September 1922; Michael Hopkinson, *Green against green: the Irish civil war* (Dublin, 1988), 188.

[7] National Archives of Ireland (NAI), Department of Taoiseach (DT), S1369/9, Mary MacSwiney: imprisonment and hunger strike, MacSwiney to Archbishop Byrne, 6 November 1922, and Archbishop Byrne to MacSwiney, 8 November 1922.

[8] Joseph Connolly to W.T. Cosgrave, 7 December 1922, cited in Ronan Fanning, Michael Kennedy, Eunan O'Halpin and Dermot Keogh (eds), *Documents on Irish foreign policy*, vol. ii, 1923–26 (Dublin 1999), 18–21.

[9] *Irish Times*, 9 November 1922.

[10] UCDA, De Valera papers, P150/658, MacSwiney to Tomás Mac Aodha, 20 November 1922.

30 NOVEMBER 1922

CUMANN NA mBAN'S TELEGRAM TO W.T. COSGRAVE

IRISH AUSTRALIANS AND THE CIVIL WAR

As the news of the deteriorating condition of Mary MacSwiney reached Australia in November 1922, the Sydney Ethna Carberry branch of Cumann na mBan swung into action in the only way available to it—by sending a cable of protest to W.T. Cosgrave. Reported in the Melbourne *Advocate* on 30 November 1922, the actions of the Sydney Cumann na mBan were directed particularly at raising local awareness about the treatment of women like MacSwiney as well as at putting pressure on the Cosgrave government from afar. The news of Mary's release from prison, and the execution of Erskine Childers, broke on the same day in Melbourne.[1] While there was widespread condemnation of the execution of Childers and the treatment of MacSwiney, Irish Australians remained divided over the civil war in Ireland throughout 1922.

Opposite: Reverend Dr Patrick Tuomey, an Irish National Association leader, surrounded by Irish Australian nationalist women, Sydney, *c.* 1925.

At the beginning of the year Irish Australians were pleased that the conflict in Ireland seemed to be over. In the main they were optimistic that the negotiated Treaty would mean most Irish people would have a similar relationship with the British Crown as was enjoyed by Australians. By this time there were only a relatively small number of Irish-born people living in Australia. The majority of the membership of various state-based Irish organisations such as the Melbourne Celtic Club, the Queensland Irish Association, or the various branches of the Hibernian Australasian Catholic Benefit Society and the Self-Determination for Ireland League of Australia were among the almost twenty percent of white Australians who were the descendants of migrants who had arrived from Ireland in the mid to late-nineteenth century.[2] The Sheehy family of Sydney was not unusual. Australian-born Madeline Margaret Sheehy was a medical student when she was president of the Sydney Cumann na mBan and signed the cable of protest to Cosgrave in 1922. That year her Irish-born father, John, was president of the Irish National Association in Sydney.[3]

Australian Irish organisations enthusiastically sent delegates from each state to the Irish Race Congress in Paris in January 1922, where the news of the growing divisions over the Treaty was received with some bewilderment. Fr Maurice O'Reilly, the Australian national delegate to the conference, while privately expressing unease over the Treaty, clashed at the conference with Mary MacSwiney; she accused him of misunderstanding the Irish situation because he 'viewed it solely from the standpoint of a British Imperialist'. Most of the rest of the Australian delegation, with the exception of the South Australian delegate T.J. Ryan, supported Michael Collins and the Treaty.[4] While the majority of Irish Australians agreed with them, along with most of the Catholic Australian hierarchy, there were a number of determined individuals in most states who agreed with T.J. Ryan. These people remained committed throughout 1922 to supporting the anti-Treaty side through fundraising, letters and telegrams of support and later by the hosting of envoys and speakers. Their most vocal spokesperson was Daniel Mannix, archbishop of Melbourne, who provoked considerable mainstream criticism for his support of the anti-Treaty side.

Taking a contrary position to Mannix, Michael Kelly, archbishop of Sydney, and James Duhig, archbishop of Brisbane, were keen to play down any divisions that might threaten the social cohesion of Irish Australian communities. Duhig's opinions on the Irish Free State were formed during his stay in Ireland in 1922, where he was present at the funerals of both

Arthur Griffith and Michael Collins. After his return to Brisbane in early 1923 he began a correspondence with W.T. Cosgrave, sending him messages of support and asking for advice about requests for funds from anti-Treaty republican groups in Ireland.[5]

News of hostilities in Ireland throughout 1922 was communicated through newspapers, letters, cables and by returning travellers. The resulting split in opinion among Irish Australians meant that former allies, friends and committee members in a range of Irish organisations were now divided, with the anti-Treaty supporters being in the minority. When anti-Treaty activist Kathleen Barry visited the eastern states of Australia on a fund-raising tour in 1924, she noted that there were still former friends who crossed the street to avoid each other in Brisbane, and she was advised not to visit Adelaide because of the intensity of divisions among Irish groups there.[6]

One of the most vocal groups supporting the anti-Treaty republicans was the Irish National Association. It was established in 1915 in Sydney by Australian-born Albert Dryer 'to assist Ireland to achieve her national destiny and to foster an Irish spirit among the Irish portion of the community', and later spread to Melbourne, Adelaide and Brisbane. In 1916 the Irish National Association passed resolutions that recognised and promoted 'Irish sovereignty' rather than supporting home rule.[7] In Sydney, a branch of Cumann na mBan was established in 1919. This group held regular fund-raising events, sending the money raised to Cumann na mBan in Dublin. Both the Sydney Irish National Association and Cumann na mBan had active cultural and social programs, and from 1922 were vocal in their political support for anti-Treaty republicans. In June 1922 the Sydney Irish National Association and Cumann na mBan published a joint protest about an article in the Sydney *Catholic Press* that had stated that the majority of Irish Australians supported the Irish Free State. Both organisations categorically denied that this was their position in their signed rebuttal.[8]

In Melbourne, Archbishop Mannix's outspoken stance against the establishment of the Irish Free State provided umbrella support to a number of anti-Treaty organisations. Fr James O'Dwyer established the Terence MacSwiney Gaelic League in 1920, running Irish language, dancing and cultural activities while supporting republican political groups in Ireland. Melbourne was also home to anti-Treaty groups such as the Irish National Association, Young Ireland Society and, from early 1923, Irish Republican Association. There was some overlap of membership between these organisations, with the Gaelic League and the Irish Republican Association working closely together. This network of organisations supported fund-raising for anti-Treaty causes and actively hosted delegations sent in 1923 and 1924 to raise funds for de Valera.[9]

Living so far from Ireland, Irish Australians in 1922 relied on news that was often out of date by the time it arrived. They were also limited in what they could do to support the efforts of both sides in the civil war. Telegrams such as those sent by the Sydney Cumann na mBan to protest the treatment of Mary MacSwiney were one of the few direct actions that they could take from such a distance. The threads of connection through such correspondence were important, especially when combined with fund-raising and public statements from Archbishop Mannix. The support shown from Australian groups to the anti-Treaty side led to two fund-raising tours from anti-Treaty republicans in 1923 and 1924, which kept the issue of Irish political divisions alive among Irish Australians. Ultimately, however, the distance, and the draining of energy from the conflict in Ireland, led to the inevitable decline of many of these politically charged organisations.

After 1926, although the Irish National Association continued in its condemnation of the Treaty, most Irish republican organisations either folded, or shifted their focus to concentrate on activities supporting local schools and charities. Madeline Margaret Sheehy worked for several years as a doctor before marrying and retiring from public engagement in Irish organisations. The Sydney Cumann na mBan continued into the 1930s, although by then it had shed the Irish name and was known as the Irish Women's Club, its focus now on local Australian matters.[10]

by Dianne Hall

FURTHER READING

Stephanie James, 'Varieties of Irish nationalism in south Australia, 1839–1950: changing terms of engagement', in Susan Arthure *et al.* (eds), *Irish South Australia: new histories and insights* (Adelaide, 2019), 192–211

Richard Reid *et al.* (eds), *To foster an Irish spirit: the Irish National Association of Australasia 1915–2015* (Sydney, 2020)

Anne-Maree Whitaker, 'The Irish Women's Club: Cumann na mBan in Sydney 1919–1935', *Journal of the Australian Catholic Historical Society* 40 (2019), 90–102

NOTES

[1] *Advocate*, 30 November 1922, 27.

[2] Elizabeth Malcolm and Dianne Hall, *A new history of the Irish in Australia* (Sydney, 2018), 3. Stephanie James, 'Varieties of Irish nationalism in South Australia, 1839–1950: changing terms of engagement', in Susan Arthure *et al.* (eds), *Irish South Australia: new histories and insights* (Adelaide, 2019), 192–211: 206–8.

[3] Anne-Maree Whitaker, 'The Irish Women's Club: Cumann na mBan in Sydney 1919–1935', *Journal of the Australian Catholic Historical Society* 40 (2019), 90–102: 99.
Jeff Kildea, 'From Go to Woe: 1915–1935', in Richard Reid *et al.* (eds), *To foster an Irish spirit: the Irish National Association of Australasia 1915–2015* (Sydney, 2020), 4–62: 49–50.

[4] Jeff Kildea, *Hugh Mahon: patriot, pressman, politician* (2 vols; Sydney, 2020), vol. 2, 246–53.

[5] Patrick O'Farrell, *The Catholic Church in Australia: a short history 1788–1967* (Melbourne, 1968), 205–9, 224–5, 232; Rodney Sullivan and Robin Sullivan, 'Archbishop James Duhig and the Queensland Irish Association, 1898–1920: exploring connections', *Journal of the Australian Catholic Historical Society* 34 (2013), 44–57. National Archives of Ireland, S1369/21, correspondence between James Duhig and W.T. Cosgrave. T.B. Boland, *James Duhig* (Brisbane, 1986), 161–2.

[6] Dianne Hall, 'Irish republican women in Australia: Kathleen Barry and Linda Kearns' tour in 1924–25', *Irish Historical Studies* 43 (163) (2019), 73–93: 76–7.

[7] Patrick O'Farrell, 'The Irish Republican Brotherhood in Australia: the 1918 internments', in Oliver MacDonagh *et al.* (eds), *Irish culture and nationalism, 1750–1950* (London, 1983), 182–93.

[8] *Catholic Press*, 15 June 1922, 11.

[9] Val Noone, *Hidden Ireland in Victoria* (Ballarat, 2012), 127. My thanks to Robert Lindsey and Val Noone for additional information on Fr O'Dwyer and the Melbourne republican groups.

[10] Whitaker, 'The Irish Women's Club', 99.

DECEMBER

6 DECEMBER 1922

THE IRISH FREE STATE CONSTITUTION BECOMES LAW

DEFINING INDEPENDENCE

The constitution of the Irish Free State became law on 6 December 1922. Under the terms of the Anglo-Irish Treaty, signed on 6 December 1921, the constitution had to come into force within a year. The third Dáil was elected as a constituent assembly on 16 June, and first considered the draft constitution on 18 September. After several amendments, it was ratified on 25 October, and received approval at Westminster on 5 December. Thus 1922 gave Sinn Féin an historic opportunity to express its values in a legal constitution. Its success in doing so would depend on how it balanced the competing claims of democracy, imperialism and nationalism.

When the constitutional committee first met on 24 January 1922, Michael Collins had pointed to a Treaty clause that conferred on the Irish Free State 'co-equal' status with Canada. Anti-treatyites saw in this formula subordination; pro-treatyites hoped for evolution. The committee subsequently held 27 meetings. Collins attended only the first. Darrell Figgis, a poet and critic, chaired in his absence. Formally, the committee consisted of Collins as chair, Figgis, vice-chairman and secretary, and eight other

men, including Hugh Kennedy (law adviser to the Provisional Government). Five committee members were legal experts, and four were civil servants. Three were former leaders of the Irish White Cross, and one, James Douglas, a Quaker businessman, would figure in peace initiatives during the civil war.

Their cosmopolitan approach was exemplified by the compilation of *Select constitutions of the world*, a volume containing the constitutions of Yugoslavia, Poland, Austria, Estonia, Czechoslovakia, Germany, the Soviet Union, Mexico, Denmark, Australia, France, Switzerland, Canada, Belgium, Norway, Sweden and the United States. It was presented to the third Dáil, by order of the Provisional Government, in September 1922. This volume was to assist the constituent assembly in its deliberation of the draft constitution that had been decided upon in June.

In its work drafting the constitution the committee also used collections of specialist documents: on functional representation, the southern unionists, the executive, the referendum, proportional representation and the judiciary. Where possible, its recommendations were kept simple and flexible, given the uncertain conditions, north and south.[1] The constitution was intended as a non-party document. The committee produced three drafts (A, B, and C), two of which were submitted to Collins on 7 March. Draft C, produced by James Murnaghan and Alfred O'Rahilly, was never taken seriously. Draft B, supported by most of the committee's members, was submitted to the British government in June, but after weeks of negotiations both sides settled for a revised draft, based on A. Published on 16 June, the day of the general election, this is the draft that was considered by the Dáil in September, although none of the original drafts were made available to it.

Dominion status under the Treaty ruled out a formal republic. Yet Article 2 of the constitution began 'All powers of government and all authority legislative, executive and judicial, in Ireland are derived from the people of Ireland'. The earliest constitutions in *Select constitutions* placed the weight of power in the executive, while those from the nineteenth century privileged legislative institutions. The more recent European constitutions tended to place more and more power in the hands of the people themselves. By 1920 most of Europe west of the Soviet Union was under democratic rule. 'Popular government' was associated with strong uni-cameralism, control of the executive, and individual and minority rights.[2] Figgis compared the new Irish state to a pyramid, with the people at the base, and the executive at the top.[3] The Irish Free State constitution provided for parliamentary control of the executive, for proportional representation, and for the use of the referendum and popular initiative. It enfranchised women under thirty, before Britain did so; the legislation simply amended the British 1918 'Representation of the People Act', replacing the references to Westminster and the United Kingdom with Dáil Éireann and Ireland.[4]

Negotiations between Hugh Kennedy on behalf of the constitutional committee and Lord Hewart for the British side in June 1922 were intended to guarantee the rights of southern unionists and to ensure that the consti-tution set no precedent for the break-up of the British empire. Hence the preliminary clause stating that any future amendment inconsistent with the Treaty's terms would be void and inoperative. This made the Treaty, not the constitution, the supreme law. Originally, Michael Collins had instructed the constitutional committee not to incorporate the terms of the Treaty into their drafts. Alfred O'Rahilly later complained that the process of founding the Irish Free State had been assimilated to that of establishing a colony.[5] In contrast, the British constitutional expert, Sir Arthur Berriedale Keith, argued that the constitution recognised the sovereignty of the people of Ireland, 'leaving utterly vague' the relations of Britain and Ireland.[6] The Free State constitution continued on the Home Rule tradition of seeing minority rights as integral to democracy. Its prescription of 'the principles of proportional representation' reflected commitments made to the south-ern unionists by Arthur Griffith during the Treaty negotiations. A similar rationale influenced the composition of the first Senate.

The constituent assembly had the formal authority to amend, ratify or reject the constitution. The Labour party naively hoped that the final document would reflect the Dáil's 1919 Democratic Programme. Yet the constitution was rushed through the assembly without major changes. The absence (due to the civil war) of anti-Treaty TDs meant that pro-Treaty Sinn Féin dominated proceedings. The main bones of contention for repub-licans were the role of the Crown in the legislative process, the office of the Governor General, and the divisive requirement for TDs to take an oath to the constitution and to the Crown. The constitution was the first test of Collins's 'stepping-stone' approach to the Treaty, but the oath tilted the country in the direction of civil war.

Partition was another bone of contention. The preamble to the 1922 constitution expressed confidence that national unity would be restored.

After the constitution's enactment, Northern Ireland could opt out of the Irish Free State, remaining within the UK. When submitting the two drafts to Collins on 7 March Figgis remarked that Northern Ireland could come in without amendment.[7] Yet Northern Ireland opted out, leaving it to the Boundary Commission to decide the final border. That body would go on to recommend minor changes. The pro-treatyites had underestimated the strength of Ulster Unionism. It could be said that while they defended the Treaty in a spirit of realism, their approach to the constitution was one of idealism. This idealism did not survive the civil war. In 1937 de Valera replaced the Irish Free State constitution with a less experimental document. Although his Bunreacht na hÉireann redefined 'the national territory' as the whole island, the border became no less permanent as a result.

by Bill Kissane

FURTHER READING

Laura Cahillane, *Drafting the Irish Free State constitution* (Manchester, 2016)

Michael Hopkinson, *Green against green: the Irish civil war* (Dublin, 1988)

Bill Kissane, *New beginnings: constitutionalism and democracy in modern Ireland* (Dublin, 2011)

NOTES

[1] National Archives of Ireland (NAI), 3/493/5, 1922 CC K5, committee's report, 7 March 1922.
[2] See, Howard Lee McBain and Lindsay Rogers, *The new constitutions of Europe* (New York, 1923).
[3] Darrell Figgis, *The Irish constitution: explained by Darrell Figgis* (Dublin, 1922), 20.
[4] UCD Archives, Mary MacSwiney papers, P48a/274, 'Representation of the People bill'.
[5] Alfred O'Rahilly, *Thoughts on the constitution* (Dublin, 1937), 7.
[6] *The Times*, 16 June 1922.
[7] NAI, K5 3/493/5 1922 CC, committee's report, 7 March 1922.

7 DECEMBER 1922

PARTITION AND POWER: UNIONIST POLITICAL CULTURE IN NORTHERN IRELAND

On the evening of 7 December 1922 the prime minister of Northern Ireland, James Craig, set sail from Belfast to deliver his parliament's decision, made only that afternoon, to opt out of the newly created Irish Free State. There had been no need to hurry. By the terms of Article 14 of the Anglo-Irish Treaty, the northern parliament had a month to make its choice, but Craig was anxious 'not to show the slightest hesitation to the world' of his government's rejection of the separatist nationalist project.[1] As one of his MPs observed in the brief debate a few hours earlier, Ulster's decision was akin to that of a lifeboat readying itself to escape a sinking ship.

That the new Irish Free State was imploding seemed self-evident. The next morning as Craig arrived in London to present his humble petition, the Free State government ordered the summary execution of four republican prisoners in Dublin in retaliation for a fatal attack on a TD the previous day, beginning a journey into the darkness of political authoritarianism, arbitrary arrest and state-sponsored murder.

It was a journey Craig knew well. Only six months earlier his own government had used similarly repressive methods to end its own undeclared civil war, after withstanding two years of violence and political opposition from southern nationalists and a recalcitrant minority within its own borders.[2]

Like the southern state, Northern Ireland was crippled both materially and psychologically by the traumatic civil war that marked its birth. Its experience was hardly unique in the context of post-war Europe, however. Most of the newly formed successor states wrestled with sizeable and troublesome minorities, and in many ways Northern Ireland had significant advantages over its continental neighbours. It had a strong industrial base, a history of representative democracy and a sizeable middle class ready to staff the new state's institutions. Added to that was the existence of a powerful neighbour ready to provide financial, political and military support in time of crisis.

Yet such advantages did not lead to compromise. In contrast to its southern neighbour, Craig's government remained in an almost permanent state of emergency, retaining its costly and repressive security apparatus and supporting tens of thousands of auxiliary police reservists. Its ageing leadership, veterans of the bitter struggles against Home Rule, contained few visionaries or progressives. Attempts to secularise the education system united both Protestant and Catholic church leaders in opposition, while initiatives to include more Catholics in the police or civil service met fierce resistance in Cabinet and from bodies such as the Ulster Protestant Voter's Defence Association, ever vigilant to protect their rights and root out 'disloyal elements' at the heart of government. The Catholic minority was to be tolerated but kept away from the levers of power. Craig's administration set about nullifying minority political influence almost immediately by targeting recalcitrant nationalist councils that refused to recognise the new Belfast regime. In September 1922 the Northern Ireland government passed into law a bill abolishing proportional representation in local council elections, redrawing boundaries with meticulous care to ensure wards would provide an overall unionist majority. Fatally, nationalists—still wedded to the doctrine of non-recognition and abstention—remained aloof from the process, allowing unionists to dictate the future political geography of the state. The result was that the number of opposition-controlled councils fell from 27 in 1920 to a mere 12 seven years later.

No nationalist of any hue took their seat in the Northern Ireland parliament until 1925. Even then the Nationalist Party, representing as it did a profoundly divided and disillusioned minority, refused to become the official opposition. Unionists remained deeply suspicious of the motives of Nationalist MPs no matter how conservative or constitutionally minded they were, leading eventually to the abandonment of proportional representation for national elections too. That bill, championed by Craig as early as 1922, was eventually enacted in February 1929, a mere three months prior to the next election; it successfully squeezed out smaller parties and reasserted unionist dominance for the next 40 years. For Craig, politics was a blunt weapon for maintaining power and crushing dissent, rather than a means of facilitating progressive democratic reform.[3]

The result was that politics began to ossify. Previously vibrant grassroots organisations withered and died. In 1925 only 8 of the 52 parliamentary seats were uncontested but by 1933 this number had risen to 33. Nationalists had been so successfully marginalised by the state that, when the new parliament buildings were opened at Stormont in 1932, they did not even bother to attend.

Craig's role then was more akin to that of a president than a prime minister, and he enjoyed majorities more secure than most European leaders of the time. This hegemony was maintained not by a programme of political reform but by a defensive and wearisome inertia. The average unionist MP was ageing, reactionary and, if the records of the parliamentary debates are anything to go by, embarrassingly inarticulate and ill-informed. Government sank into a curiously dysfunctional stasis, marked by trivial debates and inactivity. There were remarkably few private members' bills and with periods of parliamentary recess longer than those at Westminster, the parliament when it did meet spent most of its time duplicating Whitehall legislation or receiving deputations from local unionist associations concerned about the growing influence of 'disloyal elements' in their local areas.

Political complacency was reinforced by the severe financial restraints within which Northern Ireland operated. Even had there been an impetus for an energetic state-building programme, the state was effectively broke. Ironically, considering the centrality that economic arguments had played in unionist propaganda since the late nineteenth century, almost as soon as the state was founded it went into a severe economic decline.

The reason for this could not be blamed on the new border or government inefficiency. Rather, Ulster fell victim to the chronic problem of oversupply in the post-war global economy. In 1922 few people wanted what Northern Ireland was selling. Prices for linen fell to 35% of their wartime level, and unemployment in the industry rose to 32% by 1927. Shipbuilding suffered a similar fate. The number of workers at Harland and Wolff fell from a height of 30,000 during the Ulster Crisis to a mere 1,500 by 1932, while the other major shipyard in the city, Workman Clark, closed altogether. By 1922 unemployment stood at 23% of insured workers, and for the rest of the decade an average of one in five would be without a job. Endemic poverty resulted, and Northern Ireland became consistently the poorest region in the United Kingdom. In such an environment what privilege there was, both political and economic, was jealously guarded.

'Something in common'; *Punch* depicts W.T. Cosgrave and James Craig painting different futures for Ulster.

The dysfunctional nature of the northern state had much to do with limitations in the mindset of its chief architects. For all their bluster and threats of revolt, Ulster unionists had never sought, or expected to run, a parliament of their own. They had reluctantly accepted the partition idea, although with little seeming comprehension of what such a decision would entail. Certainly, as Craig made his journey that cold December night he could congratulate himself on accomplishing his overriding goal of 'saving Ulster'. While he and his colleagues had much-rehearsed ideas of what they had saved it from, however, they had little seeming interest in what exactly they had saved it for.

by Robert Lynch

FURTHER READING

Patrick Buckland, *The factory of grievances: devolved government in Northern Ireland 1921–39* (Dublin, 1979)

Bryan Follis, *A state under siege: the establishment of Northern Ireland 1920–1925* (Oxford, 1995)

Robert Lynch, *The partition of Ireland, 1918–1925* (Cambridge, 2019)

NOTES

[1] Northern Ireland parliamentary debates, vol. 2, cols. 1151–52 (27 October 1922).
[2] For events in the north-east, see, Robert Lynch, *The northern IRA and the early years of partition, 1920–1922* (Dublin, 2006).
[3] For Craig, see, *Patrick Buckland, James Craig* (Dublin, 1980).

ULSTER MUST

ULSTER WILL NOT

SOMETHING IN COMMON.

President Cosgrave. "YOU'RE VERY OBSTINATE."
Sir James Craig. "WELL, SO ARE YOU."
President Cosgrave. "I DAREN'T BE ANYTHING ELSE."
Sir James Craig. "SAME WITH ME."

8 DECEMBER 1922

ABANDONING THE RULE OF LAW: STATE EXECUTIONS DURING THE IRISH REVOLUTION

The execution without trial of Rory O'Connor, Liam Mellows, Richard Barrett and Joe McKelvey on 8 December 1922 at Mountjoy Prison was one of the most notorious events of the Irish civil war. It should be understood within the context of the Irish Free State government's execution policy, and also as part of the wider resort to executions by British governments throughout the revolutionary period.

By the autumn of 1922 the financial cost of the civil war was edging the country towards bankruptcy. At the request of the Provisional Government, the National Army issued a proclamation that, after 15 October, persons 'taken in arms' or 'attacking National Army troops' would be tried by military court and 'suffer death'. The first executions soon followed, and a legal challenge to the military courts failed.[1]

Liam Lynch wrote to the Speaker of the Dáil demanding that the executions cease or there would be immediate reprisals. His warning was ignored and three more anti-Treaty fighters were executed. On 7 December, the day after the Irish Free State came into existence, Seán Hales TD was shot dead as part of the anti-Treaty reprisal policy.

That same evening the Cabinet of the new state met and fixed upon reprisal executions of four untried prisoners. The men at Mountjoy Prison were woken and handed a typed sheet: 'being a person taken in arms against the government, you will be executed at 8am in reprisal for the assassination of Brigadier Seán Hales.'[2] They were shot at Mountjoy that morning. After the volley from the firing squad nine more bullets were needed from the supervising officers. The last to die was Joe McKelvey. 'Give me another', he asked. Another bullet was fired. 'And another.'[3]

There was no point in a trial, one minister observed sagely: the role the men had played in the Four Courts siege was well known.[4] In the Dáil debate that afternoon there were many who insisted that due process should not have been abandoned. It was pointed out that the prisoners had been in custody for months, bore no responsibility for the anti-Treaty reprisal policy, and such offences as they might have committed took place before the army proclamation created capital offences. The execution of these men represented the nadir of due process during the war. The many other executions that took place during the civil war were preceded by trial by military court. But what did that actually mean?

The military court phenomenon pervaded the Irish revolution from the outset. The principle of law, as it was then, was that the army had no jurisdiction to try civilians or anyone other than its own soldiery. In Britain this principle had subsisted for centuries and it had been maintained in colonies, save where rebellion required the military to bring in martial law to restore the status quo by trial and execution. Necessity was the guiding principle and senior army officers knew that what they did was justiciable after the conflict was over. Despite this, the suppression of rebellions in Ireland and the colonies was marked by extraordinary excesses. This history began to shape policy in Westminster and, when the Great War broke out, the Defence of the Realm Act was passed permitting trial by court martial in Ireland for capital offences in the event of 'invasion or other special military emergency'.[5] This was not martial law: it was an attempt to achieve security, but also to strictly curb the power of the military. The Easter Rising of 1916 became the first test of the legislation.

Mountjoy Prison
Dublin
8/12/22 5.a.m.

My Dearest Mother,

The time is short & much that I
would like to say must go unsaid. But you will understand
in such moments heart speaks to heart. At 3.30. this
morning we (Dick Barrett, Rory O'Connor Joe McKelvey)
& I) were informed that we were to be "executed as a
reprisal". Welcome be the will of God, for Ireland
is in his keeping despite foreign monarchs & Treaties
Though unworthy of the greatest honour that can
be paid to an Irish man or woman, I go to join
Tone & Emmett, the Fenians, Tom Clarke, Connolly.
Pearse, Kevin Barry. and Childers. My last
thoughts will be on God, and Ireland & you.

You must not grieve, Mother Darling, once
before you thought you had given me to Ireland
The reality has now come. You will bear this

General Maxwell, who was sent to Ireland to suppress the rebellion, immediately stretched the ambit of his powers to the limit. He ordered that the trials be conducted by Field General Court Martial: the most rudimentary system of trial for men at the front. He also ordered the

Opposite: Extract from letter by Liam Mellows to his mother, written in Mountjoy jail on the morning of his execution, 8 December 1922.

trials to take place *in camera* and without lawyers present. Trials and executions took place in such haste and secrecy that no legal challenge to the legality of what was done could be mounted at that time.

Afterwards Prime Minister Asquith asserted that the trials had been conducted according to law, and a test case to challenge their legality failed.[6] Recent research shows that the statutory protections conferred on prisoners—access to legal advice and to defence witnesses—were not observed. The Judge Advocate General's post-conviction review was simply bypassed. In the crisis, the law had been stretched beyond breaking point.

After the Great War, the Defence of the Realm Act was abolished but a resurgence of fighting in Ireland caused Westminster to pass the Restoration of Order in Ireland Act, which created a system of military courts that pervaded every area of life in Ireland.[7] Under this regime ten men were hanged for involvement in the insurgency, although it is now acknowledged that two of the prisoners (Patrick Maher and Thomas Whelan) had not been involved in the events that had given rise to their trials.

During the final months of the conflict, the British army lost control of much of the south and west. With the consent of Lloyd George, the army bypassed the statutory court martial regime, introducing fast-track military courts to bring about the swift execution of men 'taken in arms'. By the summer of 1921 fourteen men had been shot by firing squad and, in the Martial Law Area alone, there were forty-four men under sentence of death and dozens more awaiting trial by military courts. By a writ of habeas corpus for one of the death row prisoners, the High Court found these martial law military courts were unlawful.[8] The executions were paused and almost immediately the truce came about.

The Anglo-Irish Treaty was signed in circumstances that are well known and civil war followed; when the crisis came, the Cabinet of the Provisional Government considered whether the Treaty gave power to legislate to create military courts pending the creation of the Irish Free State. It did, explained Attorney General Hugh Kennedy. But there was a catch. Because the Irish Free State had yet to come into being, there was no Governor General to give the necessary royal assent.[9] If the Provisional Government were to proceed, it would require the personal signature of King George V to create military courts. To avoid this political embarrassment the Provisional Government decided not to enact legislation, and simply brought a motion

before the Dáil that lacked any force of law. Assurances were given that prisoners would be fairly treated and would have defence lawyers. As a result, the Army (Special Powers) Resolution (commonly and mistakenly known as the Public Safety Act) was passed by the Dáil on 28 September, but any semblance of due process was quickly abandoned. By the end of the civil war over 1,246 prisoners had been tried by military tribunals, over 400 were under sentence of death and, in addition to the Mountjoy executions, 79 men had been executed. Only a handful were ever allowed a lawyer for their trial. Patrick Hennessey's last letter home provides a compelling insight: 'We were tried at midnight…called from our cells where we were asleep, got no chance to defend ourselves'.[10]

The Mountjoy executions marked a pivotal moment in the abandonment of the rule of law. Hours before the executions were carried out, General Richard Mulcahy ordered the creation of army committees that would substantially replace military courts, expedite the trial process and make convictions easier to obtain.[11]

Mulcahy's decision probably reflected his view that the army was on the verge of a crisis. In fact, the anti-Treaty assassination campaign petered out but Mulcahy's committee system, conceived in haste, became the norm. These army committees would decide verdicts on the case papers, sometimes without hearing from the accused. For these men, there was no appeal nor any review by the Judge Advocate General and they became part of a growing bank of prisoners under sentence of death.

The criteria for choosing prisoners for execution was extraordinary: it did not depend on the perceived culpability of prisoners: anti-Treaty TDs and high-ranking officers captured with arms were not executed. The executions fell on the junior officers and rank and file.

The policy of the National Army morphed into reprisal executions—'in every case of outrage in any battalion area, three men will be executed'.[12] When troops were attacked, the army searched through the prisoners under sentence of death and singled out those who were from the locality where the ambush had taken place. Executions followed.

Fr. McMahon
Clonliffe College. Attended me. Mount Joy Prison.
He is writing to you.
                    Friday Morning 2 A.M. Dec. 8th. 1922.

To My Dearest Mother, Father, Molly, Jem, Nellie, Ellen & Baby.

I have been just called up from my old bed in cell 36
Top Landing. A little paper was read to me, which states that "I
am to be executed this morning at 8 A.M. as a reprisal for the
murder of Sean Hales". Only a few days ago when some fellow
prisoners of mine and I were speaking of the poor lads who were
executed in Beggars' Bush and wondering would it be difficult
to die in such circumstances. Well the riddle is solved for me
at any rate. The nearer we get to death the easier it is. I am
quite prepared for the last long journey. For me the best has come
but for you all. I can picture you when you receive this news
I wish you would take it as cool and resigned as I have done.
Remember it is sweet and glorious to die for one's Country.
There were three others brought out with me, Liam Mellows,
Rory O'Connor and Joe McKelvey I presume that these three great
men will also pay the full penalty for loving Ireland.
They will be a great loss to the Cause of Irish Freedom. They too
like me I'm sure regret that the Executioners should be Irish
men. In the past they were English but the Cause is the
same — holy & triumphant.
        Well I was not as good a son or as loving a brother
as I might have been. I have caused you all a lot of worry
and uneasiness but I know you will forgive me. The armies
of Ireland demand the giving up or perhaps in many
cases the breaking of some family ties & dear friendships,
but this is more than compensated for, because in the service of
our motherland with men we make acquaintanceship with
the greatest of men. men whose souls are in Communion
with the Spirits of our great martyred heroes.
        I should love to see you all but this is impossible

The justification for trials by military court rested on the contention that ordinary law had broken down and the army, as Richard Mulcahy asserted, needed to 'stand in the gap'.[13] That may have been so in the autumn of 1922 but, as the anti-Treaty faction collapsed the following spring, arguments founded on necessity evaporated. Executions nonetheless continued until well into the summer.

After the war, the government passed the Indemnity Act to protect those who had taken part in military courts and the suppression of the anti-Treaty cause. It did not render lawful what had been done, but it prevented anyone bringing a legal action in response.[14]

by Seán Enright

FURTHER READING

Colm Campbell, *Emergency law in Ireland 1918–1925* (Oxford, 1994)

Seán Enright, *The Irish civil war. Law, execution and atrocity* (Dublin, 2019)

NOTES

[1] The case in question was *R (Childers) v Adjutant General, Provisional Forces* [1923], Irish Reports (hereafter I.R.), 5.
[2] UCD Archives (UCDA), Mulcahy papers, P7/B/85, undated document.
[3] From 'Executions recalled', an account written in the 1960s by Canon John Pigott who attended the prisoners, published in *Athenry Journal* 8 (1997).
[4] Military Archives (MA), Bureau of Military History, witness statement 939, Ernest Blythe, 192.
[5] See, Defence of the Realm Act (1914), 4 and 5, Geo. 5, chapter 29. See, also The Defence of the Realm (Amendment) Act (1915), 5, Geo. 5 chapter 34 and subsequent amendments.
[6] *R v Governor of Lewes Prison ex parte Doyle* [1917], vol. 2, King's Bench reports, 254.
[7] Restoration of Order in Ireland Act (1920), 10 and 11, Geo. 5, chapter 31.
[8] *Egan v Macready* [1921], vol. 1 I.R., 265.
[9] UCDA, Mulcahy papers, P/B/7/249, advices of Hugh Kennedy, Attorney General, 15, 16 September 1922.
[10] Letter from Patrick Hennessey to his sister Julia on the eve of his execution, January 1922. Letter provided courtesy of Ellen D. Murphy (private collection).
[11] MA, DOD/A/07266, proclamation by Army Council, 7 December 1922.
[12] UCDA, Mulcahy papers, P/7/B/178, Army Council decisions, 12 February 1923.
[13] *Dáil debates*, vol. 1, cols 841–844 (27 September 1922); available at: www.oireachtas.ie/en/debates/ (accessed 22 April 2021).
[14] Indemnity Act (1923), no. 31 of 1923; signed into law on 3 August 1923.

22 DECEMBER 1922

PATRICK HOGAN'S MEMORANDUM ON LAND SEIZURES

'AGRARIAN ANARCHY': CONTAINING THE LAND WAR

On 22 December 1922 Patrick Hogan, minister for agriculture in the Irish Free State government, sent a Cabinet memorandum on 'seizures of land' to William Cosgrave, president of the Executive Council of the Irish Free State, Kevin O'Higgins, minister for home affairs, and Richard Mulcahy, minister for defence. Six days later the memorandum was again sent to Mulcahy, this time from the president's office, with an accompanying letter stating that the president 'thinks this matter is of importance'.[1] The content of this memorandum, in particular the assertion that the 'Land War is very widespread and very serious', may surprise those who associate agrarian unrest in Ireland with the late nineteenth century and who assume that the Irish land question had by this point in time been answered by land purchase acts such as the Wyndham Act of 1903.[2] As indicated by Hogan's memorandum, however, outbreaks of land agitation occurred in Ireland well after the events of 1879–82 that are generally termed the land war. These outbreaks included the period leading up to and following the sending of this memorandum.

In the spring and early summer of 1920 rural unrest was particularly pronounced, with officially returned 'agrarian outrages' higher than in any other year since 1882, but there was also notable unrest during the civil war. The dominant form that rural agitation took in the early 1920s was the seizure of land. Land let out to graziers on the eleven-month system and land under the control of the Congested Districts Board was especially targeted,[3] though even the farms of small and middling farmers were not guaranteed to be safe. Some seized land was broken up into holdings for individual farmers, non-inheriting farmers' sons or landless labourers, and some was turned into commons, occasionally referred to as 'Soviets'. A one-thousand-acre farm in County Clare belonging to H.V. McNamara, which was seized and used collectively by at least 37 small farmers and fishermen, is an example of one such commons. An immediate context for such land seizures was escalating tensions over resources because of the impact of the First World War on emigration and on beef prices. In the west of the country in particular, an already chronic land hunger that 'peasant proprietorship' of itself could not alleviate was exacerbated by restrictions on emigration; furthermore, increased beef prices ensured that land was more likely to be let out for commercial grazing than subsistence farming.

Hogan's memorandum points to a tense relationship between agrarian agitators and mainstream nationalists. In the west, land congestion had created a dissatisfaction that provided much of the energy for the War of Independence, but there was a relatively low participation in that part of the country in the war. For many within the nationalist movement, the land issue was not only a distraction from the national project but threatened to derail it. Hence direct action aimed at land redistribution was a source of considerable anxiety for both the first Dáil and the Free State government. Land was also a factor in the civil war conflict. Rural discontent was viewed by such opponents of the Treaty as Liam Mellows as a means of mobilising anti-government support, while key members of the government were hostile to an agitation that they believed was being used to undermine the authority of the Free State. Thus, a connection was made between land seizures and anti-Treaty 'irregularism', and a corresponding link formed between the defence of private property rights and the defence of the fledgling state.

Attempts to contain agrarian unrest in the early 1920s included the establishment of special land courts and of a land commission by the first Dáil,

AIREACHT TALMHUIOCHTA
(Ministry of Agriculture),

SRÁID MHUIRBHTHEAN UACH
(Upper Merrion Street),

BAILE ÁTHA CLIATH.

22nd December 1922.

M E M O R A N D U M.

SEIZURES OF LAND.

I note what General Murphy says about County Kerry.

Since I sent you the first memo. about the case of Thomas Murphy, Lisheen, Gort, I have considered this question very carefully; I have had several conferences, both with my own Inspectors and with others who would be in a position to advise, and I have come to a definite conclusions on certain aspects of it.

Of one thing I am quite certain and that is that the problem can only be dealt with by the Army, and that the measures adequate to cope with it are measures which the Government could defend only on the ground of military necessity. The Civil Authorities, that is to say the Minister for Home Affairs, would be quite powerless.

The Land War is very widespread and very serious even at present. In the past, even when it developed into large proportions, it always began in Spring. On this occasion there is a change: lands have been seized in Autumn, and there are all the signs of very serious trouble developing in the months of January and February. I know these signs from my own experience. Already people have been shot at. I have interviewed some people - stewards, owners, etc. who have been already fired at, and one who has been badly wounded - who simply left their lands derelict and are afraid to return. There is the usual knocking of walls, cattle driving, and forcible occupation. In addition there is a new development: the seizure of stock, and it is quite evident that the incidents are not isolated but part of an organised campaign.

We have explicit evidence from the letters which have been captured that the campaign is organised, but even without that evidence the general condition of affairs makes it quite clear that the Land War is coming. To produce chaos the Irregulars smashed up the transport of the country even though that was unpopular. A result which would be the same in kind though perhaps less in degree, would be produced by the wholesale seizure of land and it would have the advantage of being much more popular, in fact quite in the best traditions. The "land for the people" is almost as respectable an objective as the "Republic" and would make a much wider appeal. Moreover, almost as many abuses could be perpetrated under one pretext as the other. The up-shot of all this is that we can take it

for granted that the present land campaign, which is directed
as much against comparatively small farmers as against large
land owners, will redouble its intensity if not promptly
checked. In addition, it will make it impossible to deal
with land purchase in the year 1923, and for a long time to
come.

At present the English are quite willing to lend
us their credit for the purpose of financing land purchase
provided we make anything approaching a fair bargain with the
landlords. The landlords on their part are in the mood to
take very moderate terms indeed. While the tenant thinks
that he need never pay rent again and that he can confiscate
the landlord's land which adjoins, he will not agree to any
terms no matter how reasonable. A reduction of 50% (fifty
per cent) in his rent is no good to a tenant who is not paying
rent and who does not intend to pay rent. On the other hand,
if the tenant and the landless man are shown that things are
not all their own way, there will be no difficulty in making
a bargain and a new Land Act should be in operation in March or
April. If we miss this chance of getting English credit on
easy terms because the tenant and the landless man refuse to
see anything like reason, it will be an incalculable loss.
What is more, and perhaps even more important, it will alienate
from us all conservative support in Ireland and this will
probably have serious re-actions on the financial settlement
which we must make this year with England.

As I said, it is quite impossible to deal with
the question under the Ministry of Home Affairs as an ordinary
criminal matter. The English tried it here for twenty or
thirty years. I saw their measures in operation myself and they
were utter failures. Cattle are driven from a man's land;
the police interfere and arrest some people; they are brought
up on the next Court day before a Magistrate; all the neighbours
are in attendance; the Court is crowded, the general atmosphere
is that a few martyrs are being tried for highly moral and
religious convictions which they refuse to repudiate. There
is no evidence because, of course, the cattle are always driven
at night, or perhaps a good alibi is proved. The Magistrate
is unable to convict and the prisoners are released and carried
through the town on the shoulders of their admiring neighbours
and taken home with tar barrels lighted in front of them. That
night the owner's walls are knocked, he receives a threatening
letter, and if he has the timidity to put his cattle back on
his land they are driven again and so on until the owner either
gives up the land or is shot. Even in a case where the parties
looking for the land make the mistake of committing the first
act in the open and before witnesses and so are convicted, it
makes no difference in the long run. When they go to jail
their friends and sympathisers immediately commit criminal
injuries and don't make the mistake a second time of committing
them before witnesses. The men in jail are regarded as heroes
and martyrs and if the owner succeeds, which is very rare, in
holding the land for a time, he always succumbs either literally
or by giving up the land when they do come out of jail. This
Land War is no new thing in Ireland; the parties know every
move in the game, they are prepared to do now even more than
they ever did before, and unless we take advantage of the present
situation to meet the case we will have a sordid and fairly
bloody squabble on our hands for the next ten years.

The problem will have to be treated very carefully
because there is always the danger that any move against the
trespassers will be visited on the heads of the owners of the

and the introduction by the Free State government of a 1923 land bill focused on redis-
tributive land reform. Coercive measures
were also employed. Most notably, the Special
Infantry Corps was set up just over a month
after Hogan claimed in his memorandum that

'it is quite impossible' to deal with the seizing of land 'as an ordinary criminal matter'.[4] Kevin O'Higgins informed an army inquiry committee in 1924
that the corps was formed as a direct result of the memorandum and 'did
effective, if "rough and ready" work in stamping out agrarian anarchy and
other serious abuses existing and arising at that time'.[5] In 1923 the corps
arrested at least 173 people for 'agrarian offences'.[6] Reasons recorded for
arrest include 'interfering with land other than his own', 'breaking down
walls', 'unlawful grazing', 'illegal tillage' and 'unlawful possession'.[7] More
commonly, the corps simply cleared seized land. Those who established the
illegal commonage on McNamara's estate in Clare were initially evicted
by the Special Infantry Corps in July 1923. Following reoccupations of the
land, they were again evicted in December 1923 and May 1924.[8] Further
coercive measures included the confiscation of stock, as took place in the
case of the County Clare occupants in the December 1923 eviction; the
debarring of those involved in seizures from future land distribution; and
the paying of fines and compensation.

Notwithstanding the use of reform and coercion in the early 1920s to
stem rural discontent, agrarian unrest continued to be a feature of Irish
society, as evidenced by the anti-land annuities agitation that commenced
in 1926, and activism associated with Clann na Talmhan in the late 1930s
and early 1940s. As suggested here, land agitation is a more significant and
sustained aspect of Ireland's past than is generally acknowledged. One
way the Irish state could mark its historical importance is to open up the
untapped resource that is the Irish Land Commission archive and make its
approximately eight million documents fully accessible to all who wish to
study them.

by Heather Laird

FURTHER READING:

Fergus Campbell and Tony Varley (eds), *Land questions in modern Ireland* (Manchester, 2013)

Gavin Foster, *The Irish civil war and society: politics, class, and conflict* (Basingstoke, 2015)

NOTES

[1] Military Archives (MA), DOD.A.07869, letter from the president's office to the minister for defence, 28 December 1922. The re-sending of the memorandum to Mulcahy could indicate an initial reluctance or perceived reluctance on his part to provide the military support that Hogan had requested. Certainly, earlier communications between the Ministry for Agriculture and Ministry for Defence, stored in the same file, suggest that Mulcahy viewed some of Hogan's proposals for the stemming of rural unrest as overly harsh. The alarmist tone of the December memorandum, therefore, may in part stem from Hogan's frustration at what he judged to be an inadequate response by Mulcahy. Earlier attempts by Hogan to convince Mulcahy of the severity of the situation included the sharing of documents relating to Thomas Murphy, who is referenced at the opening of the memorandum, and whose 250-acre farm in County Galway had been seized and stocked in the latter half of 1922, possibly following a dispute with neighbours over turbary rights.
[2] MA, DOD.A.07869, Patrick Hogan, memorandum: seizures of land, 22 December 1922.
[3] This type of letting, being for less than a year, was not liable to periodical rent revisions. It suited graziers looking to lease land on a short-term basis for the fattening of cattle, but was resented by small farmers who did not have the capital to outbid them. Thus, cattle-driving, referenced in the memorandum, was a common tactic employed by agrarian agitators. This involved removing cattle from a farm and either driving them to the grazier's house, placing them on another farmer's land or leaving them on a road some distance from that farm. The Congested Districts Board, established to relieve land congestion, was targeted as it was allowing graziers to stock land in its possession.
[4] MA, DOD.A.07869, Hogan memorandum, seizures of land.
[5] MA, papers of the Army Inquiry Committee, IE.MA.AMTY.03.055, letter from Kevin O'Higgins to the army inquiry committee, 12 May 1924.
[6] Anthony Kinsella, 'The Special Infantry Corps', *Irish Sword* 20 (82) (1997), 331–45: 343.
[7] MA, CW.P.02.02.02, Special Infantry Corps returns and reports, 25 April 1923–29 September 1923.
[8] See, David Jones, 'The issue of land distribution: revisiting graziers, land reform and political conflict in Ireland', in Fergus Campbell and Tony Varley (eds), *Land questions in modern Ireland* (Manchester, 2013), 117–48: 128–29.

27 DECEMBER 1922

THE OCCUPATION OF THE IRISH CONSULATE, NEW YORK

REVOLUTIONARY DIPLOMACY

On the morning of Wednesday, 27 December 1922 the former independent nationalist and Sinn Féin MP and TD Laurence Ginnell arrived at the
offices of the Irish consulate on the tenth floor of 119 Nassau St in Lower
Manhattan, to seize them in the name of the 'Irish republic'. With Ginnell
(who reportedly produced papers signed by Éamon de Valera to back up his
claim) were Major Michael A. Kelly and John F. Finerty of the American
Association for the Recognition of the Irish Republic, and Robert Briscoe
of the IRA (recently arrived in the US on the run, and who later claimed
to have occupied the office the night before). Ginnell's next stop would, he
said, be Washington DC, to 'depose' the Irish Free State representative to
the US, Professor Timothy A. Smiddy (who was in New York at the time).

This was the scene faced by the newly appointed consul, Lindsay
Crawford (a founding member of the Independent Loyal Orange Institution
of Ireland) on his first day in the office. Crawford refused to recognise the
claim and when Smiddy himself arrived, he was told by Ginnell that the
office had been founded, and thus belonged to, the government of the Irish
Republic, which, said Ginnell, continued to function. Smiddy replied that
the Irish Free State was the successor to the independence movement, and

so 'all property and other things identified with the movement for independence went thereafter under the jurisdiction of the Irish Free State'. This was a crucial point, as in Smiddy's view 'the whole matter appears to me as a play in the suit here relating to the Irish fund'.[1]

The first Dáil Éireann had sought international recognition for Irish independence from the Paris Peace Conference, but when this was not forthcoming it pursued the same end through an international campaign of publicity and propaganda (Ginnell himself had previously represented the Republic in the US and Argentina). The Dáil never obtained the recognition that it sought, but it had one very notable overseas success: the sustained attempt to raise money for the independence movement during the US tour of Éamon de Valera in 1919–20. The first of the Dáil loan drives was launched in New York in January 1920. Eventually, $5,151,800 would be raised across the US, with 26% of that coming from New York alone. And, as of December 1922, approximately $2,500,000 of the monies raised remained in various US banks.

Smiddy had arrived in the US in March 1922 with a brief to consolidate and unify Irish American opinion in support of the Irish Free State, but he was also instructed by Michael Collins to secure the remaining funds for the Provisional Government.[2] Anti-Treaty republicans needed money, especially after the outbreak of the civil war, and, unsurprisingly, their opponents were not minded to let them have it. Smiddy, on 21 August 1922, successfully obtained an injunction to prevent any of the monies being withdrawn, and their ownership became the subject of legal wrangling, with Finerty (who was later with Ginnell at the consulate) becoming one of the counsel for the anti-Treaty side.[3] In December 1922, however, a more direct approach was taken. According to Briscoe, Smiddy was right: they were seeking the lists of subscribers to the Dáil loan.

Despite the acrimony of civil war divisions, Ginnell and Smiddy apparently debated the ownership of the office in a cordial manner. The tone changed after Muriel MacSwiney (Terence MacSwiney's widow, who was in the US on a lecture tour) and a number of others arrived at the consulate and made clear their intentions to occupy it. Smiddy pointed out that they were trespassing, but both sides agreed that neither would have recourse to force. The building owner agreed to let everyone stay overnight; Briscoe led the republican occupation, and Crawford remained as well. The consulate staff continued to work throughout the occupation, though Crawford was pessimistic about his chances of getting much sleep.[4] According to Briscoe's colourful, if not entirely reliable, account, both he and Crawford (whom he described as 'really a good fellow') slept back to back on a desk.[5] Briscoe also claimed to have obeyed an eviction order from the landlord the next day, but to have broken back in later that night; supplies were supposedly hoisted up on a rope.

On Friday, 30 December Smiddy returned to the consulate with a number of private detectives. MacSwiney called the police, but after they arrived Smiddy produced a receipt for the rent on the office (a calculated risk, he admitted, to avoid the greater risk of a legal challenge). This seemed to confirm that the Irish Free State was the rightful occupant and that the republicans were trespassing.[6] Crawford suggested that everyone vacate the office, at least until the following Tuesday, 2 January; the keys could be left with the building administrators. MacSwiney, after initially agreeing, refused to leave, but did so after Smiddy's men picked up the chair she was sitting on and began to carry it out. Smiddy returned to Washington, lest a similar incident take place there.[7]

The republicans who occupied the New York consulate may simply have been an isolated faction in an already fragmented world. According to Ginnell's wife Alice, 'all the Irish people in New York…seem to resent L.G. with the exception of Mrs. MacSwiney and Robert Briscoe'.[8] Smiddy reported that on 2 January 'fifty irregular invaders' unsuccessfully tried to gain access before going to the nearby city hall to lobby the mayor, John F. Hylan, who had bought the first Dáil bond certificate in 1919 but was dismissive of this republican claim. The next day the manager of 119 Nassau St made it clear that any pickets inside the premises would be arrested, and that was the end of the matter.[9] According to Briscoe, prior to the occupation the building was being picketed in protest at the reprisal executions of Richard Barrett, Joseph McKelvey, Liam Mellows and Rory O'Connor in Dublin on 8 December 1922. There had also been threats to the consular staff, which, along with the occupation, led Smiddy to bolster security for the nascent Irish diplomatic service in the US. His subsequent suggestions that the republicans who occupied the consulate may have had links to the Communists and 'the most violent of the Irish Reds in New York' can, perhaps, be taken as simply a sign of the times.[10]

by John Gibney

FURTHER READING

Ronan Fanning, Michael Kennedy, Dermot Keogh, Eunan O'Halpin (eds), *Documents on Irish Foreign Policy*, vol. i, *1919–1922* (Dublin, 1998); vol ii, *1922–1926* (Dublin, 2000): online at www.difp.ie

Bernadette Whelan, *United States foreign policy and Ireland: from empire to independence, 1913–29* (Dublin, 2006)

NOTES

[1] 'De Valera envoy seizes consulate', *New York Times*, 28 December 1922; Catherine M. Burns, 'The battle for the Irish consulate'; available at: www.gothamcenter.org/blog/the-battle-for-the-irish-consulate- (accessed 24 July 2020).

[2] *Documents on Irish Foreign Policy* (hereafter *DIFP*), vol. i, *1919–1922* (Dublin, 1998), document 268, Collins to Smiddy, 10 April 1922.

[3] Francis M. Carroll, *Money for Ireland: finance, diplomacy, politics and the first Dáil Éireann loans, 1919–1936* (Westport, CT, 2002), 35–44.

[4] 'Irish consul to pay', *New York Times*, 30 December 1922.

[5] Robert Briscoe, *For the life of me* (Boston and Toronto, 1958), 198.

[6] *DIFP*, vol. ii, *1923–1926* (Dublin, 2000), document 14, Smiddy to Fitzgerald, 6 January 1923.

[7] 'Free State consul ousts republicans', *New York Times*, 31 December 1922.

[8] Bureau of Military History, witness statement 982, Alice Ginnell, 67.

[9] *DIFP*, vol. ii, document 10, Smiddy to External Affairs, 3 January 1923; document 14, Smiddy to Fitzgerald, 6 January 1923.

[10] *DIFP*, vol. ii, document No. 13, Smiddy to Fitzgerald, 6 January 1923; document 18, Smiddy to Fitzgerald, 15 January 1923.

EPILOGUE

FORGETTING 1922

1922 is a worthy candidate for the most undeservedly forgotten year in contemporary Irish history. Yet, it is a strange forgetting: while key events that occurred that year have not entirely slipped out of memory, they have been eclipsed by other dates and therefore do not receive the recognition they deserve.

Ireland stands out among modern nation-states for not having a designated anniversary of its founding. Saint Patrick's Day, which in its modern form is a celebration of Irish peoplehood, does not fulfil that function (hence, on that day, leading statesmen typically go abroad on diplomatic missions to locations with substantial diaspora communities). Easter Monday, as a national holiday commemorating the failed Easter Rising, can at best mark a milestone on the path towards sovereignty. For good reason, the centennial of the Irish revolution has been memorialised through a 'Decade of Centenaries', circumventing the problem of settling on a single commemorative date, which would undoubtedly be disputed. Significantly, the various proposals occasionally floated for a designated independence celebration tellingly elide relevant dates in 1922. More generally, the year does not feature in the list of iconic dates of nationalist history (1798, 1848, 1867, 1916 and all that). It has also been left outside of the canon of unionist

A man stands in the Four Courts, holding a burned document from the Public Record Office.

history (1641, 1689–90, 1912, 1916 and all that), even though it was the year in which Northern Ireland consummated its separation from the 'South' in favour of retaining a place in the United Kingdom. In effect, 1922 has been relegated to a forgetful remembrance, whereby memory is obscured and tinged with ambivalence.

Historical oblivion is multi-layered and, when examined closely, a hierarchy of disremembering can be discerned. The founding of Saorstát Éireann, the Irish Free State, was contested from the outset by the opponents of the Anglo-Irish Treaty who sought to tarnish, if not efface, its memory. At the inaugural banquet of the (largely forgotten) Irish Race Congress held in Paris in late January 1922, Éamon de Valera provocatively proposed a toast to the Irish Republic, much to the chagrin of the pro-Treaty delegates. Indeed, in popular historical consciousness, de Valera (who was in opposition till 1932) is often erroneously remembered as the founding figure of independent Ireland, dismissively glossing over the decade of governments headed by W.T. Cosgrave and Cumann na nGaedheal, a party that was *de facto* formed at the end of 1922.

Remembrance of the civil war—with its fratricidal intra-community vehemence and hidden history of violence against women—was largely overshadowed by a glorified memory of the War of Independence. The state-choreographed funeral of Arthur Griffith (16 August 1922), who has been dubbed by Anne Dolan 'The Forgotten President', was outshone within a fortnight by the outpouring of mass grief at the funeral of Michael Collins (28 August 1922). But even this memorable event was shrouded in the discomfiting controversies of the civil war. A poorly constructed Cenotaph in memory of Griffith and Collins erected in 1923 soon fell into disrepair, to be dismantled in 1939; its replacement with a permanent monument in 1950 passed without notice.[1] The new state encountered difficulties in promoting memorialisation of its troubled foundation and, as demonstrated by David Fitzpatrick, its stifled attempts at commemoration amounted to a 'chronicle of embarrassment'.[2]

Likewise, the new autonomous statelet of Northern Ireland showed little interest in remembering 1922, which was marred by a sharp exacerbation of the sectarian violence associated with the so-called 'Belfast Pogrom', including such atrocities as the McMahon killings on 24 March. Wary of antagonising the Catholic nationalist minority and aware of having forsaken their fellow unionists outside of the six north-eastern counties, northern unionists refrained from marking the confirmation of partition that followed the formal establishment of the Irish Free State on 6 December 1922.

The dynamics of remembering and forgetting pertaining to 1922 are epitomised in the symbolism of the partial destruction of the Four Courts at the beginning of the civil war, on 30 June. Asked on the day for his response to the news of the loss of the thousands of manuscripts stored in the Treasury Records building of the Four Courts complex, Secretary of State for the Colonies Winston Churchill pragmatically quipped that 'a state without archives is better than archives without a state'.[3] The burning of the Public Record Office has been controversially decried by Tom Garvin as a deliberate 'attempt to murder the nation as a collective entity with a collective memory'.[4] Yet, it would seem that the damage to the archives was incidental rather than intended.[5]

Paradoxically, remembrance—and even forgetting—of an event can begin prior to its occurrence. There was a 'prememory' to the takeover of the Four Courts, in the sense that the anti-Treaty republican forces that occupied the buildings just before Easter 1922 were probably hoping to re-enact the spectacular takeover of the General Post Office in Easter 1916. Yet, this imitative choice of tactics was inevitably subject to 'pre-forgetting', as the episode was destined to remain in the shadow of the towering memory of the GPO, which was elevated into a national myth.[6] The demolition of much of the grand eighteenth-century building complex on Inns Quay was akin to the destruction of 'Big houses', which had commenced throughout Ireland during the War of Independence, reaching new heights in the civil war, and is another of the largely forgotten features of 1922.[7] As such, it was an act of post-colonial decommemorating that presaged the destruction of Ascendancy and imperial monuments in the following years (culminating in the blowing up of Nelson's Pillar in 1966, during the jubilee anniversary of the Easter Rising). Iconoclastic vandalism is generally regarded as an act of oblivion, but it leaves a glaring absence in the landscape that can trigger recuperative initiatives of re-commemorating.[8]

'[T]he great gap which the fire has made', was labelled by *The Irish Times* 'a memorial of destruction'. If monuments are designed to preserve memory, the haunting image of the burnt archive acquired an added symbolic resonance, inadvertently becoming a counter-monument, signifying the lamentable obliteration of historical memory. A contemporary letter to the editor expressed the yearning for restoration: 'one may hope that the destruction of the Public Record Office and the Four Courts may not prove a holocaust and that some of the records may be salvaged'.[9] This trope of a 'holocaust' (in its original Greek sense of a sacrifice by fire) would be repeated in subsequent years when people lamented the loss of archival records and expressed a hope that copies could be found.[10] The aspiration to recover lost memory would ultimately be partially fulfilled a century later with the Beyond 2022 project, a cutting-edge collaboration of the National Archives of Ireland and the UK, the Public Record Office in Northern Ireland, the Irish Manuscripts Commission and Trinity College Dublin, together with numerous other participating institutions, to create a digitalised virtual reproduction of the lost archives.[11] This is a powerful demonstration of how restored memory can counter the forgetting of 1922.

by Guy Beiner

FURTHER READING

Guy Beiner, 'Irish Studies and the dynamics of disremembering', in Marguérite Corporaal, Christopher Cusack and Ruud van den Beuken (eds), *Irish Studies and the dynamics of memory: transitions and transformations* (Oxford and Bern, 2017), 297–321

Anne Dolan, *Commemorating the Irish civil war: history and memory, 1923–2000* (Cambridge, 2003)

Ian McBride, 'Memory and national identity in modern Ireland', in Ian McBride (ed.), *History and memory in modern Ireland* (Cambridge, 2001), 1–42

NOTES

[1] Anne Dolan, *Commemorating the Irish civil war: history and memory, 1923–2000* (Cambridge, 2003), 6–120.

[2] David Fitzpatrick, 'Commemoration in the Irish Free State: a chronicle of embarrassment', in Ian McBride (ed.), *History and memory in modern Ireland* (Cambridge, 2001), 184–203.

[3] *House of Commons debates*, 30 June 1922, vol. 155, m c2558.

[4] Tom Garvin, 'The IRA's "cultural murder" at the Four Courts, 1922', *The Irish Times*, 18 May 2000, 15. In response, see, Eoin Neeson, 'No case for "cultural murder"', *The Irish Times*, 6 July 2000, 15.

[5] Michael Fewer, 'What caused the "Great Explosion"?: the battle of the Four Courts, 28–30 June 1922', *History Ireland* 27 (4) (July–August 2019), 44–7.

[6] For the concept of 'prememory', see, Guy Beiner, 'Making sense of memory: coming to terms with conceptualisations of historical remembrance', in Richard S. Grayson and Fearghal McGarry (eds), *Remembering 1916: the Easter Rising, the Somme and the politics of memory in Ireland* (Cambridge, 2016), 13–23: 21–2. For 'pre-forgetting', see, Guy Beiner, *Forgetful remembrance: social forgetting and vernacular historiography of a rebellion in Ulster* (Oxford, 2018), 46–88.

[7] Michael Hopkinson, *Green against green: the Irish civil war* (New York, 1988), 194.

[8] See Guy Beiner, 'When monuments fall: the significance of decommemorating', *Éire-Ireland* 56 (1 and 2) (2021), 37–65.

[9] *The Irish Times*, 8 July 1922, 1; 13 July 1922, 6. For the concept of 'counter-monument' (*Gegendenkmal* in German), see, Quentin Stevens *et al.*, 'Counter-monuments: the anti-monumental and the dialogic', in *Journal of Architecture* 23 (5) (2018), 718–39.

[10] *The Irish Times*, 21 September 1925, 6, and 22 May 1926, 6.

[11] See, the 'Beyond 2022: Ireland's virtual record treasury' project; it can be accessed at: beyond2022.ie (accessed 22 April 2021).

THE DEPARTURE OF ERIN.

Drawn by Bert Thomas.

John Bull (to Erin): "Well, good-bye, Erin: and I hope you'll be happy with him."

BIBLIOGRAPHY

ARCHIVAL SOURCES

American Irish Historical Society Archives, Friends of Irish Freedom papers
Archives of the Capuchin Franciscans Province of Ireland
Archives of the Pontifical Irish College, Rome, John Hagan papers
Boston College Archives, Burns Library, Thomas Clarke collection
British Library:
    Asia, Pacific and Africa Collections
    Bernard papers
Central Statistics Office, Saorstát Éireann, 1926 Census Report
Churchill College, Cambridge, Chandos papers
Cork City Library, Local Studies department
Dáil debates
Dublin Diocesan Archives, Byrne papers
European University Institute, Special Collections, League of Nations records
Garda Museum and Archives, Dublin Metropolitan Police and Civic Guard (Garda Síochána) Personnel Registers
House of Commons debates
House of Lords records
Library of Congress, Sound recordings, Éamon de Valera: St Patrick's Day address
Military Archives:
    Bureau of Military History files
    Civil War files
    Department of Defence files
    Military Service Pensions Collection
    Papers of the Army Inquiry Committee
Minutes of the Municipal Council of the city of Dublin
National Archives of Ireland:
    Board of Works files
    Census of Ireland, 1901/1911
    Department of Finance, Post-truce Compensation Claims
    Department of Foreign Affairs
    Department of the Taoiseach
    Office of the Official Film Censor
    Provisional Government Cabinet minutes

Opposite: 'The departure of Erin'; *London Opinion*, December 1922, depicts John Bull entrusting young Erin to the care of the Irish Free State.

National Archives of the United Kingdom:
    Home Office
    Records of the Colonial Office
National Library of Ireland:
    Notes from Mountjoy Jail, pamphlet volume IR 3359 P38
    Kevin O'Higgins, 'The new de Valera: a contrast and some disclosures', March
    1922, pamphlet volume IR 94109
    Seán T. Ó Ceallaigh papers
    Uncatalogued political ephemera
New York Public Library Archives and Manuscripts:
    Frank P. Walsh papers
    Maloney Collection of Irish Historical papers
Northern Ireland parliamentary debates
Parliamentary Archives, London
Public Record Office of Northern Ireland:
    Cabinet Secretariat
    Home Affairs
    Irish Unionist Alliance papers
Report of the Labour Commission to Ireland
Seanad Éireann debates
UCD Archives:
    Cumann na nGaedheal and Fine Gael party minute books
    Éamon de Valera papers
    Leinster Branch, Irish Rugby Football Union annual general meeting minutes
    Máire Comerford papers
    Moss Twomey papers
    Richard Mulcahy papers

NEWSPAPERS AND PERIODICALS

Abbotsford Post (British Columbia)
Advocate (Melbourne)
Anglo-Celt
Athlone Journal
Belfast News-Letter
Belfast Telegraph
Capital Journal (Salem, Oregon)
Catholic Press
Catholic Record (London, Ontario)
Daily Express (Waga Waga, New South Wales)
Daily News (St John's, Newfoundland)
Derry Journal

Detroit Free Press
Dublin Evening Telegraph
Donegal Democrat
Donegal News
Dungannon Democrat
El Universal
Evening Echo
Evening Herald
Evening Telegram (St John's, Newfoundland)
Evening World (New York)
Fenian
Fermanagh Herald
Freeman's Journal
Freeman's Journal (Sydney, New South Wales)
Gisborne Times
Hartford Herald (Hartford, Kentucky)
History Ireland
Illustrated London News
Irish Catholic Directory and Almanac
Irish Builder
Irish Homestead
Irish Independent
Irish Life
Irish Sword
The Irish Times
Irish Volunteer
Japan Times
Lisburn Hearld
Lisburn Standard
Montreal Gazette
The Nation
Nenagh Guardian
New Statesman
New York Herald
New York Times
New York Tribune
New Zealand Herald
Newtownards Chronicle
An t-Óglách
Paragould Soliphone (Paragould, Arkansas)
Poverty Bay Herald (New Zealand)
The Republic
Republican War Bulletin

Sligo Champion
Sunday Independent
Sunday Press
The Times
Times of India
Ulster Bulletin
Ulster Herald
Washington Times
Waterford News and Star
Weekly Irish Times
Westminster Gazette
Witness
Workers' Republic

REFERENCE

Beyond 2022: Ireland's virtual record treasury, beyond2022.ie

British Pathé, britishpathe.com/

Commission on emigration and other population problems, *Reports* (Dublin, 1955)

Corpus of Electronic Texts database, celt.ucc.ie

Dáil debates, oireachtas.ie/en/debates/find/?debateType=dail

Defence of the Realm Act (1914)

Defence of the Realm (Amendment) Act (1915)

Fine Ghaedheal, *Proceedings of the Irish Race Congress in Paris, January 1922.*

Hansard House of Commons reports, hansard.parliament.uk/commons

Indemnity Act (1923)

Irish Film and TV Research Online, www.tcd.ie/Irishfilm

Irish Reports

Kilmainham Gaol graffiti, kilmainhamgaolgraffiti.com/

King's Bench reports

Nobel Prize in Literature, 1923 lecture, www.nobelprize.org/prizes/literature/1923/
     yeats/lecture/

Restoration of Order in Ireland Act (1920)

Saorstát Éireann, Census Report 1926, cso.ie/en/census/censusvolumes1926to1991/
     historicalreports/census1926reports/

Seanad debates, oireachtas.ie/en/debates/find/?debateType=Seanad

The Sir Arnold Bax website, arnoldbax.com/

BOOKS AND ARTICLES

Addams, Jane 1930 *The second twenty years at Hull-House*. New York. Macmillan.

Alford, C.F. 2016 *Trauma, culture and PTSD*. New York. Palgrave Macmillan.

Andrews, C.S. 2001 *Dublin made me* (originally published 1979). Dublin. Dufour Editions.

Banerjee, Sikata 2012 *Muscular nationalism: gender, violence and empire in India and Ireland, 1914–2004*. New York and London. New York University Press.

Bardon, Jonathan 1992 *A history of Ulster*. Belfast. Blackstaff Press.

Bax, Arnold 1952 Foreword to Aloys Fleischmann (ed.), *Music in Ireland. A symposium*, iii–iv. Cork. Cork University Press.

Beatty, Aidan 2016 *Masculinity and power in Irish nationalism, 1884–1938*. London. Palgrave Macmillan.

Beiner, Guy 2016 'Making sense of memory: coming to terms with conceptualisations of historical remembrance', in Richard S. Grayson and Fearghal McGarry (eds), *Remembering 1916: the Easter Rising, the Somme and the politics of memory in Ireland*, 13–23. Cambridge. Cambridge University Press.

Beiner, Guy 2017 'Irish Studies and the dynamics of disremembering', in Marguérite Corporaal, Christopher Cusack and Ruud van den Beuken (eds), *Irish Studies and the dynamics of memory: transitions and transformations*, 297–321. Oxford and Bern. Peter Lang.

Beiner, Guy 2018 *Forgetful remembrance: social forgetting and vernacular historiography of a rebellion in Ulster*. Oxford. Oxford University Press.

Ben-Ze'ev, Efrat, Ginio, Ruth and Winter, Jay (eds), 2010 *Shadows of war: a social history of silence in the twentieth century*. Cambridge. Cambridge University Press.

Bence-Jones, Mark 1978 *Burke's guide to country houses* (3 vols), vol. i: *Ireland*. London. Burke's Peerage.

Bew, Paul 2016 *Churchill and Ireland*. Oxford. Oxford University Press.

Bielenberg, Andy 2013 'Exodus: the emigration of southern Irish Protestants during the Irish War of Independence and the civil war', *Past & Present* 218 (1) (February), 199–233.

Boland, T.B. 1986 *James Duhig*. Brisbane. University of Queensland Press.

Borgonovo, John 2013 *The battle for Cork: July–August 1922*. Cork. Mercier Press.

Borgonovo, John 2020 'Cumann na mBan, martial women and the Irish civil war, 1922–1923', in Linda Connolly (ed.), *Women and the Irish revolution: feminism, activism, violence*, 68–84. Dublin. Irish Academic Press.

Bourke, Joanne 2000 'Effeminacy, ethnicity and the end of trauma: the sufferings of "shell-shocked" men in Great Britain and Ireland, 1914–39', *Journal of Contemporary History* 35 (1) (January), 57–69.

Bourke, Richard 2017 'Reflections on the political thought of the Irish revolution', *Transactions of the Royal Historical Society* 27, 175–91.

Bourke, Richard 2020 'Political and religious ideas of the Irish revolution', *History of European Ideas* 46 (7), 997–1008.

Briscoe, Robert 1958 *For the life of me*. Boston. Little, Brown.

Brooks, Tim 2020 'The minstrel show on records', in *The Blackface minstrel show in mass media: 20th century performances on radio, records, film and television*. Jefferson, North Carolina. McFarland and Company.

Brothers, Thomas 2014 *Louis Armstrong, master of modernism*. New York. W.W. Norton and Company.

Brown, Howard G. 2018 *Mass violence and the self: from the French wars of religion to the Paris Commune*. Ithaca, NY. Cornell University Press.

Brown, Terence 2001 *The life of W.B. Yeats: a critical biography* (originally published 1999). Dublin. Gill and Macmillan.

Browne, William J. 1981 *Eighty-four years a Newfoundlander: memoirs of William J. Browne*. St John's, Newfoundland. W.J. Browne.

Bruce, Steve 2007 *Paisley: religion and politics in Northern Ireland*. Oxford. Oxford University Press.

Brundage, David 2016 *Irish nationalists in America: the politics of exile, 1798–1998*. New York. Oxford University Press.

Brundage, David 2016 'The Easter Rising and New York's anticolonial nationalists', in Miriam Nyhan Grey (ed.), *Ireland's allies: America and the 1916 Easter Rising*, 347–59. Dublin. UCD Press.

Buckland, Patrick 1979 *The factory of grievances: devolved government in Northern Ireland, 1921–1939*. Dublin. Gill and Macmillan.

Buckland, Patrick 1980 *James Craig: Lord Craigavon*. Dublin. Gill and Macmillan.

Byrne, Susan 2020 '"Keeping company with the enemy": gender and sexual violence against women during the Irish War of Independence and civil war, 1919–1923', *Women's History Review*, 108–25.

Cahillane, Laura 2016 *Drafting the Irish Free State constitution*. Manchester. Manchester University Press.

Campbell, Colm 1994 *Emergency law in Ireland 1918–1925*. Oxford. Clarendon Press.

Campbell, Fergus and Varley, Tony (eds) 2013 *Land questions in modern Ireland*. Manchester. Manchester University Press.

Carroll, Francis M. 2002 *Money for Ireland: finance, diplomacy, politics, and the First Dáil Éireann loans, 1919–1936*. Westport, CT. Praeger Publishers.

Carroll, Stuart (ed.), 2007 *Cultures of violence: interpersonal violence in historical perspective*. Basingstoke. Palgrave Macmillan.

Casement, Roger 1914 *The crime against Ireland*. New York.

Childers, Erskine 1911 *The framework of home rule*. London. Edward Arnold.

Clark, Gemma 2014 *Everyday violence in the Irish civil war*. Cambridge. Cambridge University Press.

Clark, Gemma 2017 'Violence in the Irish civil war', in John Crowley, Donal Ó Drisceoil and Mike Murphy (eds), *Atlas of the Irish revolution*, 732–5. Cork. Cork University Press.

Clark, Gemma 2020 'Violence against women in the Irish civil war, 1922–3: gender-based harm in global perspective', *Irish Historical Studies* 44 (165) (May), 75–90.

Clarke, Kathleen 1991 (Helen Litton ed.), *Revolutionary woman: my fight for Irish freedom*. Dublin. O'Brien Press.

Coleman, Marie 2015 'Violence against women during the Irish War of Independence, 1919–21', in Diarmaid Ferriter and Susannah Riordan (eds), *Years of turbulence: the Irish revolution and its aftermath*, 137–56. Dublin. UCD Press.

Coleman, Marie and Murphy, William 2009 'Mellows, William Joseph (Liam)', in James McGuire and James Quinn (eds), *Dictionary of Irish biography*, 477–9. Cambridge. Cambridge University Press.

Collins, Stephen and Meehan, Ciara 2020 *Saving the state: Fine Gael from Collins to Varadkar*. Dublin. Gill.

Commission on Emigration and Other Population Problems, 1955 *Reports*. Dublin. Stationery Office.

Conlon, Lil 1969 *Cumann na mBan and the women of Ireland, 1913–25*. Kilkenny. Kilkenny People Ltd.

Connolly, James 1914 *Labour in Irish history*. Dublin. Maunsel and Company.

Connolly, Linda 2021 'Sexual violence in the Irish civil war: a forgotten war crime?', *Women's History Review* 30 (1), 126–43.

Costello, Peter and Farmar, Tony 1992 *The very heart of the city: the story of Denis Guiney and Clerys*. Dublin. Clery and Company.

Cousins, Mel 2013 *The birth of Irish social welfare in Ireland, 1922–1952*. Dublin.

Crawford, Lyndsay 1920 *The problem of Ulster*. New York. Protestant Friends of Ireland.

Cronin, Mike and Adair, Daryl 2002 *The wearing of the green: a history of St Patrick's Day*. Oxford and New York. Routledge.

Cronin, Mike 2004 'The Irish Free State and Aonach Tailteann', in Alan Bairner (ed.), *Sport and the Irish: histories, identities, issues*, 53–84. Dublin. UCD Press.

Cronin, Seán 1972 *The McGarrity papers*. Tralee. Anvil Books.

Cullen, Fintan and Kennedy, Róisín (eds), 2021 *Sources in Irish art 2. A reader*. Cork. Cork University Press.

Cullingford, Elizabeth 1981 *Yeats, Ireland and fascism*. London. Macmillan.

Cunningham, Niall 2013 '"The doctrine of vicarious punishment": space, religion and the Belfast Troubles of 1920–22', *Journal of Historical Geography* 40, 52–66.

Curran, Joseph M. 1980 *The birth of the Irish Free State, 1921–1923*. Tuscaloosa, AL. University of Alabama Press.

Daly, Mary E. 1992 *Industrial development and Irish national identity, 1922–1939*. Syracuse, NY. Syracuse University Press.

Daly, Mary E. 2006 'Marriage, fertility and women's lives in twentieth-century Ireland', *Women's History Review* 15, 571–85.

Dawley, Alan 2003 *Changing the world: American progressives in war and revolution*. Princeton, NJ. Princeton University Press.

de Búrca, Padraig and Boyle, John 1922 *Free State or Republic? Pen pictures of the historic treaty session of Dáil Éireann*. Dublin. Talbot Press.

de Nie, Michael 2004 *The eternal Paddy: Irish identity and the British press, 1798–1882*. Madison, WI. University of Wisconsin Press.

Delaney, Enda and McGarry, Fearghal 2020 'Introduction: a global history of the Irish revolution', *Irish Historical Studies* 44 (165), 1–10.

Dervan, Michael (ed.), 2016 *The invisible art: a century of music in Ireland, 1916–2016*. Dublin. New Island.

Dicey, A.V. 1913 *A fool's paradise*. London. John Murray.

Dolan, Anne 2003 *Commemorating the Irish civil war: history and memory, 1923–2000*. Cambridge. Cambridge University Press.

Dolan, Anne 2018 'Politics, economy and society in the Irish Free State, 1922–1939', in Thomas Bartlett (ed.), *The Cambridge history of Ireland*. Volume iv, *1800 to the present*, 323–48. Cambridge. Cambridge University Press.

Dolan, Anne and Murphy, William 2018 *Michael Collins, the man and the revolution*. Cork. Collins Press.

Dolan Stover, Justin 2017 'Families, vulnerability and sexual violence during the Irish revolution', in Jennifer Evans and Ciara Meehan (eds), *Perceptions of pregnancy from the seventeenth to the twentieth century*, 57–75. London. Palgrave Macmillan.

Donnelly, James S., Jr, 2012 'Big House burnings in county Cork during the Irish revolution, 1920–21', *Éire-Ireland* 47 (3 and 4) (Fall/Winter), 141–97.

Dooley, Terence 2001 *The decline of the big house in Ireland: a study of Irish landed families, 1860–1960*. Dublin. Wolfhound Press.

Dooley, Terence 2004 *'The land for the people': the land question in independent Ireland*. Dublin. UCD Press.

Dooley, Terence and Ridgway, Christopher (eds), 2011 *The Irish country house: its past, present and future*. Dublin. Four Courts Press.

Dorney, John 2017 *The civil war in Dublin: the fight for the Irish capital, 1922–1924*. Dublin. Merrion Press.

Dubois, Laurent 2012 *Haiti: the aftershocks of history*. New York. Henry Holt-Metropolitan Books.

Earner-Byrne, Lindsey 2015 'The rape of Mary M: a microhistory of sexual violence and moral redemption in 1920s Ireland', *Journal of the History of Sexuality* 24 (1) (January), 75–98.

Earner-Byrne, Lindsey 2017 *Letters of the Catholic poor: poverty in independent Ireland, 1920–1940*. Cambridge. Cambridge University Press.

English, Richard 1994 *Radicals and the republic: socialist republicanism in the Irish Free State, 1925–1937*. Oxford. Clarendon Press.

Enright, Seán 2019 *The Irish civil war. Law, execution and atrocity*. Dublin. Merrion Press.

Expert Advisory Group on Centenary Commemorations 2019 *Guidance from the Expert Advisory Group on Commemorations to support the state's approach to the remembrance of significant historical events over the remainder of the decade of centenaries.* Dublin. Stationery Office.

Fallon, Charlotte H. 1986 *Soul of fire: a biography of Mary MacSwiney*. Cork. Mercier Press.

Fanning, Ronan 1978 *The Irish Department of Finance 1922–58*. Dublin. Institute of Public Administration.

Fanning, Ronan 1983 *Independent Ireland*. Dublin. Helicon.

Fanning, Ronan 2013 *Fatal Path. British government and Irish revolution 1910–1922*. London. Faber and Faber.

Fanning, Ronan, Kennedy, Michael, Crowe, Catriona, Keogh, Dermot and O'Halpin, Eunan (eds), 1998 *Documents on Irish Foreign Policy*, vol. i, *1919–22*. Dublin. Royal Irish Academy.

Fanning, Ronan, Kennedy, Michael, O'Halpin, Eunan and Keogh, Dermot (eds), 1999 *Documents on Irish foreign policy*, vol. ii, *1923–26*. Dublin. Royal Irish Academy.

Farmar, Tony 2010 *Privileged lives: a social history of middle-class Ireland, 1888–1989*. Dublin. A. & A. Farmar.

Farrell, Michael 1983 *Arming the Protestants: the formation of the Ulster Special Constabulary and the Royal Ulster Constabulary, 1920–27*. London and Cork. Pluto Press and Brandon.

Fedorowich, Kent 1996 'The problems of disbandment: The Royal Irish Constabulary and imperial migration, 1919–29', *Irish Historical Studies* 30 (117), 88–110.

Ferriter, Diarmaid 2011 'Birth of a nation: the Treaty that transformed Ireland', *The Irish Times*, 3 December.

Ferriter, Diarmaid 2015 *A nation and not a rabble: the Irish revolution 1913–1923*. London. Profile Books.

Fewer, Michael 2019 'What caused the "Great Explosion"? The battle of the Four Courts, 28–30 June 1922', *History Ireland* 27 (4) (July–August), 44–7.

Figgis, Darrell 1922 *The Irish constitution: explained by Darrell Figgis*. Dublin. Mellifont Press.

Fitzpatrick, David 1980 'Strikes in Ireland', *Saothar* 6, 26–39.

Fitzpatrick, David 1984 *Irish emigration, 1801–1921*. Dublin. Economic and Social History Society of Ireland.

Fitzpatrick, David 1998 *The two Irelands 1912–1939*. Oxford. Oxford University Press.

Fitzpatrick, David 2001 'Commemoration in the Irish Free State: a chronicle of embarrassment', in Ian McBride (ed.), *History and memory in modern Ireland*, 184–203. Cambridge. Cambridge University Press.

Fitzpatrick, David 2002 'The Orange Order and the border', *Irish Historical Studies* 33 (129) (May), 52–67.

Flanagan, Frances 2015 *Remembering the revolution: dissent, culture and nationalism in the Irish Free State*. Oxford. Oxford University Press.

Follis, Brian 1995 *A state under siege: the establishment of Northern Ireland, 1920–25*. Oxford. Clarendon Press.

Foreman, Lewis (ed.), 1992 *Farewell, my youth and other writings by Arnold Bax* (originally published 1943). Farnham. Scholar Press.

Fortescue, John 1933 *Author and curator: an autobiography*. Edinburgh, London. Blackwood.

Foster, Gavin 2015 *The Irish civil war and society: politics, class, and conflict*. London. Palgrave Macmillan.

Foster, R.F. 1988 *Modern Ireland. 1600–1972*. London. Penguin.

Foster, R.F. 1989 'Varieties of Irishness', in Maurna Crozier (ed.), *Cultural traditions in Northern Ireland*, 5–24. Belfast. Queen's University.

Foster, R.F. 2003 *W.B. Yeats, A life:* vol. ii, *the arch-poet, 1915–1939*. Oxford. Oxford University Press.

Foster, R.F. 2014 *Vivid faces. The revolutionary generation in Ireland 1890–1923*. London. Penguin.

Foster, R.F. 2019 '"When all is ruin once again": Yeats and Thoor Ballylee', in Hermione Lee and Kate Kennedy (eds), *Lives of houses*, 217–31. Oxford and Princeton, NJ. Princeton University Press.

Frawley, Oona (ed), 2021 *Women and the Decade of Commemorations*. Bloomington, IN. Indiana University press.

Gallagher, Frank 1965 *The Anglo-Irish Treaty*. London. Hutchinson.

Gannon, Darragh 2016 *Proclaiming a Republic. Ireland, 1916 and the National Collection*. Dublin. Irish Academic Press.

Gannon, Darragh 2020 'Addressing the Irish world: Éamon de Valera's "Cuban policy" as a global case study', *Irish Historical Studies* 44 (165) (May), 41–56.

Gannon, Seán William 2018 *The Irish imperial service: policing Palestine and administering the empire, 1922–1966*. London. Palgrave Macmillan.

Garnham, Neal 2002 'Fox hunting', in Sean J. Connolly (ed.), *The Oxford companion to Irish history*, 214–5. Oxford. Oxford University Press.

Garvin, Tom 1996 *1922: the birth of Irish democracy*. Dublin. Gill and Macmillan.

Garvin, Tom 2000 'The IRA's "cultural murder" at the Four Courts, 1922', *The Irish Times*, 6 July, 15.

Gillis, Liz 2011 *The fall of Dublin*. Cork. Mercier Press.

Gilmore, George, *et al.*, 1934 *The Irish Republican Congress* (reprinted 1974). Cork. Cork Workers' Club.

Glennon, Kieran 2013 *From pogrom to civil war: Tom Glennon and the Belfast IRA*. Cork. Mercier Press.

Goltermann, Svenja 2010 'On silence, madness, and lassitude: negotiating the past in post-war West Germany', in Efrat Ben-Ze'ev, Ruth Ginio and Jay Winter (eds), *Shadows of war: a social history of silence in the twentieth century*, 91–112. Cambridge. Cambridge University Press.

Grant, Adrian 2018 *Derry: the Irish revolution, 1912–23*. Dublin. Four Courts Press.

Greaves, C.D. 2004 *Liam Mellows and the Irish revolution*. London. Lawrence and Wishart.

Grayson, Richard and McGarry, Fearghal (eds), 2016 *Remembering 1916: the Easter Rising, the Somme and the politics of memory in Ireland*. Cambridge. Cambridge University Press.

Griffith, Arthur 1904 *The resurrection of Hungary: a parallel for Ireland*. Dublin. Whelan and Son.

Gurley Flynn, Elizabeth 1973 *The rebel girl: an autobiography* (reprint of 1955 edn). New York. International Publishers.

Gwynn, Stephen 1921 *The Irish situation*. London. Jonathan Cape.

Hall, Dianne 2019 'Irish republican women in Australia: Kathleen Barry and Linda Kearns' tour in 1924–25', *Irish Historical Studies* 43 (163), 73–93.

Harari, Yuval 2005 'Martial illusions', *Journal of Military History*, 69 (1) (January), 43–72.

Hart, Peter 1992 'Michael Collins and the assassination of Sir Henry Wilson', *Irish Historical Studies* 28 (110) (November), 150–70.

Hart, Peter 1998 *The IRA and its enemies: violence and community in Cork, 1916–1923*. Oxford. Clarendon Press.

Hassett, Joseph 1986 *Yeats and the poetics of hate*. New York. St Martin's Press. Dublin. Gill and Macmillan.

Heaney, Mavis (ed.), 2004 *To God be the glory. The personal memoirs of Rev. William P. Nicholson*. Belfast. Ambassador Publications.

Heaney, Seamus 1995 *Crediting poetry: the Nobel lecture 1995*. Oldcastle. Gallery Press.

Henebry, Richard 1903 *Irish music: being an examination of the matter of scales, modes, and keys, with practical instructions and examples for players*. Dublin. An Cló Chumann.

Higgins, Michael D. 2017 'Foreword', in John Crowley *et al.*, *Atlas of the Irish revolution*, xiii–xiv. Cork. Cork University Press.

Hogan, David [Frank Gallagher], 1953 *The four glorious years*. Dublin. Irish Press.

Holmes, Andrew R. 2013 'Revivalism and fundamentalism in Ulster: W.P. Nicholson in context', in D.W. Bebbington and David Ceri Jones (eds), *Evangelicalism and fundamentalism: the experience of the United Kingdom during the twentieth century*, 253–72. Oxford. Oxford University Press.

Hopkinson, Michael 1988 *Green against green: the Irish Civil War* (reprinted 2004). Dublin. Gill and Macmillan.

Hopkinson, Michael (ed.), 1998 *Frank Henderson's Easter Rising. Recollections of a Dublin Volunteer*. Cork. Cork University Press.

Hopkinson, Michael (ed.) 1999 *The last days of Dublin Castle: the Mark Sturgis diaries*. Dublin. Irish Academic Press.

Hughes, Brian 2016 *Defying the IRA? Intimidation, coercion, and communities during the Irish revolution*. Liverpool. Liverpool University press.

Hughes, Brian 2021 'The disbanded Royal Irish Constabulary and forced migration, 1922–31', *Irish Studies Review* 29 (2), 212–28.

Hughes, Brian and Morrissey, Conor (eds), 2020 *Southern Irish loyalism, 1912–1949*. Liverpool. Liverpool University Press.

Hunt, Nigel C. 2010 *Memory, war and trauma*. Cambridge. Cambridge University Press.

Irwin, Archibald 1922 'Is there a revival in Ulster?', *The Witness*, 24 November, 5.

James, Stephanie 2019 'Varieties of Irish nationalism in south Australia, 1839–1950: changing terms of engagement', in Susan Arthure *et al.* (eds), *Irish South Australia: new histories and insights*, 192–211. Adelaide. Wakefield Press.

Jeffery, Keith 2000 *Ireland and the Great War*. Cambridge. Cambridge University Press.

Jeffery, Keith 2006 *Field Marshal Sir Henry Wilson: a political soldier*. Oxford. Oxford University Press.

Jolivet, Simon 2011 'Entre nationalismes Irlandais et Canadien-français: les intrigues Québécoises de la Self Determination for Ireland League of Canada and Newfoundland', *Canadian Historical Review* 92 (1), 43–68.

Jones, David 2013 'The issue of land distribution: revisiting graziers, land reform and political conflict in Ireland', in Fergus Campbell and Tony Varley (eds), *Land questions in modern Ireland*, 117–48. Manchester. Manchester University Press.

Jones, Heather 2021 *For king and country. The British monarchy and the First World War*. Cambridge. Cambridge University Press.

Kalyvas, Stathis N. 2006 *The logic of violence in civil war*. Cambridge. Cambridge University Press.

Kanter, Douglas and Walsh, Patrick (eds), 2019 *Taxation, politics, and protest in Ireland, 1662–2016*. London. Palgrave Macmillan.

Kelly, Brendan 2014 *Ada English: patriot and psychiatrist*. Dublin. Irish Academic Press.

Kennedy, Róisín 2016 'Art and uncertainty: painting in Ireland 1912–1932', in Brendan Rooney (ed.), *Creating history: stories of Ireland in art*, 154–71. Dublin. Irish Academic Press.

Kennedy, Róisín 2020 *Art and the nation state: the reception of modern art in Ireland*. Liverpool. Liverpool University Press.

Kenny, Colum 2020 *The enigma of Arthur Griffith: 'Father of us all'*. Dublin. Irish Academic Press.

Kettle, T.M. 1912 *The open secret of Ireland*. London. W.J. Ham-Smith.

Keown, Gerard 2016 *First of the small nations: the beginnings of Irish foreign policy in the interwar years, 1919–1932*. Oxford. Oxford University Press.

Kerr, Michael 2006 *Imposing power-sharing: conflict and coexistence in Northern Ireland and Lebanon*. Dublin. Irish Academic Press.

Kildea, Jeff 2020 *Hugh Mahon: patriot, pressman, politician* (2 vols). Sydney. Anchor Books.

Kildea, Jeff 2020 'From Go to Woe: 1915–1935', in Richard Reid *et al.* (eds), *To foster an Irish spirit: the Irish National Association of Australasia 1915–2015*, 4–62. Sydney. Anchor Books.

Kinsella, Anthony 1997 'The Special Infantry Corps', *Irish Sword* 20 (82), 331–45.

Kissane, Bill 2005 *The politics of the Irish civil war*. Oxford. Oxford University Press.

Kissane, Bill 2011 *New beginnings: constitutionalism and democracy in modern Ireland*. Dublin. UCD Press.

Klein, Axel 2016 'No state for music', in Michael Dervan (ed.), *The invisible art: a century of music in Ireland, 1916–2016*, 47–68. Dublin. New Island.

Klein, Axel 2019 *Bird of time. The music of Swan Hennessy*. Mainz. Schott Buch.

Kleinrichert, Denise 2001 *Republican internment and the prison ship Argenta 1922*. Dublin. Irish Academic Press.

Knirck, Jason 2006 *Imagining Ireland's independence: the debates over the Anglo-Irish Treaty of 1921*. Plymouth and Lanham, MD. Rowman and Littlefield.

Knirck, Jason 2006 *Women of the Dáil: gender, republicanism and the Anglo-Irish Treaty*. Dublin. Irish Academic Press.

Knirck, Jason 2007 'The Dominion of Ireland: the Anglo-Irish Treaty in an imperial context', *Éire-Ireland* 42 (1 and 2), 229–45.

Knirck, Jason 2014 *Afterimage of the revolution. Cumann na nGaedheal and Irish politics, 1922–1932*. Madison, WI. University of Wisconsin Press.

Kreilkamp, Vera 2004 'Fiction and empire: the Irish novel', in Kevin Kenny (ed.), *Ireland and the British Empire*, 154–81. Oxford. Oxford University Press.

Laffan, Michael 1999 *The resurrection of Ireland: the Sinn Féin party, 1916–1923*. Cambridge. Cambridge University Press.

Laffan, Michael 2009 'Griffith, Arthur Joseph', in James McGuire and James Quinn (eds), *Dictionary of Irish biography*, 277–86. Cambridge. Cambridge University Press.

Laffan, Michael 2014 *Judging W.T. Cosgrave*. Dublin. Royal Irish Academy.

Lavery, John 1940 *The life of a painter*. London. Little, Brown.

Lawlor, Pearse 2011 *The outrages 1920–1922*. Cork. Mercier Press.

Leary, Peter 2016 *Unapproved routes: histories of the Irish border 1922–1972*. Oxford. Oxford University Press.

Lee, J.J. 1989 *Ireland 1912–1985. Politics and society*. Cambridge. Cambridge University Press.

Lee McBain, Howard and Rogers, Lindsay 1923 *The new constitutions of Europe*. New York. Doubleday.

Loughlin, James 2007 *The British monarchy and Ireland, 1800 to the present*. Cambridge. Cambridge University Press.

Lynch, Robert 2004 'The Clones affray, 1922: massacre or invasion?', *History Ireland* 12 (3) (Autumn), 33–7.

Lynch, Robert 2006 *The northern IRA and the early years of partition, 1920–1922*. Dublin. Irish Academic Press.

Lynch, Robert 2010 'Explaining the Altnaveigh massacre', *Éire-Ireland* 45 (Winter), 184–210.

Lynch, Robert 2019 *The partition of Ireland 1918–1925*. Cambridge. Cambridge University Press.

Lynd, Robert 1919 *Ireland a nation*. London. Grant Richards.

Lyons, F.S.L. 1973 *Ireland since the Famine* (originally published 1971). London. Fontana Press.

McAtackney, Laura 2019 'Material and intangible interventions as future-making heritage at Kilmainham Gaol, Dublin', *Journal of Contemporary Archaeology* 6 (1), 120–35.

McAuliffe, Mary 2018 '"An idea has gone abroad that all women are against the Treaty": Cumann na Saoirse and pro-Treaty Women, 1922–3', in Mícheál Ó Fathartaigh and Liam Weeks (eds), *The Treaty: debating and establishing the Irish state*, 160–82. Newbridge. Irish Academic Press.

McAuliffe, Mary 2020 *Margaret Skinnider*. Dublin. UCD Press.

McAuliffe, Mary 2020 'The homefront as battlefront: women, violence and the domestic space during war in Ireland, 1919–1921', in Linda Connolly (ed.), *Women and the Irish revolution: feminism, activism, violence*, 164–82. Dublin. Irish Academic Press.

McBride, Ian 2001 'Memory and national identity in modern Ireland', in Ian McBride (ed.), *History and memory in modern Ireland*, 1–42. Cambridge. Cambridge University Press.

McCabe, M.P. 2013 *For God and Ireland: the fight for moral superiority in Ireland, 1922–1932*. Dublin. Irish Academic Press.

McCarthy, Cal 2014 *Cumann na mBan and the Irish revolution* (originally published 2007). Cork. Collins Press.

McCarthy, Patrick 1999 'The twilight years: the Irish regiments, 1919–1922', *Irish Sword* 21 (85), 314–35.

McClintock, Anne 1993 'Family feuds: gender, nationalism and the family', *Feminist Review* 44 (Summer), 61–80.

McConville, Sean 2014 *Irish political prisoners 1920–62: pilgrimage of desolation*. London. Routledge.

McCook, Alistair 2004 *Days of thunder: the history of the Ulster Grand Prix*. Belfast. Gill and Macmillan.

McCoole, Sinéad 2003 *No ordinary women: Irish female activists in the revolutionary years, 1900–1923*. Dublin. O'Brien Press.

McCoole, Sinéad 2010 *Passion and politics. Sir John Lavery: the salon revisited*. Dublin. Dublin City Gallery, The Hugh Lane.

McCourt, Frank 1996 *Angela's ashes*. New York. Scribner.

McCullagh, David 2017 *Éamon de Valera*, vol. 1, *Rise, 1882–1932*. Dublin. Gill and Macmillan.

McGahern, John 1990 *Amongst women*. London. Faber and Faber.

McGarry, Fearghal 2010 *The Rising. Ireland: Easter 1916*. Oxford. Oxford University Press.

McGee, Owen 2015 *Arthur Griffith*. Sallins. Irish Academic Press.

McGrath, Charles Ivar 2019 'Politics, parliament, patriot opinion, and the Irish national debt in the age of Jonathan Swift', in Douglas Kanter and Patrick Walsh (eds), *Taxation, politics, and protest in Ireland, 1662–2016*, 43–87. London. Palgrave Macmillan.

McLaughlin, Robert 2013 *Irish Canadian conflict and the struggle for Irish independence, 1912–1925*. Toronto. University of Toronto Press.

McNamara, Conor 2019 *Liam Mellows, soldier of the Republic: selected writings, 1914–1922*. Newbridge. Irish Academic Press.

McNeill, Ronald 1922 *Ulster's stand for Union*. London. John Murray.

Macardle, Dorothy 1937 *The Irish Republic*. London. Victor Gollancz.

Magill, Christopher 2020 *Political conflict in East Ulster, 1920–22: revolution and reprisal*. Woodbridge. Boydell Press.

Maguire, Martin 2008 *The civil service and the revolution in Ireland, 1912–38. 'Shaking the blood-stained hand of Mr Collins'*. Manchester. Manchester University Press.

Malcolm, Elizabeth and Hall, Dianne 2018 *A new history of the Irish in Australia*. Sydney. NewSouth Publishing.

Mannion, Patrick 2018 *A land of dreams: ethnicity, nationalism, and the Irish in Newfoundland, Nova Scotia, and Maine, 1880–1923*. Montreal. McGill-Queen's University Press.

Mannion, Patrick and McGarry, Fearghal (eds), 2022 *The Irish revolution: a global history*. New York. New York University Press.

Mansergh, Nicholas 1991 *The unresolved question: the Anglo-Irish settlement and its undoing, 1912–1972*. New Haven. Yale University Press.

Meehan, Ciara 2010 *The Cosgrave party: a history of Cumann na nGaedheal, 1923–1933*. Dublin. Royal Irish Academy.

Mellows, Liam 2019 'The Irish Republic is the people's republic', in Conor McNamara, *Liam Mellows, soldier of the republic: selected writings, 1914–1922*, 133–6. Newbridge. Irish Academic Press.

Mishkin, Tracy 1998 *The Harlem and Irish renaissances: language, identity and representation*. Gainsville, FL. University of Florida Press.

Mitchell, Arthur 1995 *Revolutionary government in Ireland: Dáil Éireann, 1919–22*. Dublin. Gill and Macmillan.

Mooney Eichaker, Joanne 2003 *Irish republican women in America: lecture tours, 1916–1925*. Dublin. Irish Academic Press.

Moore, Cormac 2019 *Birth of the border: the impact of partition in Ireland*. Newbridge. Merion Press.

Moorhouse, H.F. 1996 'One state, several countries: soccer and nationality in a "United" Kingdom', in J.A. Mangan (ed.), *Tribal identities: nationalism, Europe, sport*, 55–74. London. Frank Cass.

Moran, D.P. 2006 *The philosophy of Irish Ireland* (originally published 1905, *The Leader/*James Duffy & Co). Dublin. UCD Press.

Morrissey, T.J. 2010 *Edward J. Byrne 1872–1941: the forgotten archbishop of Dublin*. Dublin. Columba Press.

Moulton, Mo 2014 *Ireland and the Irish in interwar England*. Cambridge. Cambridge University Press.

Mulcahy, Risteárd 1999 *Richard Mulcahy (1886–1971): a family memoir*. Dublin. Aurelian Press.

Murphy, William 2014 *Political imprisonment and the Irish 1912–1921*. Oxford. Oxford University Press.

Murray, Damien 2018 *Irish nationalists in Boston: Catholicism and conflict, 1900–1928*. Washington, D.C. The Catholic University of America Press.

Murray, Patrick 2000 *Oracles of God: the Roman Catholic Church and Irish politics, 1922–37*. Dublin. UCD Press.

Mytton, Rebecca 2020 Revolutionary masculinities in the IRA, 1916–1923. Unpublished Ph.D. thesis. University of Sheffield.

Nally, T.H. 1922 *The Aonach Tailteann and the Tailteann Games: their origin, history and development*. Dublin. Talbot Press.

Nash, Catherine, Reid, Bryonie and Graham, Brian 2013 *Partitioned lives: the Irish borderlands*. Farnham. Ashgate.

Neeson, Eoin 2000 'No case for "cultural murder"', *The Irish Times*, 6 July, 15.

Noone, Val 2012 *Hidden Ireland in Victoria*. Ballarat. Ballarat Heritage Services.

Norton, Christopher 2007 'An earnest endeavour for peace: unionist opinion and the Craig/Collins peace pact of 30 March 1922', *Études Irlandais* 32 (1), 91–108.

O'Callaghan, Liam 2011 *Rugby in Munster: a social and cultural history*. Cork. Cork University Press.

O Cathaoir, Brendan 1997 'An Irishman's Diary', *The Irish Times*, 27 May.

O'Donnell, Peadar 1932 *The gates flew open*. London. Cape.

O'Dwyer, Rory 2010 *The Bastille of Ireland: Kilmainham Gaol: from ruin to restoration*. Dublin. History Press.

Ó Drisceoil, Donal 2001 *Peadar O'Donnell*. Cork. Cork University Press.

O'Farrell, Patrick 1968 *The Catholic Church in Australia: a short history 1788–1967*. Melbourne. Nelson.

O'Farrell, Patrick 1983 'The Irish Republican Brotherhood in Australia: the 1918 internments', in Oliver MacDonagh *et al.* (eds), *Irish culture and nationalism, 1750–1950*, 182–93. London. Palgrave Macmillan.

O'Halpin, Eunan and Ó Corráin, Daithí 2020 *The dead of the Irish revolution*. New Haven. Yale University Press.

O'Hegarty, P.S. 2015 *The victory of Sinn Féin: how it won it and how it used it* (originally published 1924, Talbot Press). Dublin. UCD Press.

O'Higgins, Kevin 1923 *The Catholic layman in public life*. Dublin. Catholic Truth Society.

O'Leary, Brendan 2006 'Foreword', in Michael Kerr, *Imposing power-sharing: conflict and coexistence in Northern Ireland and Lebanon*, xvii–xxxv. Dublin. Irish Academic Press.

O'Malley, Cormac K.H. and Dolan, Anne (eds), 2007 *'No surrender here!'. The civil war papers of Ernie O'Malley*. Dublin. Lilliput Press.

O'Malley, Kate 2008 *Ireland, India and empire: Indo-Irish radical connections, 1919–1964*. Manchester. Manchester University Press.

O'Neil, Timothy M. 2015 'Reframing the Republic: republican socioeconomic thought and the road to Fianna Fáil, 1923–26', in Mel Farrell, Jason Knirck and Ciara Meehan (eds), *A formative decade: Ireland in the 1920s*, 157–76. Dublin. Irish Academic Press.

O'Rahilly, Alfred 1937 *Thoughts on the constitution*. Dublin. Browne and Nolan.

O'Riordan, Anne 2015 *East Galway agrarian agitation and the burning of Ballydugan House*. Dublin. Four Courts Press.

Ó Ruairc, Pádraig Óg 2010 *The battle for Limerick city*. Cork. Mercier Press.

O'Sullivan, Niamh 2014 *Written in stone: the graffiti in Kilmainham Jail* (originally published 2009). Dublin. Liberties Press.

Ó Siadhail, Pádraig 2003 'The Self-Determination for Ireland League, 1920–1922: some notes on the league in Nova Scotia', *An Nasc* 15, 15–30.

Ozseker, Okan 2019 *Forging the border: Donegal and Derry in times of revolution, 1911–1925*. Newbridge. Irish Academic Press.

Parkinson, Alan F. 2004 *Belfast's unholy war*. Dublin. Four Courts Press.

Parlett, Graham 2017 'The background to In Memoriam', 9 March, The Sir Arnold Bax Website: http://arnoldbax.com/the-background-to-in-memoriam/ (accessed 26 August 2020).

Patterson, Henry 1997 *The politics of illusion: a political history of the IRA*. London. Serif.

Paul-Dubois, Louis François Alphonse 1907 *L'Irlande contemporaine et la question Irlandaise*. Paris. Perrin.

Philips, W. Alison 1923 *The revolution in Ireland, 1906–1923*. London. Longmans, Green.

Phoenix, Eamon 1994 *Northern nationalism: nationalist politics, partition and the Catholic minority in Northern Ireland, 1890–1940*. Belfast. Ulster Historical Foundation.

Pickering, Michael 2008 *Blackface minstrelsy in Britain*. Hampshire. Ashgate Publishing.

Pigott, John 1997 'Executions recalled', *Athenry Journal* 8. Available at: athenryparishheritage.com/executions-recalled-1922-by-canon-john-pigott/ (accessed 28 June 2021).

Plunkett, Horace 1904 *Ireland in the new century*. London. J. Murray.

Power, Bill 2000 *White knights, dark earls: the rise and fall of an Anglo-Irish dynasty*. Cork. Collins Press.

Prager, Jeffrey 1986 *Building democracy in Ireland*. Cambridge. Cambridge University Press.

Privilege, John 2009 *Michael Logue and the Catholic Church in Ireland, 1879–1925*. Manchester. Manchester University Press.

Puirséil, Niamh 2007 *The Irish Labour Party, 1922–73*. Dublin. UCD Press.

Rains, Stephanie 2010 *Commodity culture and social class in Dublin, 1850–1916*. Dublin. Irish Academic Press.

Raven Hill, L. 1922 'Our special artist in Ulster', *Illustrated London News*, 1 April, 464.

Redmond, John 1960 *Church, state and industry in East Belfast, 1827–1929*. Belfast. John Aiken & Son.

Regan, John M. 1999 *The Irish counter-revolution, 1921–1936: treatyite politics and settlement in independent Ireland*. Dublin. Gill and Macmillan.

Regan, John 2007 'Southern Irish nationalism as a historical problem', *Historical Journal*, 5 (1), 197–223.

Reid, Richard, *et al.* (eds), 2020 *To foster an Irish spirit: the Irish National Association of Australasia 1915–2015*. Sydney. Anchor Books.

Reilly, Ciaran J. 2011 'The burning of country houses in Co. Offaly, 1920–3', in Terence Dooley and Christopher Ridgway (eds), *The Irish country house: its past, present and future*, 110–33. Dublin. Four Courts Press.

Reizbaum, Marilyn 2010 'Urban legends', *Éire-Ireland* 45 (1 and 2) (Spring/Summer), 242–65.

Riordan, Susannah 2018 'Politics, economy, society: Northern Ireland, 1920–1939', in Thomas Bartlett (ed.), *The Cambridge history of Ireland*. Volume IV. *1800 to the present*, 296–98. Cambridge. Cambridge University Press.

Rockett, Kevin 1987 'The silent period', in Kevin Rockett, Luke Gibbons and John Hill, *Cinema and Ireland*, 23–9 (reprinted 2014). London. Croom Helm.

Rockett, Kevin with Rockett, Emer 2004 *Irish film censorship: a cultural journey from silent cinema to internet pornography*. Dublin. Four Courts Press.

Rouse, Paul 2015 *Sport and Ireland: a history*. Oxford. Oxford University press.

Ruskin, John 1877 *St Mark's rest. The history of Venice*. New York. John Wiley.

Russell, George 1901 'Nationality and imperialism', in Augusta Gregory (ed.), *Ideals in Ireland*, 15–24. London. Unicorn.

Ryan, Louise 2000 '"Drunken Tans": representations of sex and violence in the Anglo-Irish War (1919–21)', *Feminist Review* 66, 73–94.

Ryan, Louise 2002 *Gender, identity and the Irish Press, 1922–1937: embodying the nation*. New York. E. Mellen Press.

Ryan, Meda 2012 *Liam Lynch: the real chief* (originally published 1986). Cork. Mercier Press.

Shea, Patrick 1981 *Voices and the sound of drums: an Irish autobiography*. Galway. Blackstaff Press.

Sheridan, Clare 1923 *In many places*. London. Jonathan Cape.

Shortall, William 2020 Art and the Irish Free State—visualizing nationhood (1922–34). Unpublished Ph.D. thesis. Trinity College Dublin.

Silvestri, Michael 2009 *Ireland and India: nationalism, empire and memory*. Basingstoke. Palgrave Macmillan.

Stevens, Quentin, *et al.*, 2018 'Counter-monuments: the anti-monumental and the dialogic', in *Journal of Architecture*, 23 (5), 718–39.

Stopford Green, Alice 1911 *Irish nationality*. London. H. Holt and Company.

Sullivan, Rodney and Sullivan, Robin 2013 'Archbishop James Duhig and the Queensland Irish Association, 1898–1920: exploring connections', *Journal of the Australian Catholic Historical Society* 34, 44–57.

Terrazas Gallego, Melania (ed.) 2020 *Trauma and identity in contemporary Irish culture*. Berlin. Peter Lang.

Townshend, Charles 2002 'Historiography', in Joost Augusteijn, *The Irish revolution, 1913–1923*, 1–16. Basingstoke. Palgrave.

Townshend, Charles 2013 *The Republic: the fight for Irish independence, 1918–1923*. London. Allen Lane.

Tynan, Jane 2015 'The unmilitary appearance of the 1916 rebels', in Lisa Godson and Joanna Brück (eds), *Making 1916: material and visual culture of the Easter Rising*, 25–33. Liverpool. Liverpool University Press.

Tynan, Jane and Godson, Lisa (eds) 2019 *Understanding uniform: clothing and discipline in the modern world*. London. Bloomsbury Academic.

Valente, Joseph 2010 *The myth of manliness in Irish nationalist culture, 1880–1922*. Urbana-Champaign, IL. University of Illinois Press.

Valente, Joseph 2010 'Editor's introduction', *Éire-Ireland* 45 (1 and 2) (Spring/Summer), 5–10.

Van Esbeck, Edmund 1974 *One hundred years of Irish rugby*. Dublin. Gill and Macmillan.

W.B.R., 1923 'An Ulster artist', *The Ulster Bulletin* 1 (3) (July), 14.

Wade, Allan 1954 *The Letters of W.B. Yeats*. London. Robert Hart-Davis.

Walker, Brian 2020 'Voices opposing violence', *The Irish Times*, 9 June.

Walsh, Frank P. 1922 'American imperialism', *The Nation*, 1 February, 115–16.

Walsh, Frank P. 1922 'Catholic economics', *The Nation*, 8 February.

Walsh, Maurice 2015 *Bitter freedom: Ireland in a revolutionary world, 1918–1923*. London. Faber and Faber.

Walshe, Pat 1994 *Irish republicanism and socialism: the politics of the republican movement 1905–1994*. Belfast. Athol Press.

Ward, Margaret 1995 *Unmanageable revolutionaries: women and Irish nationalism*. Dublin. Pluto Press.

Weeks, Liam and Ó Fathartaigh, Mícheál (eds) 2018 *The Treaty: debating and establishing the Irish state*. Newbridge. Irish Academic Press.

Weldon Johnson, James 1922 'Preface', *The book of American Negro poetry*, vii–xxxvii. New York. Harcourt, Brace and Company.

Wells, R.A. 2001 'Transatlantic revivalism and Ulster identity: the career of W.P. Nicholson', in Patrick Fitzgerald and Steve Ickringill (eds), *Atlantic crossroads: historical connections between Scotland, Ulster and North America*, 99–113. Newtownards. Colourpoint.

Whitaker, Anne-Maree 2019 'The Irish Women's Club: Cumann na mBan in Sydney 1919–1935', *Journal of the Australian Catholic Historical Society* 40, 90–102.

White, Gerry 2017 'Free State versus Republic: the opposing armed forces in the civil war', in John Crowley, Donal Ó Drisceoil and Mike Murphy, *Atlas of the Irish revolution*, 691–7. Cork. Cork University Press.

White, Harry 2016 'The invisible art review—a mosaic of music brought to light', *The Irish Times*, 10 December.

Wilk, Gavin 2014 *Transatlantic defiance: the militant Irish republican movement in America, 1923–45*. Manchester. Manchester University Press.

Wilson, Tim 2010 '"The most terrible assassination that has yet stained the name of Belfast": the McMahon murders in context', *Irish Historical Studies* 37 (145) (May), 83–106.

Wilson, Tim 2016 'The strange death of loyalist Monaghan, 1912–21', in Senia Pašeta (ed.), *Uncertain futures: essays about the Irish past for Roy Foster*, 174–87. Oxford. Oxford University Press.

Wright, Frank 1987 *Northern Ireland: a comparative analysis*. Dublin. Gill and Macmillan.

Yeates, Padraig 2012 *A city in turmoil: Dublin 1919–1921*. Dublin. Gill and Macmillan.

Yeates, Padraig 2015 *A city in civil war, Dublin 1921–4*. Dublin. Gill and Macmillan.

Yeats, Jack B. 1922 *Modern aspects of Irish art*. Dublin. Cumann Léigheacht an Phobail.

Yeats, W.B. 1923 'Meditations in time of civil war', *The London Mercury* 7 (January), 232–38 and *The Dial* 74 (1) (January 1923), 50–56.

Yeats, W.B. 1925 'The Irish dramatic movement: Nobel Lecture, 15 December 1923', in *The bounty of Sweden*. Dublin. Cuala Press.

Yeats, W.B. 1928 *The tower*. London. Macmillan.

Yeats, W.B. (ed.) 1936 *The Oxford book of modern verse*. New York. Oxford University Press.

Zimbo, Ted 2019 *McCallions in the IRA*. Privately published.

IMAGE CREDITS

26   Reproduced courtesy of Melbourne Diocesan Historical Commission.

35   Photo by Boris Lipnitzky, via Getty Images/Roger Viollet; © Getty Images.

36   International Music Score Library Project (Petrucci Music Library); public domain.

41   Library of Congress, Prints and Photographs Division, BIOG FILE-Walsh, Frank P.; courtesy of Library of Congress.

50   The International Center of Photography (ICP), accession No. 1045.1990; gift of Daniel Cowin, 1990, reproduced courtesy of ICP.

56   NLI, Hogan-Wilson Collection, HOGW 87; courtesy of the National Library of Ireland.

58   NLI, 'To hold as 'twere': 17 caricatures, BB554; courtesy of the National Library of Ireland.

62   Reproduced courtesy of Laura McAtackney.

63   Reproduced courtesy of Laura McAtackney.

68   Ulster Museum Collection, BELUM.Y3940; © National Museums Northern Ireland.

73   NLI, Ephemera collection, EPH G20; courtesy of the National Library of Ireland.

80   NLI, Prints and Drawing, 3061 TX; courtesy of the National Library of Ireland.

83   NLI, Ephemera collection, EPH B6; courtesy of the National Library of Ireland.

88   Photo by Bettmann/Getty Images; © Getty Images.

94   Dublin Diocesan Archives, Byrne papers, Charity cases, box 1: 1921–26. Reproduced courtesy of Dublin Diocesan Archives.

96   Royal Society of Antiquaries Ireland, DDC, no. 44; reproduced courtesy of Royal Society of Antiquaries Ireland.

99   Photo by Bettmann/Getty Images; © Getty Images.

105   UCDA, Éamon de Valera papers, P150/3487; reproduced by kind permission of UCD Archives.

108   Irish Republican History Museum Conway Mill; reproduced courtesy of Joe Baker.

116   UCDA Desmond FitzGerald Collection: P80/PH/144; reproduced by kind permission of UCD Archives.

117   UCDA Desmond FitzGerald Collection: P80/PH/157; reproduced by kind permission of UCD Archives.

123   Thoor Ballylee Society; reproduced with permission.

134   In private ownership; reproduced by permission.

138   British Pathé, 1920: 'Side lights on Sinn Fein—May Connelly punished'; reproduced courtesy of British Pathé.

142–3   NLI, Hogan-Wilson Collection, HOGW 55; courtesy of the National Library of Ireland.

145   *An tÓglach*, 24 June 1922; courtesy of Military Archives.

300–01   NLI, Hugh Kennedy collection, KEN 1; courtesy of the National Library of Ireland.

309   *Punch*, Bernard Partridge Cartoons, EPH D161; © Punch Limited.

312   Capuchin Archives, 1922, civil war collection; courtesy of the Irish Capuchin Provincial Archives.

315   Capuchin Archives, 1922: civil war collection; courtesy of the Irish Capuchin Provincial Archives.

319–20   NAI, Department of the Taoiseach, TSCH/3/S1943; courtesy of the National Archives of Ireland.

324–5   LOC, National Photo Company collection, LC-F8-37603; courtesy of the Library of Congress.

330   UCDA, Desmond FitzGerald photograph collection, P80/PH/33; reproduced by kind permission of UCD Archives.

334   NLI, Ephemera collection, EPH C476; courtesy of the National Library of Ireland.

370   Irish Newspaper Archives, courtesy of National Library of Ireland.

CONTRIBUTORS

AIDAN BEATTY
is originally from Galway and
now teaches at the Honors
College of the University of
Pittsburgh. He is the author
of *Masculinity and power in
Irish nationalism* (Palgrave
Macmillan, 2016) and co-editor
of *Irish questions and Jewish
questions: crossovers in culture*
(Syracuse University Press,
2018). His work has appeared in
the *Journal of Modern History*,
Irish Historical Studies and the
Journal of Jewish Studies.

GUY BEINER
is the Sullivan Chair in Irish
Studies at Boston College and
professor of modern history
at Ben-Gurion University of
the Negev. His books on Irish
history and memory include
*Remembering the year of the
French: Irish folk history and*
social memory (University
of Wisconsin Press, 2007)
and *Forgetful remembrance:
social forgetting and vernacular
historiography of a rebellion
in Ulster* (Oxford University
Press, 2018). He is the editor
of *Pandemic re-awakenings:
the forgotten and unforgotten
'Spanish' Flu of 1918–1919*
(Oxford University Press, 2021).

JOHN BORGONOVO
is a lecturer in the School of
History at University College
Cork. He has published
extensively on diverse aspects of
revolutionary Ireland, including
the civil war. He co-edited the
award-winning *Atlas of the Irish
Revolution* (Cork University
Press, 2017), and wrote the civil
war monograph, *The battle for
Cork: July–August 1922* (Mercier
Press, 2011).

RICHARD BOURKE

is professor of the History of
Political Thought and a fellow of
King's College at the University
of Cambridge. He has published
on the political ideas of the
Enlightenment and on modern
Irish history. His publications
include *Peace in Ireland: the war
of ideas* (Pimlico, rev. edn 2012)
and *Empire and revolution: the
political thought of Edmund Burke*
(Princeton University Press,
2015).

JOANNA BRÜCK

is professor of Archaeology at
University College Dublin. She
co-edited the volume *Making
1916: material and visual culture
of the Easter Rising* (Liverpool
University Press, 2015) with Lisa
Godson, and she is currently
conducting archaeological survey
and excavation at Frongoch in
North Wales, the camp where some
1,800 Irish men were interned in
the aftermath of the Rising.

DAVID BRUNDAGE

is professor of History at the
University of California, Santa
Cruz and the author of *Irish
nationalists in America: the politics
of exile, 1798–1998* (Oxford
University Press, 2016). His

current book project is entitled
*New York against empire:
challenging British colonialism
in a time of war and revolution,
1910–1927.*

GEMMA CLARK

is senior lecturer in British and
Irish History at the University
of Exeter. Since her first book,
*Everyday violence in the Irish civil
war* (Cambridge University Press,
2014), she has published further
on conflict and violence, including
gender-based harm and arson.
Gemma is currently writing a
history of fire as an Irish (and
global) protest tool.

MARIE COLEMAN

a History professor at Queen's
University Belfast, is the author
of a number of books and
articles on modern Irish history,
including *County Longford and
the Irish revolution, 1910–1923*
(Irish Academic Press, 2003), *The
Irish sweep: a history of the Irish
hospitals sweepstake, 1930–1987*
(UCD Press, 2009) and *The Irish
revolution, 1916–1923* (Routledge,
2013). Her current research
interests include the award of
military service pensions to
veterans of the Irish revolution,
the violence experienced by

women during the period and the Protestant experience of revolution in southern Ireland.

ENDA DELANEY

is a professor at the University of Edinburgh, where he holds a Personal Chair in Modern History. He has published extensively on the history of modern Ireland and the global Irish diaspora, including *The Great Irish Famine: a history in four lives* (Gill and Macmillan, 2014) and *The Irish in post-war Britain* (Oxford University Press, 2007).

ANNE DOLAN

is associate professor in Modern Irish History in the Department of History, Trinity College Dublin. She is author of *Commemorating the Irish civil war: history and memory 1923–2000* (Cambridge University Press, 2003) and, with William Murphy, *Michael Collins: the man and the revolution* (Collins Press, 2018).

TERENCE DOOLEY

is professor of History and director of the Centre for the Study of Historic Irish Houses and Estates, History Department, Maynooth University. His book

on country house burnings and the experience of the Irish aristocracy in war and revolution, 1914–23 will be published by Yale University Press in 2022.

LINDSEY EARNER-BYRNE

holds the SALI Chair of Irish Gender History at University College Cork. She has published on Irish social, gender and welfare history with an emphasis on the intersections between policy and lived experience. Her most recent book, co-authored with Diane Urquhart, explores the history of abortion focusing on differences and commonalities of experience on the island of Ireland.

SEÁN ENRIGHT

is a Circuit judge and a legal historian of the Irish revolutionary period 1914–23, with a specialism in the legal system and the capital trials that took place at that time. His books include *Easter Rising 1916: the trials* (Irish Academic Press, 2013); *After the Rising: soldiers, lawyers and trials of the Irish revolution* (Merrion Press, 2016); *The trial of civilians by military courts—Ireland 1921* (Irish Academic Press, 2012); *The Irish civil war. Law, execution and atrocity* (Merrion Press, 2019).

DIARMAID FERRITER
is professor of Modern Irish
History at University College
Dublin and author of numerous
books, most recently *The border:
the legacy of a century of Anglo-
Irish politics* (Profile Books, 2019)
and *Between two hells: the Irish
civil war* (Profile Books, 2021).
He is a regular television and
radio broadcaster and a weekly
columnist with *The Irish Times*.

GAVIN FOSTER
is associate professor in Irish
Studies at Concordia University.
In addition to publishing
numerous articles, essays and
chapters on aspects of the Irish
revolutionary period, he is the
author of *The Irish civil war and
society: politics, class, and conflict*
(Palgrave Macmillan, 2015).

R.F. (ROY) FOSTER
is emeritus professor of Irish
History at Oxford and of Irish
History and Literature at Queen
Mary University of London. His
many prizewinning books include
*Modern Ireland 1600–1972; Paddy
and Mr Punch: connections in Irish
and English history* (Penguin,
1995); *The Irish story: telling
tales and making it up in Ireland*
(Penguin, 2001); the two-volume

authorised biography of W.B.
Yeats (Oxford University Press,
1998, 2005); *Vivid Faces: the
revolutionary generation in Ireland
1890–1923* (Penguin, 2014); and
On Seamus Heaney (Princeton
University Press, 2020). He is also
a well-known cultural
commentator and critic.

DARRAGH GANNON
is AHRC research fellow at
Queen's University Belfast
and ICUF Beacon fellow at the
University of Toronto. He has
published widely on the Irish
diaspora and the Irish revolution,
including *Proclaiming a republic:
Ireland, 1916 and the National
Collection* (Irish Academic Press,
2016) and *Conflict, diaspora,
and empire: Irish nationalism
in Great Britain, 1912–1922*
(Cambridge University Press,
2022). He is currently completing
a monograph entitled *Worlds
of revolution: Ireland's 'global
moment', 1919–1923*.

JOHN GIBNEY
is assistant editor with the Royal
Irish Academy's *Documents on
Irish Foreign Policy* series. His
books include *The shadow of a
year: the 1641 rebellion in Irish
history and memory* (University of
Wisconsin Press, 2013) and *A short*

history of Ireland, 1500–2000 (Yale University Press, 2017). He is the co-author, with Michael Kennedy and Kate O'Malley, of *Ireland: a voice among the nations* (Royal Irish Academy, 2019), and, with Kate O'Malley, of *The Handover: Dublin Castle and the British withdrawal from Ireland, 1922* (Royal Irish Academy, 2022).

LISA GODSON
is programme leader of the MA in Design History and Material Culture at the National College of Art and Design, Dublin. She is a cultural historian with a particular focus on material culture and architecture. Her publications include *Uniform: clothing and discipline in the modern world* (Bloomsbury Academic, 2019); *Modern religious architecture in Germany, Ireland and beyond* (Bloomsbury Visual Arts, 2019); and *Making 1916: visual and material culture of the Easter Rising* (Liverpool University Press, 2015). Her monograph *How the crowd felt: public ritual, memory and religion in the Irish Free State* is forthcoming.

DIANNE HALL
is associate professor in History at Victoria University, Melbourne.

She has written extensively on the history of the Irish in Australia, including *A new history of the Irish in Australia* with Elizabeth Malcolm, published by NewSouth and Cork University Press in 2018/19.

BRIAN HANLEY
is assistant professor in twentieth-century Irish History at Trinity College Dublin. He has written widely on Irish republicanism and is currently examining the global impact of the Irish Revolution. His most recent book is *The impact of the Troubles on the Republic of Ireland, 1968–79* (Manchester University Press, 2018).

ANDREW R. HOLMES
is reader in History at Queen's University Belfast. He has published extensively in the history of Protestantism and evangelicalism in Ireland, including *The Irish Presbyterian mind: conservative theology, evangelical experience, and modern criticism 1830–1930* (Oxford University Press, 2018). With Gladys Ganiel, he is currently editing *The Oxford handbook of religion in modern Ireland*.

BRIAN HUGHES

lectures in History at Mary Immaculate College, University of Limerick. His publications include *Defying the IRA? Intimidation, coercion, and communities during the Irish Revolution* (Liverpool University Press, 2016) and, with Conor Morrissey (eds), *Southern Irish loyalism, 1912–1949* (Liverpool University Press, 2020). He is currently writing a book on Dublin for Four Courts Press's *Irish Revolution, 1912–23* series.

HEATHER JONES

is professor of Modern and Contemporary European History at University College London. She is the author of *Violence against prisoners of war in the First World War: Britain, France and Germany, 1914–1920* (Cambridge University Press, 2011) and *For king and country: the British monarchy and the First World War* (Cambridge University Press, 2021) and over 50 chapters and articles on the Great War era.

RÓISÍN KENNEDY

is lecturer in the School of Art History and Cultural Policy at University College Dublin. She is co-editor of *Sources in Irish*

Art 2. A reader, published by Cork University Press in 2021. Her other recent publication is *Art and the Nation State. The reception of Modern Art in Ireland* (Liverpool University Press, 2021).

BILL KISSANE

was born in Ireland and educated at Trinity College Dublin (BA, MA) and the London School of Economics (MSc, PhD). He is currently associate professor of Politics at the LSE. Among his books are *The politics of the Irish civil war* (Oxford University Press, 2005), and *Nations torn asunder: the challenge of civil war* (Oxford University Press, 2016).

JASON KNIRCK

is a professor of History at Central Washington University. His research focuses on the political culture of the Irish revolution, including intersections of revolutionary politics with notions of gender, dissent and empire. His most recent book is *Afterimage of the Revolution: Cumann na nGaedheal and Irish politics, 1922–32* (University of Wisconsin Press, 2014).

HEATHER LAIRD

is a lecturer in English at University College Cork. Her research interests include theories and practices of resistance, particularly as they relate to land usage; critical/radical historical frameworks; and Irish culture since the early nineteenth century. She is the author of *Subversive law in Ireland* (Four Courts Press, 2005) and *Commemoration* (Cork University Press, 2018), and an editor of the book series Síreacht: Longings for another Ireland.

PETER LEARY

is a vice chancellor's fellow in History at Oxford Brookes University and author of *Unapproved routes: histories of the Irish border, 1922–72* (Oxford University Press, 2016), winner of the American Conference for Irish Studies Donald Murphy Prize. His articles on the Irish border have appeared in various publications, including *History Workshop Journal, Folklore* and *The Guardian*.

ROBERT LYNCH

has taught and researched at various universities across Britain and Ireland, including Stirling, Oxford, Trinity College Dublin, Warwick and Queen's University Belfast. He has published numerous books and articles on the history of Ulster in the twentieth century, with particular focus on partition and the establishment of Northern Ireland. He currently lives and works in Glasgow, Scotland.

BREANDÁN MAC SUIBHNE

is a historian of society and culture of modern Ireland at the National University of Ireland, Galway, where he leads Acadamh na hOllscolaíochta Gaeilge. Among recent publications are *The end of outrage: post-Famine adjustment in rural Ireland* (Oxford University Press, 2017) and *Subjects lacking words? The grey ʒone of the Great Famine* (Quinnipiac University Press, 2017).

LAURA McATACKNEY

is an associate professor in the Department of Archaeology and Heritage Studies at Århus University in Denmark and docent in Contemporary Historical Archaeology at Oulu University in Finland. Her research involves exploring the material remains of political imprisonment, colonialism and urban segregation, often through the lens of gender and/or class, in Ireland and the Caribbean.

MARY McAULIFFE
is a historian and assistant
professor in Gender Studies at
UCD. She recently published a
biography of the Scottish-born
Irish revolutionary and feminist,
Margaret Skinnider (UCD
Press, 2020), and is currently
researching and writing on
gendered and sexual violence
during the Irish revolutionary
period, to be published in 2022.

DAVID McCULLAGH
is a journalist with Ireland's
public service broadcaster, RTÉ,
and author of a history of the
first Inter-Party government, *A
makeshift majority* (Institute of
Public Administration, 1998), a
biography of John A. Costello,
The reluctant Taoiseach (Gill
and Macmillan, 2010), and a
recent two-volume biography of
Éamon de Valera, *Volume 1: Rise,
1882–1932* and *Volume 2: Rule,
1932–1975* (Gill, 2017, 2018).

FEARGHAL McGARRY
is professor of Modern Irish
History at Queen's University
Belfast and a member of the
Royal Irish Academy. His books
include *The Abbey rebels of
1916: a lost revolution* (Gill and
Macmillan, 2015) and *The Rising.*

Ireland. Easter 1916 (Oxford
University Press, 2016 edn). He
recently led the major AHRC
project, A Global History of Irish
Revolution, 1916–23. His next
book will explore anxieties about
modernity in interwar Ireland.

**ANNE-MARIE
McINERNEY**
is a librarian who is based
in Dublin City Library and
Archive. She received a PhD
in Modern Irish History from
Trinity College Dublin in 2015
and previously worked as both a
teaching assistant and researcher.
She is currently working on a
publication covering military
imprisonment in Ireland during
the 1920s and 1930s.

MARTIN MAGUIRE,
formerly senior lecturer in the
Department of Humanities,
Dundalk Institute of Technology,
is now visiting research fellow
at both the Trinity College
Dublin Research Centre for
Contemporary Irish History and
the University College Dublin
Geary Institute. He has published
on the civil service experience of
revolution in Ireland. Current
research is on civil service trade
unions in independent Ireland.

PATRICK MANNION
is research fellow in Irish History at the University of Edinburgh, and his first book, *A land of dreams: ethnicity, nationalism, and the Irish in Newfoundland, Nova Scotia, and Maine, 1880–1923*, was published by McGill-Queen's University Press in 2018.

LAURENCE MARLEY
is a lecturer in modern Irish and British history at the National University of Ireland, Galway. His publications include *Michael Davitt: freelance radical and frondeur* (Four Courts Press, 2007), and (edited) *The British Labour Party and twentieth-century Ireland* (Manchester University Press, 2016). He is a former co-editor of *Saothar*, journal of the Irish Labour History Society.

CIARA MEEHAN
is reader in History at the University of Hertfordshire. She is the author of *The Cosgrave party: a history of Cumann na nGaedheal* (Royal Irish Academy, 2010) and *A just society for Ireland? 1964–1987* (Palgrave Macmillan, 2013). Most recently, she co-wrote *Saving the state: Fine Gael from Collins to Varadkar* with Stephen Collins (Gill, 2020).

CAOIMHE NIC DHÁIBHÉID
is senior lecturer in Modern History at the University of Sheffield, and has previously held research posts at the University of St Andrews, Fitzwilliam College Cambridge and Queen's University Belfast. Her research interests include the history of Irish republicanism and the comparative history of political violence, and her current research project, which is funded by the Leverhulme Trust, is titled 'Emotions and the Irish Revolution'.

DAITHÍ Ó CORRÁIN
lectures in the School of History and Geography, Dublin City University. He has published widely on Irish Catholicism, including contributions to the *Cambridge history of Ireland* (Cambridge University Press, 2018) and the *Oxford history of British and Irish Catholicism* (Oxford University Press, 2022). He is co-author of *The dead of the Irish revolution* (Yale University Press, 2020), and co-editor of the Four Courts Press *The Irish Revolution, 1912–23* series.

EUNAN O'HALPIN

MRIA FTCD is professor emeritus of Contemporary Irish History at Trinity College Dublin. Among his publications are *Head of the civil service: a study of Sir Warren Fisher* (Routledge, 1989), *Defending Ireland: the Irish state and its enemies since 1922* (Oxford University Press, 1999), *Kevin Barry: an Irish rebel in life and death* (Merrion Press, 2020), and (with Daithí Ó Corráin), *The dead of the Irish revolution* (Yale University Press, 2020).

STEPHEN O'NEILL

is an Irish Research Council Enterprise Postdoctoral Fellow at Trinity College Dublin and the Irish Museum of Modern Art. His *Irish culture and partition 1920–1955* will be published by Liverpool University Press in 2022. From 2019 to 2020 he was the National Endowment for the Humanities Fellow at the University of Notre Dame's Keough-Naughton Institute for Irish Studies.

KEVIN ROCKETT

is the former professor of Film Studies, and is now fellow emeritus at Trinity College Dublin, where he was also director of Irish Film & TV Research Online (www.tcd.ie/Irishfilm). He is author or co-author of nine books on the history of Irish cinema and the cinemas of the Irish diaspora.

PAUL ROUSE

is a professor in the School of History at University College Dublin. He has written extensively on the history of Irish sport. His books include *Sport and Ireland: a history* (Oxford University Press, 2015) and *The hurlers: the first All-Ireland Championship and the making of modern hurling* (Penguin, 2018).

DAMIAN SHIELS

is a conflict archaeologist and historian. He has undertaken archaeological analysis at a number of revolutionary-era sites, including the first archaeological analysis of an Irish revolutionary landscape, which focused on the operational area of an IRA company in Cork. He established the Landscapes of Revolution Archaeology project and has published and lectured widely on Irish conflict archaeology.

MICHAEL SILVESTRI

is professor of History at Clemson University. He is the author of *Ireland and India: nationalism, empire and memory* (Palgrave Macmillan, 2009) and *Policing 'Bengali Terrorism' in India and the world: imperial intelligence and revolutionary nationalism, 1905–1939* (Palgrave Macmillan, 2019), and a co-author of *Britain since 1688: a nation in the world* (Routledge, 2014).

ELAINE SISSON

is a cultural historian and senior lecturer in Visual Culture at the National Film School, Institute of Art, Design and Technology. She has broadcast and published widely on early twentieth-century Irish visual and literary culture. Her research into Irish modernism and bohemian culture, incorporating theatre and costume design, cinema and popular performance, is explored in a forthcoming book on the Irish Free State.

FIONNUALA WALSH

is assistant professor of Modern Irish History at University College Dublin. She completed her PhD and Irish Research Council postdoctoral fellowship at Trinity College Dublin. Her first monograph *Irish women and the Great War* was published by Cambridge University Press in 2020. She is the secretary of the Women's History Association of Ireland.

HARRY WHITE

is professor of Musicology at University College Dublin and a fellow of the Royal Irish Academy of Music. His most recent book is *The musical discourse of servitude. Authority, autonomy and the work-concept in Fux, Bach and Handel* (Oxford University Press, 2020).

TIM WILSON

directs the Centre for the Study of Terrorism and Political Violence (CSTPV) at St Andrews University. He is the author of both *Frontiers of violence: conflict and identity in Ulster and Upper Silesia, 1918–1922* (Oxford University Press, 2010) and *Killing strangers: how political violence became modern* (Oxford University Press, 2020). As an Englishman writing on Irish history, he pleads the excuse that he finds English history really very dull indeed.

Overleaf: Anti-Treaty cartoon by Grace Gifford Plunkett depicting Arthur Griffith and Michael Collins struggling to keep the Irish Free State afloat.